THIS IS WHERE YOU BELONG

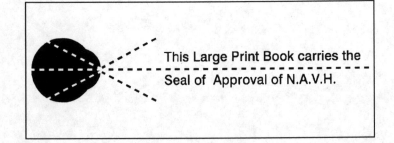

This Large Print Book carries the
Seal of Approval of N.A.V.H.

THIS IS WHERE YOU BELONG

THE ART AND SCIENCE OF LOVING THE PLACE YOU LIVE

MELODY WARNICK

THORNDIKE PRESS

A part of Gale, Cengage Learning

GALE
CENGAGE Learning·

Farmington Hills, Mich • San Francisco • New York • Waterville, Maine
Meriden, Conn • Mason, Ohio • Chicago

GALE
CENGAGE Learning

LIBRARY OF CONGRESS CATALOGING-IN-PUBLICATION DATA

Names: Warnick, Melody, author.
Title: This is where you belong : the art and science of loving the place you live /
  by Melody Warnick.
Description: Large Print edition. | Waterville : Thorndike Press, 2016. | Series:
  Thorndike Press Large Print lifestyles | Includes index.
Identifiers: LCCN 2016028142 | ISBN 9781410493989 (hardcover) | ISBN 1410493989
  (hardcover)
Subjects: LCSH: Place attachment. | Place attachment—Psychological aspects. |
  Environmental psychology. | Neighborhoods—Psychological aspects. | Human
  beings—Effect of environment on. | Large type books.
Classification: LCC BF353 .W37 2016b | DDC 155.9/4—dc23
LC record available at https://lccn.loc.gov/2016028142

Published in 2016 by arrangement with Viking, an imprint of Penguin
Publishing Group, a division of Penguin Random House LLC

Printed in Mexico
1 2 3 4 5 6 7 20 19 18 17 16

For Quinn.
You're my favorite.

A place belongs forever to whoever claims it hardest, remembers it most obsessively, wrenches it from itself, shapes it, renders it, loves it so radically that he remakes it in his own image.

— Joan Didion

CONTENTS

CHAPTER ONE:
THE LOST ART
OF STAYING PUT

At some point during my family's move from Texas to Virginia, the thought crossed my mind that I should have set fire to all our belongings rather than wrestle them into another moving truck. It was embarrassing, really, how much we'd accumulated. Back in college, all my worldly possessions fit into a Subaru station wagon. A husband, two kids, and a million purchases later, our house was a clown car, disgorging a laughably steady stream of stuff. Four mattresses. Five bicycles. Fifteen chairs. A rolled-up Pottery Barn rug. Boxes and boxes of books. How was it possible that we owned all this? Wasn't a bonfire the most prudent course of action here? Much easier to torch everything and start over from scratch.

Now, of course, it was too late. I watched as the twenty-eight-foot truck juddered to a stop in the driveway of our new rental house. My husband, Quinn, raised the rear gate and scanned the Tetris stacks at the back of the load for collapsed cardboard. Then he turned to the two burly guys we'd hired off craigslist for $270. "Okay," he said. "Let's do this." All of us, down to five-year-old Ruby, took turns lugging boxes up the porch steps, invariably scraping our knuckles as we squeezed through the front door.

Welcome to Blacksburg, Virginia.

In one fell swoop we had reinvented our lives. You could see the evidence of this physical and metaphorical 1,200-mile shift in our house, a FEMA disaster zone of disassembled bed frames and legless tables. With every book we slid back into a bookcase, every pot lid we shoved into a drawer, we'd feel like we were putting things back together again. Like we could re-create our old life from Austin in this new space if we only found the right spot for the sofas and the side tables.

Really, nothing would be the same ever again. Our family now lived in a town where we'd never lived before and knew absolutely no one. Frankly, that was kind of the point.

We'd come to Blacksburg for the same reason many Americans move long distances: a job. At least, that was the story we told people when they asked why we were abandoning Austin after only two years in favor of an obscure college town in the folds of the Blue Ridge Mountains. "Quinn scored the English professor dream job," we explained. "It's an opportunity too good to pass up."

In reality, moving was our thing. The average American can expect to move 11.7 times before he or she dies. In my case, Virginia marked post-college move #6, the fifth state I'd lived in after a childhood spent in a single cul-de-sac in Southern California, and I'd come to see each new city in a new state as an irresistible blank slate. Moving offered absolution for whatever failures I'd amassed in my present town: the disappointing friendships, the inescapable, guilt-inducing commitments, the taunting list of unfinished home renovation projects. Each time the moving truck pulled away from the curb, these petty vexations and regrets vanished. Thus freed and forgiven, I'd relish the prospect of beginning again in the next city. Things would definitely be better this time. *I* would be better in Blacksburg.

Specifically, I would amass a well-curated collection of affectionate but not emotionally needy friends. I'd meditate. I'd take up gardening and yoga. I'd cook more, with ingredients like organic bok choy. (My kids would like it now.) I'd write with precision and emotional depth. I'd make more money doing it. Having completely sworn off mindless hours frittered away on Facebook, I'd read the *New Yorker* cover to cover every week. No more fussing at my kids or kvetching to my husband. In Blacksburg, I'd be more pleasant, more patient, more clever. Happier.

I believed so thoroughly in the healing power of geography — what a friend called "the geographic cure" — that I didn't bother to make plans for how these changes would occur. By stirring up the better angels of my nature, the right place would simply complete me.

I realize this sounds like magical thinking. "Wherever you go, you take yourself with you," a therapist might have scolded (if I'd had one). And yet my life *did* change from city to city, dramatically so. How could it not, when so many quotidian details depended on where I was, from the supermarket where I bought my groceries to the friends we traded babysitting with?

Plus, there's true psychic power in a clean slate. "The time of moving introduces so much upheaval into our customary habits that change becomes far easier," points out the author Gretchen Rubin. "In one study of people trying to make a change — such as changes in career or education, relationships, addictive behaviors, or health behaviors including dieting — 36 percent of successful changes were associated with a move to a new place." Want to lose weight? Stop drinking? Start working out? A new city presses the reset button, forcing you to at least temporarily abandon old patterns of thought and environmental triggers. The Melody I was in Virginia would not, fingers crossed, turn out to be the Melody I was in Texas.

Not that I hadn't liked Austin. Moving there in 2010 had been like scoring a seat at the middle school popular table. "You're so lucky!" our friends squealed. "It's such a great city!" They rhapsodized about Austin's music scene, running trails, and impressive urban bat population, assuring us that we'd adore it as passionately as they did when they went to college/vacationed/attended the SXSW conference there. Convinced, we bought a house in the southwestern suburbs of the city. Never mind that my first visit to the city was our house-hunting trip. We were going to commit.

Except when we rolled into town after the Fourth of July, Austin was mired in a soul-sucking heat wave that turned out to be not a heat wave at all, just summer in Texas.

15

The air quivered with mosquitoes. Air conditioners rattled and clanked, the only sound in the otherwise empty neighborhood streets. Why hadn't anyone warned us how sweltering it would be? Or that we'd have to navigate curling ribbons of freeway to get downtown? Or that the high-rise sprawl of Austin's 816,000 residents would make us long for the quiet solitude of Iowa, the state we'd just left?

We'd gone to Austin expecting perfection. How dare Austin not be perfect? Then, since it wasn't, the insidious thought came that maybe life would be perfect, or at least better, if I lived somewhere else.

In each town I'd lived in as an adult — Silver Spring, Maryland; St. George, Utah; Ames, Iowa; Austin, Texas — I'd followed the same pattern. What started as *This is the place!* would be edged out over time by geographic FOMO, or fear of missing out, a vague dread that someplace better existed in the world and I didn't live there.

Late at night, Quinn and I would lie in bed and quiz each other about where we would live if we could go anywhere at all. *Would you prefer a big city or a small town? Do you like the mountains, the plains, or the coast? How important is low cost of living? Good schools? A short commute?* Clicking through Realtor.com listings was my midthirties suburbanite version of crystal meth — a filthy habit I couldn't quit. *This is the last time,* I'd tell myself, and then I'd creep online again to ogle Victorians in Corvallis, Oregon, or cut-rate bungalows in Lawrence, Kansas. On trips I'd load up on the free real estate guides at gas stations and ask Quinn, "Would you live in Oklahoma City? What if I told you we could buy a three-bedroom brick ranch there for $95,000?"

Once Quinn applied for a faculty job at Virginia Tech, I channeled my discontent into hours spent hunting online for details about Blacksburg, studying the Flickr photos and Wikipedia entries like they were the Magic 8 Ball about to pop up a message about my future. ("Signs point to yes.") I slotted each tiny bit of data into a list of pros and cons. Blacksburg had four-season weather. Austin's two seasons were hot and hotter. Blacksburg had 42,000 residents, Austin too many.

Two years earlier, I'd gone through the same obsessive process before we moved to Texas. The way I was now devising elaborate fantasies about the small-town simplicity of Blacksburg's historic downtown, with its restored movie theater and hip vegetarian restaurant, I'd once daydreamed about the adrenaline rush of urban life in Austin. The trick was, I couldn't fantasize about Austin anymore once we'd moved there. Prosaic, annoying reality kept heaving into view. And so my imagined version of Blacksburg became the remedy for everything that was wrong with my life, mostly because I couldn't prove otherwise. More than anything, that was what I loved about a new city: the thrill of possibility.

In the end, the pro/con lists didn't matter as much as Blacksburg's untested promise. Up went the For Sale sign. Out came the packing tape. I was leaving one of the coolest cities in America for a small southwest Virginia town I had never set foot in before. My friends in Austin looked at me like I had taken leave of my senses. But I had faith. This move would fix everything.

So, sure, we moved to Blacksburg for a job. But really we moved because Quinn and I desperately wanted to believe that settling in our best possible town could make us whole and happy and maybe slightly superhuman. That going there we would find some missing part of ourselves. As in any great hero quest, there would be moments of challenge and defeat (see: packing and unpacking), but we would triumph in the end.

With the moving truck finally unloaded, I paid the craigslist guys, then hurled myself onto a couch I hadn't seen since Austin and waited for Blacksburg to woo me.

And waited.

Almost immediately, I realized my mistake. The day after we moved in, it started to rain, and it didn't stop for a week. Someone let slip that the town's nickname is Bleaksburg. The girls moped. Quinn and I argued. Even after we'd unloaded the boxes and recycled the cardboard, I couldn't figure out my way around our rental house. *Where do the cereal bowls go?* I kept asking myself. *Think hard — where did I put the stamps?* At Kroger I roamed the aisles, a lost soul searching for black beans.

As it turned out, the imaginary Blacksburg I'd invented in my mind was not at all the same place as the very real Blacksburg where I now lived. Life in a smaller town was supposed to be simpler, but nothing was easy, not even the easy stuff. Filling out forms at the new doctor's office, I remembered, with consternation, that not only did I have no one's name to put on the "Emergency Contact" line, I couldn't remember my own address. At the hardware store, I asked the clerk about getting new door keys cut, and he burbled his reply in an Appalachian accent so thick I had to ask him to repeat himself.

In those first few weeks, strangers kept asking me what I thought of Blacksburg. "Ooh, you moved here from Texas?" said the librarian who issued my new library card. "That's a long way. What do you think of our town?"

"It's nice," I murmured, stifling the urge to scream, "This library is smaller than my old library! We had better restaurants in Austin! Your mountains make me claustrophobic! Your trees give me anxiety! It rains too much! There's nothing to do! I don't know anyone! I never will!"

I know the drill. Of course you feel upended by moving to a new city. You're rattled by your lack of basic life skills. You don't know where the post office is or when to drag the garbage can to the curb. You can also feel intensely alone. I heard one woman describe her move to Pennsylvania from Minnesota this way: "There was a real sense of grief, because I realized, oh my gosh, no one within a ninety-mile radius would care if I died." Abruptly you've gone from being known to being no one. Moving to a new place can make you feel as if you've lost your very self.

Was it inevitable, then, this slide into thinking life would be better elsewhere? Would I slowly slip back, like a serial adulterer, to real estate listings in Indiana and Michigan? Or would Blacksburg manage to win my affection quickly, before Quinn and I decided to try our luck elsewhere? Anyone will tell you that it takes at least six months and often three or four years to adjust to a new city. I suspected my feelings for my town would improve in time — I just wasn't sure I had the patience to wait it out.

I turned thirty-six the day we arrived in Blacksburg. Moving so often had begun to make me feel like a failure as an adult, like I was missing some fundamental grit that allowed me to commit to a place the way I'd committed to a marriage and a career. My family's average stay in any city to that point was 3.2 years. I was starting to lose confidence in our ability to live anywhere for long.

THE ONES WHO NEVER STOP MOVING

As lonely as moving sometimes feels, it's a shared loneliness. Americans have long been among the world's most insistently mobile people. Each year around 12 percent of us move — a national game of musical chairs with 36 million players. To get a sense of the scale of it, imagine every single resident of the twenty-five largest cities in the country — New York, Los Angeles, Chicago, Houston, and so on — boxing up the bed linens and pulling up stakes.

We aren't the only people who live this nomadically. Norwegians and Finns move almost as much; New Zealanders outpace us by a hair. But in countries like China and Germany, only about 5 percent of the population has moved in the past five years. In the United States, 35 percent of us have.

Why do we move so much? If you plot the reasons in a spreadsheet, the way the census does, you see that moving is largely driven by sensible, bank-account-enhancing life changes like a new job or a lower cost of living elsewhere. Americans are as restless in employment as we are in geography, switching workplaces about every four and a half years. Often, we chase our new gigs around the country.

Yet during the recession, economists gnashed their teeth in frustration that people wouldn't follow the money to towns with lower unemployment rates, like Midland, Texas, or Omaha, Nebraska. If moving to a new city or state promised to dramatically improve your financial prospects, would you go? You'd likely want to know *where* the job was first. Most of us sense instinctively that income, housing prices, and cost of living are only part of the story. We want to be sure we're heading somewhere we wouldn't mind living.

According to one survey, two-thirds of college-educated Millennials say they'd pick the city where they want to live first, *then* find the job to get them there. The startling realization: To many of us, place matters more than paycheck.

Once I started asking around, I heard some incredible stories of people's efforts to settle in a place they would love. I spoke with a woman named Holly Doggett who, in 2003, realized that she and her husband, Daryl Turicek, wanted to live somewhere other than Washington, D.C. So Holly and Daryl quit their jobs, bought a Sunline camper, and embarked on a year-long, 61,592-mile road trip through America's forty-eight contiguous states, on the hunt for a city that had four seasons, a small-town feel, and enough of a job market that they could find work as Web designers.

On the way, they logged factors both hard (size, crime rate) and squishy (restaurant quality, gut feeling) in a spreadsheet, eventually paring it to a short list that included Ann Arbor, Michigan; Missoula, Montana; and Asheville, North Carolina. "We never found one city that we knew instantly, 'This is the one,' " Holly told me. "There were a lot of places where we thought we could be happy."

Ultimately, they chose Portland, Maine. They had no census-approved family-, work-, or housing-related reasons to go there. They knew no one and had no jobs lined up. And still, in September 2004, they wheeled their Sunline into the Wild Duck Campground in nearby Scarborough and started searching for an apartment. Ten years later, they're still in Portland.

The Excel spreadsheet forty-year-old Ben Bristoll made when he decided to escape the small town in upstate New York where he'd lived for eighteen years was even more exhaustive, a cascading list of thirty-eight candidate cities that Ben checked for the qualities he considered most vital in a town, like low housing costs, the proximity of family, the number of vegan restaurants, and the prevalence of Lyme disease. Harrisonburg, Virginia, looked particularly promising after a shoestring visit; so did Burlington, Vermont. Then he came to Roanoke, Virginia, during a January heat wave and rode his bike around the greenways in a T-shirt. *Okay, you got me,* Ben thought. *I'm going to move here.* In 2012, he did.

We always want the postscript to stories like these to be "and they lived happily ever after." Though only some of us will actually move in a given year, mulling the possibilities is practically a national pastime, especially because of this long-standing habit of conflating geography and happiness. As Eric Weiner points out in *The Geography of Bliss,* "We speak of searching for happiness, of finding contentment, as if these were locations in an atlas, actual places that we could visit if only we had the proper map and the right navigational skills. Anyone who has taken a vacation to, say, some Caribbean island and had flash through their mind the uninvited thought *I could be happy here* knows what I mean."

If the idea that a place can make us happy is a fantasy, it's both sweet and pervasive. Most Americans, it seems, spend an inordinate amount of time thinking about where we wish we lived. On trips, we peer at For Sale signs in resort towns. We plot ways to buy a second home in a town we like better than our own; every year, about seven hundred thousand of us do.

Lacking the wherewithal to cruise the

country in an RV, we instead cruise social media for the click-bait of city rankings. The *Huffington Post* has run hundreds of stories with titles like "The Top 12 Cities for Millennials to Live, Work, and Play," "The Top 10 Cities for Getting Rich," "The Best Cities for Boomers to Pre-Retire," "10 Best Cities for Art Lovers," and, usefully, "The Top 10 Cities for Mistresses." Websites like Livability.com and BestPlaces.net offer "Best Place to Live" and "City Finder" tools. Print publications as varied as *Money, Outside, Bicycling,* and *Forbes* regularly weigh in on the nation's top cities to live, work, and play in, while an entire glossy magazine covers the matter of *Where to Retire.*

Meanwhile, the website City-Data, which is like a Yelp for towns, attracts 22 million unique visitors a month — about as many as the TED website — to its extensive network of forums dedicated to analyzing, debating, and crowing about America's cities. In over fifteen thousand posts a day, members parse the relative virtues of Tupelo, Mississippi, and Trout Lake, Michigan, and add an avalanche of opinion to threads with titles like "Relocating to Flagstaff — thoughts?" or "Is southside Fort Wayne really that bad?"

Each state gets its own forum. The most popular, with over 1.7 million posts, belongs to Texas. One particularly virulent thread, started in 2007 by a user named deeptrance, begins, "Texans, let's admit it, no matter where we live, there are only 2 REAL cities in this state, DFW and H-town. Yeah, San Antonio, Austin and El Paso are cities but they're not CITIES, am I right?" The replies, 12,939 of them and counting, have been viewed 1.2 million times.

That we're thinking long and hard about where we live makes sense, since geography dictates or correlates with so much about our lives. Some of a place's effects are obvious: You probably have the friends and partner you have because at some point you lived in the same city. Others are more startling. The Stanford economist Raj Chetty made waves in 2014 by pointing out how decisively geography seems to influence our earnings. According to his exhaustive study of federal income tax records for 40 million children and their parents, a person's odds of rising from the bottom income bracket to the top change dramatically depending on where he or she grows up. If you were raised in Williston, North Dakota, for instance, you're far more likely to make that financial ascent than if you grew up in Valdosta, Georgia. Only 4.4 percent of poor children from Charlotte, North Carolina, became wealthier than their parents; 12.9 percent of children from San Jose, California, did.

The federal government had already launched a series of place-based policies and initiatives back in 2009, in response to ongoing debates about the primacy of place in the land of opportunity. The Chetty data added fuel to that fire. I heard one White House staffer say that if she had a dollar for every time she'd heard Chetty mentioned in Washington lately, she'd have a pretty large amount to help struggling communities. Referring to the disheartening inequality among Americans from different parts of the country, Barack Obama remarked that "a person's zip code shouldn't decide their destiny."

In so many ways, though, it does. Another study found a geographical "marriage effect" that says you're 10 percent less likely to marry if you grew up in a city like New York or Chicago. There's a happiness effect; Gallup-Healthways' annual Well-Being Index shows that you're far more likely to consider yourself happy if you live in Sarasota, Florida, instead of, say, Youngstown, Ohio.

Physical health and longevity link to the places we've lived, as well. Consider Fairfax County, Virginia, whose male residents live, on average, for eighty-one years, the longest life expectancy of any place in the country, according to a 2013 study. Meanwhile, in McDowell County, West Virginia, 340 miles away, a man can expect to live to be just sixty-four years old. Along with quizzing patients about medical history, more and more doctors are asking about mobility history, with the idea that where we've spent our lives can have an enormous impact on our propensity for illnesses like cancer and asthma. Like it or not, geography may well be destiny, an idea I've always believed, maybe to the extreme. It was why I moved so much. Was there an off chance I could do better somewhere else? Let's go!

The first time Quinn and I made a long-haul move it was from Provo, Utah, to Silver Spring, Maryland. We were bright and shiny twenty-three-year-old newlyweds, just out of college, and nothing seemed so romantic, so like a scene from an old-timey movie, as huddling inside the cab of a U-Haul, listening to the radio stations flicker past Albuquerque and Memphis. We hadn't even bothered to line up an apartment in Maryland, but who cared? Neither of us had ever lived east of the Mississippi, and we felt deliriously footloose. *Look at how unfettered we are! No ties to keep us anywhere!*

All these years later, being seminomadic had started to take a heavy toll. Maybe I was just older and crabbier, thirteen years more likely to get a bum back from lifting a sofa bed, but the move to Blacksburg had exhausted me. I'd yearned for the romance of a new geography. Now that I had it, I felt mostly anxious and lonely.

Our children were getting older, too. Ella would be a fifth grader. Ruby was getting ready to start kindergarten. Funny, living in Maryland in 2001, we'd scrimped and bought our first house two months before Ella was born, on the basis that it didn't feel "real" enough to bring an infant home to a one-bedroom apartment across from the Metro station. Stability and security were what children required! Only a solid brick colonial would do! Eleven months later, our money pit of a 1940s fixer-upper drove us not only to sell the house but to leave the state altogether. We didn't stay in Maryland long enough to notch a single growth spurt on a door frame, let alone introduce our daughter to the kids with whom she might one day graduate from high school.

That was when I became obsessed with searching for alternate-reality lives in other cities. Quinn and I kept moving and moving, dragging our daughters along for the ride — to a new job in Utah, grad school in Iowa, a job in Texas, and now another job in Virginia. Ella ended up attending three different elementary schools in three states. In Austin, she dutifully recited the Texas pledge — "I pledge allegiance to thee, Texas, one state under God, one and indivisible" — even though we clearly weren't loyal to Texas. Meanwhile, Ruby, who was born in Ames, Iowa, can't remember that town at all.

Most parents worry about how moving affects our children, and we're probably right to. University of Virginia sociologist Shigehiro Oishi and University of Toronto Mississauga psychologist Ulrich Schimmack followed 7,100 adults over ten years and found that introverts who had moved around a lot as children tended to struggle more as adults. They reported lower life satisfaction and fewer social relationships, and they were more likely to die before a ten-year follow-up appointment. Of course, another study found that college freshmen who had been "Movers" as kids made more new friends during the first two months of school than "Stayers." Many highly mobile children do fine. Quinn had lived in twelve houses in five states before he graduated from high school, and he's not a complete basket case.

But at some point, I wondered, shouldn't responsible parents pick a place and stay there? What is home, after all, if not the house where you took your first steps, the front porch where you played Barbies with the girl from across the street, the street you rode your bike up and down? In a 2002 study, Victoria Derr, now an environmental designer at the University of Colorado Boulder, interviewed children in New Mexico about their experience of place. One ten-year-old boy described the hill by his house as "my big mountain," saying, "This is the best place." "He knows where he comes from," writes Derr, "he knows he has a place he belongs, and this knowing seems to give him confidence, rootedness, and stability." When I considered my own one-house childhood in Fullerton, California — precisely the secure growing-up experience I wasn't giving Ella and Ruby — I felt like I had irrevocably messed up as a parent.

My first few weeks in Blacksburg forced me to a realization: I wanted to settle down somewhere. For the sake of my children, I needed to try. I just wasn't sure I wanted my forever home to be Blacksburg, a town I didn't hate, but didn't particularly love, either. Then I found a game changer in a place not too far away: West Virginia.

ROOTED

According to Google Maps, Lorado, West Virginia, the town where Gertie Moore has lived her entire life, doesn't exist. "At the red light in Man, set your odometer," she instructed me over the phone. "Go eleven miles and take a right on Davy Branch Road." I could call her again if I got lost, she said, but I'd have to drive back to Highway 10 to do it, since the valley that leads to Gertie's house blocks out nearly all cell phone coverage.

I was heading to West Virginia on assignment for *Reader's Digest,* to report on the fortieth anniversary of the Buffalo Creek flood. In 1972, a coal slurry dam collapsed at the top of the valley where Gertie lives, unleashing a wall of viscous black water into the coal company towns below. Having lived through the flood, Gertie had become a de facto town historian, and she'd agreed to show me around.

After I found her modular house on the far side of the train tracks, Gertie offered to take me on a driving tour of the area, starting with the grassy plot of land at the top of her road — the site of the house where she was born. A few doors down was the two-room home her family moved into next, followed by the place Gertie moved as a newlywed, then the slightly larger house she and her husband rented after children came. Every few years she slid a couple dozen feet closer to the main highway where the coal trucks rumbled past.

"You've lived on the same street your whole life?" I asked.

"Yep. They named the road after me, because everybody knows Gertie."

Gertie, who is a sprightly seventy-two and wears her hair in champagne curls, drove me in her blue minivan past the soaring steel tubes of the coal processing plant to the top of the hollow where the road petered into nothing much and the houses slumped together in defeat. Then we turned around and followed the creek past the Buffalo Foodland grocery store into the big town of Man (population: 733), with its narrow streets and frozen-in-time pizza restaurant. For twenty-nine years, Gertie had driven a school bus on these roads, and she kept up a drawling narration of the lives of people long since gone: the pastor of the church who used to live here, the "real countrified" woman who sat in her rocking chair there.

Everything about this place — its smallness, its sheer mountain walls, its sad trailer houses trying to be respectable — filled me with claustrophobia. There was no sign of the disaster beyond the official State of West Virginia historical marker that declared Buffalo Creek the site of one of the worst floods in the United States. The creek itself shimmered innocently under a canopy of trees. Still I felt a creeping anxiety passing by it.

I couldn't understand why Gertie lived here. Moving came so easily to me. Why didn't she move? Pack up for Charleston? Start over somewhere else? Why live in Lorado after a flood killed 125 people and skinned the valley floor with coal tar? Even when her husband succumbed to black lung, widowing her at age thirty-five with five small children, Gertie stayed. Maybe she had no choice but to live here, I thought. Maybe being born and raised in Appalachian coal country meant she didn't have other options.

Yet there was something noble in the way Gertie presided over her hometown, surrounded by people to whom she'd made herself useful, like the now-grown children who once rode her school bus, or the neighbor woman she took to Walmart every other week for quilt fabric. Most of her extended family lived within twenty miles. Grandkids slept at her place regularly; she'd added a room to her house for just that purpose. A niece had recently helped her remodel her kitchen into a gleamingly modern affair, complete with white cabinets and a subway tile backsplash. "Have you heard of Pinterest?" Gertie asked me when I admired it. "That's where we got all our ideas."

My last day in Lorado, Gertie asked me how I was getting home. "You're not going all the way back through Man, are you?" When I told her I was planning on it, she said, "Come on, I'll show you the back way." The back way turned out to be a boulder-strewn dirt road that wound across vertiginous mountain passes to catch the highway farther south. Gertie barreled up it like her minivan was a monster truck, with me timidly revving my Mazda behind her. Finally she stopped and let me pull alongside her. "You can find your way okay now," she said. "Just keep going." She pulled a three-point turn and headed home.

I wanted to feel sorry for her, living where she did. Instead, I felt like she had figured out something I hadn't. In Lorado, Gertie's life was geographically narrow, but deep in things that mattered, like relationships. Gertie knew everyone for fifteen miles, and everyone knew her.

I don't want to romanticize the very real challenges of where she lives. In 2015, West Virginia came in dead last, for the sixth year in a row, in Gallup's poll of statewide well-being levels. But where people like me would have skipped town fast at the first sign of trouble, Gertie dug down and claimed the town's worst history as her own. Why? Because this is where she belongs.

More than six in ten adults move to a new community at least once in their lives, but the truth is that often they don't go very far. A Pew Research Center study found that 57 percent of Americans have never lived outside their home state. More remarkable, 37 percent have never left their hometown. For a country that prides itself on its happily mobile populace, that more than a third of American adults still live where they grew up seems . . . shocking. To the modern imagination, people who never leave their hometown are viewed with suspicion — seen as unadventurous at best, pathetic at worst. (A telling 2013 headline from the *Onion* reads, "Unambitious Loser with

Happy, Fulfilling Life Still Lives in Hometown.") Sure, we think, you can have a nice life in your hometown, but why would you want to?

In his book *Who's Your City?* the demographer Richard Florida divides people into three categories: the mobile, the stuck, and the rooted. "We tend to focus on the first two: the mobile, who can pick up and move to opportunity, and the stuck, who lack the resources to leave where they are," Florida says. "But we cannot forget about the rooted — those who have the means and opportunity to move, but choose to stay." Why do they choose to stay? Because they're content where they are.

From the outside, it can be tough to tell the difference. If I hadn't spent time with her, I would have assumed that Gertie Moore was stuck in that West Virginia coal mining hollow. Except she wants to live there. She's never considered moving. For all its faults, Gertie chose Lorado, and that makes her rooted.

Meanwhile, I drove back to Blacksburg, where I knew no one and felt not the least bit at home. I began to wonder if in all these years of waiting for a town to wallop me over the head with its made-for-me glory, I'd had it all wrong. What if a place becomes the right place only by our choosing to love it?

THE POWER OF PLACE ATTACHMENT

Humans are instinctively driven to form connections with places. "To be rooted," the philosopher Simone Weil wrote, "is perhaps the most important and least recognized need of the human soul." In 1947, the poet W. H. Auden coined the charming term "topophilia," from the Greek roots *topos,* or place, and *philia,* meaning love, to describe the sense of being connected to one's environment. The biologists, anthropologists, sociologists, and urban planners who study it alternately call it things like "place identity," "geopiety," "person-place bonding," "environmental embeddedness," or "at-homeness."

The most common term, and the one I like best, is "place attachment," because it suggests the affectionate, almost familial connection that can form between us and where we live. You mostly know it when you feel it, which you probably have. When you roll into your town and sigh, "It's good to be home," that's a product of place attachment. So is feeling drawn as if by magic to a particular city, never wanting to leave the place where you grew up, or never wanting to leave the place you live right now.

If all this sounds a bit touchy-feely, it is. Like happiness, place attachment exists partly as emotion and partly as a pattern of thought, which makes it difficult to quantify. But over the years researchers have developed a "place attachment scale" of statements they use to gauge the sensation. Study participants are usually asked to rank their agreement on a scale from 1 to 5, but for the sake of simplicity, you can assess your own place attachment by answering each of the questions below "true" or "false" about the town or city where you live:

1. I feel like I belong in this community.
2. I've lived here a long time.
3. I know a lot of people here.
4. I know my way around.
5. I feel comfortable here.
6. The friendships and associations I have with other people in this town mean a lot to me.
7. I feel rooted here.
8. I like to tell people about where I live.
9. I grew up here.
10. I rely on where I live to do the stuff

I care about most.

11. If I could live anywhere in the world, I would live here.
12. If something exciting were happening in this community, I'd want to be involved.
13. I'm really interested in knowing what's going on here.
14. My town isn't perfect, but there are a lot of things that make me love it.
15. The people who live here are my kind of people.
16. I hope that my kids live here even after I'm gone.
17. I feel loyal to this community.
18. I like to attend events that are happening in my town.
19. Where I live tells you a lot about who I am as a person.
20. I care about the future success of this town.
21. I don't want to move anytime soon.
22. I can rely on people in this town to help me.
23. There is no other place I'd rather live.
24. It feels like home.

The more times you answer "true," the more likely you are to be attached to your town. Marking nineteen or more "true" answers, which puts you in the top quartile, indicates that you probably feel strongly connected to where you live. Six or fewer, on the other hand, suggests that you live somewhere unfamiliar or in a town you're not particularly over the moon about. And if you're not very place attached you may be saying to yourself, *Clearly place attachment feels nice. But why should I care? Will it actually make my life better?*

According to place attachment research, the answer is a resounding yes. Studies show that when you pit Stayers — long-term residents of a place — against chronic Movers, the Stayers are generally far more social. They're more likely to volunteer or, say, help the environment by buying a habitat preservation license plate. A study by biologists and anthropologists at Harvard, Princeton, and Binghamton universities found, unsurprisingly, that teens who didn't move around a lot, and whose neighbors didn't move away, either, had more friends.

So where we live matters, and staying where we live matters. But *liking* where we live? Feeling satisfied? Or even better, feeling connected, engaged, a little bit in love with our city? That's the kind of place attachment whose effects extend far beyond the standard "no place like home" frisson, pleasant as it may be.

Physically, when we're happy where we live and like the people who live around us, we're less anxious, less likely to suffer heart attacks or strokes, and less likely to complain about ailments. In a study conducted in Tokyo, elderly Japanese women who were attached to the neighborhood where they lived were more likely to be alive five years down the road than women who didn't care one way or another. For women who liked where they lived and also interacted with their neighbors, their chance of survival shot up by an additional 6 percent. Other researchers have linked place attachment to a general sense of well-being.

Being loved also happens to be excellent medicine for towns themselves. In a multi-year study, Gallup and the Knight Foundation, a nonprofit that promotes community engagement, surveyed twenty-six thousand residents of twenty-six American communities, from Boulder, Colorado, to Myrtle Beach, South Carolina, about how much they loved the city where they lived. The rather astounding result: Even in the Great Recession, the happier residents were with their town, the more the town prospered economically.

Researchers who measure place attachment don't try to examine the objective magnificence of one's city — the soaring beauty of its skyscrapers and statues, the leafy depths of its parks. That would be like measuring a couple's love for each other by posting their photos on Hot or Not. Instead, scientists study residents' emotions by asking whether or not their town *feels* like home. When it comes to place attachment, our towns are what we think they are. That means your city doesn't need to be the Platonic ideal of a city, in the same way you (thankfully) don't have to be particularly gorgeous, clever, or wealthy to love and be loved. Like Gertie Moore in Lorado, West Virginia, you can adore a place that makes your friends shudder and still accrue the physical, emotional, and social benefits of place attachment. Your town just has to make *you* happy.

That psychic felicity between you and your city is something experts call "person-environment fit," a term that gets bandied about mostly by human resources experts talking about workplace culture but has just as much to do with how we fit in with our cities. My friend Amber, for example, adores living in Austin, Texas, and if you know anything about the kind of person she is —

she once streaked her hair with fuchsia and goes to concerts in smoky clubs on week-nights — you understand why. If Austin, Texas, were a guy, you would set Amber up with him on a blind date.

That's not such an outlandish metaphor. As the place consultant Katherine Loflin told me, "People are on a search to find their place the same way they're on a search to find a partner or a spouse. If you care about where you live, and it is one of the things that pushes you and compels your decision making, you have to think of it as a personal relationship."

The corollary to person-environment fit is that not every city works for every person. City-Data's belligerent forum discussions attest to the fact that no single town makes all its residents deliriously happy. Two people's experience of the same place can be vastly different. But what happens if you end up in a town that feels like an OkCupid match gone wrong, the way Blacksburg did to me? Should I wait it out till I could agree with the "I've lived here a long time" state-ment on the place attachment scale, hoping that, *Fiddler on the Roof* style, loyalty and patience would eventually turn an arranged marriage into something resembling affec-tion?

Researchers suspect that a primary factor in whether we feel at home in a town is the length of our stay there. (Peak season for place attachment: three to five years after moving.) That would involve waiting. And in those early days in Blacksburg, I didn't feel equipped to wait that long. In three to five years I might be gone, trying unsatisfactorily to settle somewhere else, so busy moving that I never bothered to find a forever place.

Was it possible to get the rewards of place attachment without the long-haul commitment? To test whether I could feel at home in Blacksburg, or any city I landed in, not five or ten years from now, but *now*?

I know what a ridiculous fast-food-style sentiment that is: *I want to be rooted this instant, dang it!* But something I hit on in the place attachment research suggested that it might not be such a crazy idea. According to anthropologist Setha Low and psychologist Irwin Altman, both pioneering place attachment researchers, place attachment is emotion and belief *combined with action or behavior.* Put more simply, place attachment is a process. It's the way we imbue places with meaning and memory. That suggested that loving my town and feeling more rooted in Blacksburg, here and now, was something I could *do.* I could make it happen.

As psychologists discovered in the 1970s, our actions can shape our emotions. (Consider the studies that have shown that forcing yourself to smile, even when you don't feel like it, reduces stress and ultimately makes you happier.) So I formed a hypothesis: By performing behaviors that had been linked to place attachment, or that produced place attachment feelings in others, I could proactively make myself love where I lived, even without love-at-first-sight attraction.

First, I had to figure out what place attachment behaviors looked like. I read dozens of studies by psychologists, sociologists, natural resource managers, and other researchers who were looking into the nature of place attachment, particularly how it develops and how it affects us. I spoke with a small army of experts, including a woman who's made a career out of helping cities fashion themselves into more attractive places to live. I traveled with a team of community branders to find out how they marketed middle-of-nowhere towns. I visited a woman who's turned her life upside down to build a community arts center in her tiny town. Looking for anecdotal evidence, I talked with more than a hundred

Movers and Stayers about what drew them to their town, made them fall in love with it, and then made them stay.

I also looked at the spreading movement of "placemaking," an umbrella term for the ways citizens are trying to make their communities more livable. One of the most notable placemakers, Tony Hsieh, has arguably become more famous for dedicating vast amounts of his personal fortune to reinventing a struggling neighborhood two miles from the Strip in Las Vegas than he was for founding the shoe retailing giant Zappos. Through the Downtown Project, he's bought up real estate; bankrolled festivals, a theater, a private school, and co-working spaces; and recruited small-business owners to his newfangled live-work-play utopia.

Hsieh treats his neighborhood like the largest start-up incubator you've ever seen, where "return on community" is just as important as return on investment. Why? Because he wants to love where he lives. As Hsieh has said, "I want to live where there are places I enjoy hanging out in and people I enjoy being around." Dan Gilbert, the billionaire owner of mortgage lender Quicken Loans, is working similar magic in his hometown of Detroit, where he's become a local hero for pouring millions into downtown revitalization.

Placemaking has become common enough that major corporations, government entities, and nonprofits, including Southwest Airlines and the National Endowment for the Arts, have spent millions of dollars on placemaking projects in the past five years. Recently, the Pratt Institute and Ohio State University started offering courses in placemaking for community arts leaders.

Often, though, the people restoring a city's run-down buildings, building bike lanes, and planning festivals are just average residents with day jobs and piddly bank accounts who happen to want to make their city better. Placemaking has gone guerrilla. Ethan Kent, a senior vice president with the nonprofit Project for Public Spaces, told me that Americans are emerging from an era of thinking of towns and cities as products for residents to consume. "Now," he says, "the energy is more around the idea that the cities that succeed are the ones that allow people to help create them. That's how they become better places, but also how people are going to become more attached to them. When people help create their place, they see themselves reflected in it. It reflects their values and personalities and becomes more an extension of themselves."

If you want to love your town, I decided, you should act like someone who loves your town. So what I wanted to know from all these consultants, researchers, placemakers, Movers, and Stayers, was this: How did people who loved their towns behave? Where did they spend their time? What were they doing, even unwittingly, to feel more connected to their city? I was looking for ideas I could apply in Blacksburg and that others could do wherever they live. Because I wanted to create a road map of rootedness, I needed to find out: What could I do to feel happier living here?

Some of the suggestions I got I couldn't afford to do (buy a house). Some were too time-consuming or headache inducing (run for mayor, open a community center). Some were flat-out impossible (build a time machine and move to Blacksburg thirty years ago). But eventually I managed to distill what I'd learned into a master list of ten basic place attachment behaviors that were relatively doable and potentially enjoyable and that I hoped would help me put down roots.

1. Walk more.
2. Buy local.

3. Get to know my neighbors.
4. Do fun stuff.
5. Explore nature.
6. Volunteer.
7. Eat local.
8. Become more political.
9. Create something new.
10. Stay loyal through hard times.

Here was my methodology: For each item on the list, I'd commit to one or two simple Love Where You Live experiments. I would, for instance, attend a cash mob downtown. I'd hike more. I'd march in a town parade. I made sure that the experiments were relatively small and quick; they were less daunting that way. As Carol Coletta, vice president of the Knight Foundation, which funds placemaking ventures across the country, reminded me, "The hundreds of actions taken every day by thousands of people living in a city or a community help determine the future of that community. When I walk out my door and there's a piece of trash, do I pick it up? Do I plant flowers? Do I say hello to people? Do I walk? Do I sit on my porch? It sounds so small, but those are things that have a lot to do with the quality of life in a city, and once you can get people doing those things and realizing the impact that collectively they have, that's where the magic is."

Small actions mattered. They could change a city, and they could also, I hoped, change the way *I* felt in my city. Maybe loving where you lived was a small thing, too, not as paramount in the grand scheme of happiness as, say, a terrific marriage or a job you adore or a good relationship with your teenager. Yet marriages and jobs and child rearing happened somewhere. They belonged to a particular place.

Our cities nourish us and challenge us, encourage us and hurt us and test our patience. At their best they bring us joy. For good or ill, places always, always form the landscape of our daily lives, and it made sense that becoming more satisfied with the *where* of my life could have positive trickle-down effects for the *who, what,* and *how.*

My friend Jen, who as an army wife knows a thing or two about moving, told me, "It is an incredibly conscious decision to love where you live. I have seen so many families become miserable because they hate where they are when they move to a new place. You *have* to choose to love it."

That would be the goal of my Love Where You Live experiments: to choose to love where I was. I wanted the solidly affectionate bond of place attachment, with the rewards that went along with it: stable relationships, secure children, good health, and, for that matter, a nicer town. If my hypothesis wasn't completely off base, by acting like someone who loved Blacksburg, I would actually start to attach to Blacksburg. By sheer force of will, I would belong where I lived, enough to want to stay put, at least for a while.

Since there are a few studies that suggest that the first two to four years of living somewhere make the most impact on how much attachment you feel, I couldn't delay my Love Where You Live experiments — nor did I want to. The more uprooted I felt, the more I longed to be moored in place. In a world that's supposedly flat, loving where we live still matters, even when we move a lot. Maybe especially when we move a lot.

CHAPTER TWO:
LACE UP YOUR SNEAKERS

Once, for a magazine article I was writing, I interviewed a woman who had completely ditched her car for family bicycles. "What's your favorite thing about getting around by bike?" I asked, assuming she'd say, "All the calories I burn" or "The way I'm saving the planet." What she said instead was "Riding a bike is fun." The litany of daily errands that are stultifying or stressful by car became exhilarating on a bike. Fetching the forgotten gallon of milk from the grocery store wasn't a hassle. It was freeing.

In the kinds of circles where people talk about cities and towns and how to make them better, walking and biking are having a moment. That's a huge turnabout for a nation where car culture has reigned for decades. In 1998, 83 percent of our trips were by car; only 10 percent happened on foot. The number of children who lived within a mile of their school and walked or biked there had, by 2009, fallen to only 35 percent.

So it was notable when in 2013, for the first time, the National Association of Realtors found that car-centric suburbs were out. In: mixed-use, quasi-urban developments where residents could stroll from apartment to dry cleaner to restaurant. Sixty percent of home buyers wanted walkable, bikeable neighborhoods.

To lure this 60 percent, cities and towns are cranking out urban redesign plans that emphasize greenways and bike lanes. In Indianapolis, for instance, luxury condo complexes are blooming near the city's Cultural Trail, a $62.5 million walking and biking pathway modeled after ones in Copenhagen and Paris. New York City has doubled its number of bike lanes since 2006. In Minneapolis, demand for bikeable housing along the Midtown Greenway, a rails-to-trails path, is so high that one condominium building, VÉLO North Loop, named each of its floor plans for bicycle brands (the Schwinn, the Cannondale). The online brochure juxtaposes stock photographs of smiling twentysomethings with pictures of beach cruisers and racing cycles. One image shows two bikes tangled in the sheets of a queen-sized bed, as if to say,

"Cyclists have more sex."

On that particular point, I will refrain from comment. What is clear, though, is that one of walking and biking's fundamental benefits applies to everyone, but particularly Movers like me: It helps us figure out where the heck we are, and we need to do that to stand any chance of becoming place attached.

Here's a simple exercise: Think about the last time you were on vacation in an unfamiliar city. How did you get around? Google Maps? The soothing directional whispers of Siri? What if someone deposited you at a random street corner? How would you figure out how to get home?

In Blacksburg, I spent months slightly lost, either because I didn't know where my destination was or because I couldn't figure out how to get there from here. (And Blacksburg is no Austin, with its confounding frontage roads, and certainly no Los Angeles or New York.) Knowing where we are in the world and where everything else is in relation to us is the first, fundamental part of feeling like we belong in a place. Without it, we're literally disoriented — without orientation — a deeply unsettling feeling.

In a new city, the most basic navigation

requires front-of-mind brain space, the prime mental real estate you usually allocate to higher-level thinking, like solving a work problem or choosing which BBC series to watch on Netflix. Basically, you're using a gigabyte of RAM on a job that should normally take ten megabytes. That's a poor allocation of resources, and it means there's less memory than normal to spare for other tasks, leaving Movers in a state of perpetual muddledom. My friend Vanessa told me it took six months in her new city before she could stop actively giving herself step-by-step directions (*Okay, turn left here*) every time she left the house.

Eventually, when we've come to know a place well, daily navigation descends, pleasingly, into the unconscious realm again. Muscle memory kicks in. One minute you're on the freeway, the next you're in your driveway, and you can barely remember how you got there. Home is the place where you know how to shortcut past a knot of traffic or speed to work entirely on back roads. (Or maybe home is the town where your body instinctively knows how to get to the nearest Starbucks.)

Scientists call the way we learn to navigate a place "mental mapping." In the 1940s, a behavioral psychologist named Edward Tolman found that rats who first aimlessly explored a maze developed cognitive maps that helped them quickly scamper through it later. Chimpanzees have shown the same ability. In a 1978 experiment, psychologist Emil Menzel carried a chimp around a field, showing him where researchers had hidden food. When Menzel walked to the edge of the field and set the chimp down, the animal beelined straight to the hidden food, because on the walk-through he'd formed a mental map of where the prize was. He knew just how to get there. Meanwhile, five chimps who hadn't been shown the hiding spot in advance wandered, lost.

Maybe if they'd given those five chimps a smartphone, they would have figured it out. GPS-enabled devices make a fabulous second brain; one in four Americans, myself included, use their phone to get directions almost daily. But over time our technology can rob us of our ability to figure out directions on our own. "Navigating, keeping track of one's position and building up a mental map by experience is a very challenging process for our brains, involving memory (remembering landmarks, for instance) as well as complex cognitive processes (like calculating distances, rotating angles, approximating spatial relations)," says Julia Frankenstein, a psychologist at the Center for Cognitive Science at the University of Freiburg. "Stop doing these things, and it'll be harder to pick them back up later."

Before I moved to Blacksburg, I spent months studying the town on Google Maps Street View. As maps go, Street View is a pretty serious step down in the poetry department. Nothing to unfurl, no romance. But thanks to a fleet of Google cars with their fancy, roof-mounted cameras, I could fake-stroll my future city, mouse-clicking through residential neighborhoods like a newfangled Peeping Tom. Over time I Street Viewed so much that I was pretty sure if you dropped me in a parking lot in the middle of Blacksburg I'd be able to find my way anywhere.

What I realized when I finally moved here was that Street View made Blacksburg familiar, but in a bizarro-world way. These were the same places I'd traveled online, but the dimensions were wonky. Buildings were taller, more upright — my new city as pop-up book. And there were so many hills! What had Street View done with all the hills? The mental map of my town that I'd spent months crafting in 2-D was rendered totally pointless by the 3-D, real-life version. My sense of geography withered. I was lost.

Like Tolman's rats, humans most effectively acquire our cognitive maps of a town by exploring it. Google Street View doesn't do the trick. We have to be there physically, trying out the back roads, learning where things are. You can do that in a car, of course, and most people do, but some research suggests that our mental maps are more accurate when we walk or bike places.

When Bruce Appleyard, a professor of city planning at San Diego State University, asked a group of nine- and ten-year-olds to draw maps of their neighborhoods, he discovered something interesting. Kids who lived in a suburb where they primarily traveled by car had no idea how the streets in their community connected or where their best friend's house was in relation to their own. What Appleyard calls the "windshield perspective" prevented them from developing a sense of local geography.

Meanwhile, the children who walked or biked a lot drew much more detailed maps. They pointed out more places to play and added trees and homes. Their maps were also more correct. The kids understood how streets fit together, how this one led to the elementary school and that one led to the playground.

Yes, but kids don't drive, you say; they only navigate when they walk or bike. But the results line up with another study in the Netherlands that found that college students who walked or biked around their campus and town had a better sense of its geography than students who rode public transit. In other words, if you really want to figure out where you live, the quickest way to do that is under your own steam.

Within a few days of moving to Blacksburg, I started walking in Grissom/Highland, the neighborhood in the hills behind my rental house. Mostly I was after exercise and thirty minutes of fresh air, but as it turned out, tramping up and down the streets of split-levels and neocolonials put me at the perfect pace to pay attention to where I was.

"One's destination is never a place," said Henry Miller, "but rather a new way of looking at things." These walks were like a Zen practice in being present. I noticed the bacon-and-egg smells that wafted out of open windows and the plastic flamingos that populated a neighbor's lawn. I breathed in the evergreen that reminded me of summer camp. By clarifying how each street jigsawed into the next, my daily walks allowed me to build my mental map of Blacksburg piece by piece.

Jeff Speck, a city planner and author of *Walkable City* — a key source for this chapter — told me that the way you get around determines your relationship to your environment by determining what you see. Driving a car, you're so focused on not killing yourself or others that you only notice the big stuff, like road signs. Biking allows you to experience your place's topography and weather (*Hills! And it's raining now!*), but you're still going too fast to notice minutiae. "Only walking," says Speck, "is an invitation to socialize, as well as the slowest productive pace for observing the details of the buildings, landscape, humans, and other animals around you."

The 3.5 miles per hour I manage on foot would make me tear my hair out in a car. But the slowness is the point. Walking is more than transportation; it's experience. You admire a baby in a stroller on the bike trail. You have a conversation with the guy walking his husky. Even the simplest elements of a walk can take on the quality of poetry: The warblers sing. The grass sways.

All these things combined create a sense of where we are. As the novelist Alexander

McCall Smith writes, "Regular maps [have]
few surprises: their contour lines re[veal]
where the Andes are, and are reasonably
clear. More precious, though, are the unpublished maps we make ourselves, of our
city, our place, our daily world, our life;
those maps of our private world we use
every day; here I was happy, in that place I
left my coat behind after a party, that is
where I met my love."

Each jolt of memory becomes a geoloca-
tion marker that we press into our mental
map of where we live. Little by little, we pin
ourselves into place.

STOP COMMUTING

One of the first people to tap this underground seam of interest in walking and biking was a tech entrepreneur named Matt
Lerner. A Microsoft refugee, in 2007 he
whipped up a beta version of a website
called Walk Score with fellow entrepreneur
Mike Mathieu. As a kid, Lerner says, "I just
thought that cities were either cool or not
and you didn't have much control over it."
Later he realized that the cities he thought
of as cool were all more or less walkable.
Walkability was one of the things that *made*
a place cool. But did everyone think so? He
e-mailed the link to the beta Walk Score to

fifteen friends for feedback. "The next day," he says, "we had 150,000 unique visitors on the site."

The idea behind Walk Score is pretty ingenious. Using Google Maps, Walk Score awards points to an address based on its distance from a range of businesses and amenities: schools, libraries, parks, grocery stores, restaurants, gyms, and so on. If your house is within a five-minute walk of at least one place in each of thirteen categories, it scores a perfect 100, making it "a Walker's Paradise" where you don't need a car to get around. The New York City neighborhoods of Little Italy and Chinatown pull down perfect 100s. Downtown San Francisco scores a 99. Topeka, Kansas, where Matt Lerner grew up, scores a 33 ("Car-Dependent City," in Walk Score parlance).

Walk Scores have become such a real estate phenomenon that the site now churns out about 20 million Walk Scores a day, many by way of its Walk Score Professional version, which is available on over thirty thousand real estate sites, including the two largest, Zillow and Trulia. "For my buyers," says Stephanie Somers, a Philadelphia real estate agent, "walkability is almost equal to price as the most important criterion."

My rental house in Blacksburg earns a

respectable Walk Score of 55: "Somewhat Walkable." That means that I'm 0.2 miles from Cafe Mekong, 0.4 miles from First Citizens Bank, and 0.8 miles from Dunkin' Donuts (the kind that's in the back of a gas station mini-mart, though I'm not sure Walk Score knows that). In less than ten minutes, I can grab frozen pot stickers at the international food market, macarons at Our Daily Bread bakery, or a new pair of running shoes at Blue Ridge Mountain Sports. This convenience is no accident. Every time we move, I angle to land in a walkable neighborhood, comforted to know that if the world ended, I could still mosey my way around my city, gathering socks and soap for the apocalypse.

Everyone has their own reasons for wanting walkability. As a former Brooklynite, my friend Kate wanted to normalize fresh air and self-propelled transportation for her two kids, even after the family moved to Providence, Rhode Island. "We looked at many houses that weren't really walkable to anything and nixed them," she said. "It was one of our first criteria."

Suzanne picked her neighborhood in Southern California because she wanted to be close enough to the action of downtown that she'd never need a designated driver.

"My friends and I walk everywhere on the weekends — my nail place, the grocery store, restaurants, bars. The location was my number one requirement in renting my house."

Then there was my friend Amy, who hunted for an apartment in a walkable neighborhood when her husband's four-mile commute to work was regularly taking ninety minutes in rush-hour Seattle traffic. "He was exhausted and I saw no reason to have his time be spent like that. So we broke our lease early and moved closer."

Walking seems like it makes people happier with the place they live, but does it? To figure that out, let's look at the opposite of a walkable town: a town where you're trapped behind the wheel of your car for hours every day. When two Swiss economists, Bruno Frey and Alois Stutzer, asked people, "How satisfied are you with your life?" the answer among commuters was "Not very." A one-hour drive each way to work diminished life satisfaction so drastically that commuters would have to make 40 percent more money at their jobs to be as happy as noncommuters. "For many people," Frey and Stutzer write, "commuting seems to encompass stress that does not pay off."

There's more bad news. In one study, researchers attached electrodes to the heads of volunteers and found that battling rush-hour traffic or crowded trains sent commuters' heart rates soaring and flooded their bodies with the stress hormone cortisol. Biologically, riot police facing angry mobs are less freaked out.

And the longer people spend behind the wheel every day, the more miserable they are. Measuring the results of an eighteen-year longitudinal study of British commuters, researchers found that each successive minute stuck in traffic steadily sucks the joy out of you. On the other hand, when a former car commuter switches to walking to work, his happiness levels go up as much as if he'd gotten a raise or fallen in love.

Why? I think it's the walking itself. People who walk regularly are better at creative thinking. They're more likely to volunteer and trust their neighbors. They have more energy. And it almost goes without saying that they're healthier — less likely to be overweight or obese, to struggle with diabetes or high blood pressure. The effects are so profound that Vancouver, Canada, set an ambitious goal to earn a Walk Score of at least 70 in every last one of its neighborhoods by 2025.

More than a hundred other cities are courting a culture of biking and walking by launching Open Streets initiatives. For a day or an afternoon, cities like Parkersburg, West Virginia, and Edmond, Oklahoma, close a section of city streets to car traffic. The asphalt becomes a biking, walking, and Rollerblading free-for-all. San Francisco's monthly Sunday Streets draw up to seventy-five thousand pedestrians. In other places, pop-up bike lanes, removable curb bump-outs, and other small-scale interventions aim to make biking and walking safer, at least temporarily.

People who walk a lot feel better about their lives, and one of the principles I was coming to understand about loving where you live is that feeling good in general often translates to feeling good about where you live. When you're happy, for whatever reason, you also happen to be happy in the place you live. There is a subtle difference — happy people can feel meh about their town — but there's a spillover effect, since it's easier to have a pleasant attitude about your surroundings if you're in a good mood in general.

If you're a Mover, choosing a walkable city, or a walkable neighborhood in your city, can improve your happiness in your new place and thus your chances of becoming firmly place attached. Unfortunately, a lot of us can't afford the price tag. Because three in four millennials want to live where they don't need a car to get around, neighborhoods with higher Walk Scores tend to be more desirable, and thus more expensive.

After studying tens of thousands of real estate transactions in fifteen cities, economist Joe Cortright, in a project for the nonprofit CEOs for Cities, found that houses with above-average Walk Scores commanded up to $34,000 more than homes in less-walkable neighborhoods. In Tucson, Arizona, for instance, a house with a Walk Score of 66 — in the seventy-fifth percentile for the area — fetches an average of $10,841 more than a house with a score of 51. Even a relatively moderate Walk Score of 55 jacks up real estate prices in most cities. "If we're looking to shore up value in local housing markets," says Cortright, "it appears that promoting more walkable neighborhoods is one way to do so."

That's bad news for home buyers. But if you want to love where you live, you'd be better served forgoing the granite countertops and spending your money to land in a neighborhood where you can walk or bike to most of the places you need to go. "When you look at Americans' day-to-day activity," says Dan Buettner, author of *Thrive: Finding Happiness the Blue Zones Way,* "the top two things we hate the most on a day-to-day basis [are], number one, housework, and number two, the daily commute in our cars. . . . [So] it's an easy way for us to get happier: Move closer to your place of work."

Even when we do live close enough to walk, however, we don't always do it. Sometimes we need a little nudge.

MAKE YOUR TOWN WALKABLE

The historic Boylan Heights neighborhood of Raleigh, North Carolina, curls like a cat in the center of the city. Only a few railroad tracks separate its leafy streets of bungalows from a menacing warehouse district and the 752 felons of Raleigh's Central Prison. Now Matt Tomasulo wanted me to cross those tracks.

We were heading from his coworking space, an old warehouse with Japanese lanterns fluttering from the ceiling and a sound system piping in the Avett Brothers (Walk Score: 79), to downtown Raleigh. The route should have taken us over the Boylan Street overpass bridge. But Matt asked, "How would you feel about taking a secret path?" and we left the roadway. Fording some tall grass, we eventually dead-ended in a thick bed of gravel. Two sets of train tracks floated there like noodles on broth. Matt forged ahead.

"Are these tracks still in use?" I asked nervously.

"Oh yeah," Matt replied.

No worries, though. His shortcut had been rubber-stamped by no less than the former mayor of Raleigh himself, Charles Meeker, who lives in Boylan Heights. "One day I saw him walking down here in his suit," Matt said. "He's a lawyer downtown. He told me he'd been taking this path every day for years." Besides, this route shaves six minutes off Matt's daily walking commute. He's not going to abandon it over a minor concern like safety.

I was walking with Matt, a thirty-two-year-old who wears Hawaiian shirts ironically, because he was an unexpected rising star in placemaking, known for creating a project that, simply and cheaply, helps cities get their residents to walk more. That is a bigger deal than you'd think. After all, telling you to move to a more walkable town is cold comfort if you've already parked your minivan in suburbia. Even urban environments aren't always truly walkable. As Fred Kent, founder of the Project for Public

Spaces, often says, "If you plan cities for cars and traffic, you get cars and traffic. If you plan for people and places, you get people and places." Heavy-duty urban design is required to engineer the mixed-use streetscapes, sidewalks, crosswalks, tree cover, and public spaces that provide *Walkable City* author Jeff Speck's four great pillars of walkability:

Walks must be useful.
Walks must be safe.
Walks must be comfortable.
Walks must be interesting.

Some of Walk Score's heavy hitters, like New York, seem to have stumbled into the magic combination by happy accident (although even New York has made efforts in recent years to increase its walkability and bikeability). In cities that missed the boat, efforts to change things after the fact have often been misguided.

In 1977, Raleigh closed downtown Fayetteville Street to cars and converted it into a pedestrian mall, but instead of attracting the expected foot traffic, the retail businesses along Fayetteville slowly asphyxiated for lack of customers. Like 89 percent of pedestrian malls, it eventually failed. When the city reopened Fayetteville Street to automobiles in 2006, it did so with a multimillion-dollar plan to change the street in some of the ways Jeff Speck recommends, by making Fayetteville feel populated and lively at least eighteen hours a day.

When Matt Tomasulo moved to Raleigh in 2007 for graduate school in landscape architecture at North Carolina State University, what shocked him was how few people walked. Right away he loved the city, but his friends kept decamping for Brooklyn or San Francisco. What did those places have that Raleigh didn't? The answer he kept returning to: feet on the street.

He had spent a semester abroad in Copenhagen and seen how walkers and cyclists enlivened the city. If Raleigh could convince people who worked downtown to live there, eat there, and hang out there, Matt figured, shops and restaurants would thrive and multiply. The domino effect might not make Raleigh the new Brooklyn, but it could help the city create its own southern version of the "ballet of the good city sidewalk" that urban activist Jane Jacobs wrote about in *The Death and Life of Great American Cities.* In Matt's mind, change hinged on getting people to walk.

At his downtown apartment building,

Matt started asking his neighbors if they ever walked to the supermarket to pick up a gallon of milk or a jar of peanut butter. "No way," they scoffed. "It's too far."

It wasn't really. It was just a half mile. Matt had timed the walk himself and it took only twelve minutes. The problem, he guessed, was less the actual distance than the *idea* of the distance. In a city like New York, going ten blocks on foot from Grand Central to Rockefeller Center is a fact of life. In Raleigh, a ten-block walk was a nonstarter. "It was a perception thing," Matt told me. "I was like, what if we try to shift that perception? You say to someone, 'Would you walk a half mile?' they say no. But if you say, 'Would you walk for ten minutes?' they say yes."

But how to do that? Thinking about it, Matt remembered reading about a project called PARK(ing) Day. One afternoon in 2005, a few designers from the San Francisco design studio Rebar dropped their coins into a parking meter on Mission Street in the city's South of Market district. They rolled sod into the six-by-twenty-foot streetside space, set out a bench and a potted tree, and called it a park. People lay on the grass. Some sat on the bench to read the *San Francisco Chronicle*. Two hours later, when the meter expired, they rolled it all up and left.

At the time, 70 percent of San Francisco's outdoor space downtown was devoted to parking. In a slightly wacky way, PARK(ing) Day drew attention to the need for more spaces for humans. Within a few years, the City of San Francisco worked with Rebar to develop a permit process for permanently converting a parking space into a miniature public plaza. There are now more than thirty such parklets in San Francisco and dozens more around the world. PARK(ing) Day itself is re-created each year on the third Friday in September. In 2011, the last year the creators gathered participation data, 975 parking spaces in 162 cities across the world were turned into parks for a day — or until the meters expired.

Matt had never heard of "tactical urbanism," a term coined for the kind of small-scale, fly-by-night projects that average citizens like the Rebar designers were implementing to make their cities more livable. But he was fascinated by "this idea of a temporary, DIY thing that was transitioning into policy." Before long he had his own idea for an urban intervention that would, if all went well, make people realize how easy it was to walk around Raleigh.

After dark fell on a cold January night in 2012, Matt and a few friends approached the intersection of Wilmington and Hargett in downtown Raleigh, dressed in black like ninjas. Working fast, they pulled corrugated cardboard signs from the back of a buddy's van and lashed them to streetlamps and traffic signal poles with plastic zip ties.

Matt's tactical urbanism project was a set of twenty-seven way-finding signs with messages such as "It's a 16 Minute Walk to Seaboard Station," "It's a 9 Minute Walk to the NC Belltower," or "It's 17 Minutes by Foot to Oakwood Cemetery." Each featured an arrow pointing the correct way and a QR code that a passerby could scan for step-by-step directions. Matt called the project "Walk Raleigh."

He'd designed the signs on his laptop over Christmas break, then paid $300 to have them printed professionally. However, he'd gone through precisely zero official channels. Without permits, this was, technically speaking, illegal. So when a police officer approached as Matt hung a sign, he froze.

"What's that?" the cop asked.

Heart thumping, Matt mustered a breezy reply. "Oh, they're just directional signs for people."

The cop leaned in for a long, slow look.

"Okay," he said at last and wandered off.

For weeks after that, no one seemed to even notice Walk Raleigh. Then, in February, a local pointed the project out to the *Atlantic Cities* blog. Soon the BBC, *Scientific American, Sierra* magazine, and the *Huffington Post* all ran enthusiastic stories that had the unintended consequence of tipping the City of Raleigh off to the signs' presence. In the grand tradition of responsive local governments, city employees took the signs down. Matt collected 1,255 signatures on a digital petition. The signs went back up. Ultimately, the city council voted to turn Walk Raleigh into "an educational pilot program for the city." The signs stayed.

On the Thursday evening Matt and I took our shortcut through the Warehouse District, downtown Raleigh thrummed with the noise and energy of people blowing off steam after work. Because not many people scanned the QR codes, it was hard to get a sense of how many pedestrians actually read the signs, let alone responded to them. (Matt's experimenting with sensors and other ways to measure traffic.) The Walk Raleigh signs themselves were long gone, dissolved by weather and the high-fives of drunks, who, according to Matt, are inexplicably drawn to hitting them. But their echoes seemed to remain. "This area used to be a ghost town," Matt said.

Now, we passed a popular Laotian restaurant and an Irish bar with outdoor seating. Across the street, kids ran the mandala paths of Moore Park while their parents waited out the heat under the trees. We'd walked a mile but the streets were so full of things to see — our walk so useful, comfortable, interesting, and, apart from the train tracks, safe — that I'd barely noticed.

Waiting to cross the intersection by the Morning Times, a coffee house whose café tables were spread with mugs and laptops, I asked Matt my million-dollar question: "Does walking make people feel more attached to their towns?"

He replied without hesitation. "Absolutely. I think that it helps people discover the character of where they live and why they like it. Otherwise it's a faceless kind of experience. You don't come into contact with anybody. Even having the comfort of being social and being around other people is so healthy. It's fun to walk down the street and say hi to people." As if to demonstrate, Matt greeted several friends on the sidewalk as we headed back to Boylan Heights.

Not every place can be downtown Raleigh, let alone downtown Brooklyn. What if you live in a place where walking is weird or where there aren't well-marked sidewalks? Matt was bullish. Walk anyway, he said. "It might not be enjoyable yet, but when people see you walking, they say, 'Hey, I can walk here. That's a thing.'"

ARRANGE AN URBAN INTERVENTION

When Walk Raleigh took off, Matt launched a Kickstarter campaign for a project that would let anyone, anywhere, create custom-ized way-finding signs for where they live. On WalkYourCity.org, all you had to do was type in what you wanted the signs to say and pay $25 each to have them printed and sent to you. Three thousand Walk [Your City] signs have now been hung on every continent but Antarctica, each speaking of a rich local culture ripe for exploration. In Hyderabad, India: "It is a 17 minute walk to Moazam Jahi." In Buenos Aires: "Son 10 minutos caminando al jardín botánico."

Raleigh's official way-finding signs, which were only three years old when Matt de-buted Walk Raleigh, cost $1.3 million. A set of forty Walk Raleigh signs costs around $1,000, so downtown development corpora-tions and arts organizations use the signs as a cheap way to drum up foot traffic. When Mount Hope, West Virginia (population

1,500), hired Matt to tack up seventy customized way-finding signs, it was like the circus had come to town. They had never seen so many people out walking.

Walking was the best way I knew to ease into a city. Wasn't encouraging other people to walk the next step? Because Blacksburg was a college town, people walked here more than most. Virginia Tech students drummed a constant rhythm of home–campus, campus–home. On fall weekends when the football team played, the downtown sidewalks flooded with foot traffic. Some of the neighborhoods close to campus, like Miller Southside, earned hefty Walk Scores (80: "Very walkable!").

So deciding that Matt Tomasulo's Walk [Your City] signs were tailor-made for my first Love Where You Live experiment wasn't a matter of admonishing Blacksburgians (though the tussle for on-street parking spots proved that most of us didn't walk as much as we could). Mostly I wanted to try out placemaking, and Matt's online sign templates made transforming my town for the better idiotproof. Then Matt started throwing around phrases like "mapping city assets" and "creating campaign nodes," and I started to wonder.

Before you can make signs at WalkYour

City.org, you have to identify where people are likely to start walking — an origin — and where you want them to go, a destination like a museum or a park. Origins and destinations have to be matched up. Sign locations must be plotted onto a map of city streets. You have to figure out which way the arrows on the signs will point. It seemed . . . complicated.

Worse, Matt told me I should collaborate with other people. Official people. For his original Walk Raleigh experiment, he'd gone renegade (and escaped police interference by the skin of his teeth). Now, he said, "I really recommend that you work with the city government and get some buy-in."

What? No! I knew exactly zero city officials who could run Walk [Your City] up the flagpole for me. A public meeting would mire the whole idea in bureaucracy. Anyway, what about the "guerrilla" aspect of Matt's system of "guerrilla way-finding"? *Forget what other people want,* I thought. *I'm going to do this myself.*

Filled with righteous resistance, I logged onto WalkYourCity.org and clicked "Make a Sign." An hour later, I'd charged $125 to my credit card. My five signs were slated for delivery within a week.

When the cardboard box came, however,

I couldn't bring myself to open it. I mean, it was easy to be all "I'm fighting the man" when I was just staring at my computer in my house. But what if a cop came by when I was putting them up and my explanations didn't seem as legit as Matt's did? To help me move past my mounting sense of dread, I recruited help from Laura, a fellow mom and writer I'd met working the cash registers at the elementary school book fair. She wrote restaurant reviews. Logical conclusion: She was not averse to pissing people off.

We started early on a Thursday morning at the northern terminus of the Huckleberry Trail, a six-mile rails-to-trails pathway through Blacksburg. I held an "It Is a 6 Minute Walk to Farm-Fresh Fruits and Veggies" sign whose QR code map directed pedestrians to the farmers' market at Market Square Park. Laura strained to zip-tie it to a post. Then, out of the corner of my eye, I saw a man in neon yellow gliding toward us on his bike. *Bike cop!* I thought. *We're busted!* As fear adrenaline started spiking through my body, the cyclist slow-mo tumbled to the side. "Man, I can't get the hang of these clips," he groused. A few seconds later, his buddies joined him, and they sped off for a morning bike ride.

My nervous giggling took on a hysterical edge.

Laura and I walked the neat grid system of downtown streets and furtively attached the four remaining signs at the proper street corners. Only a handful of college students were on the sidewalks, too absorbed in their smartphones to notice us, let alone inquire after the state of our city permits. Near the crosswalk by Souvlaki, the Greek greasy spoon, we lashed the "It Is a 15 Minute Walk to a Nice Bench by the Duck Pond" sign. "It Is a 9 Minute Walk to a Great Public Library" went by the streetlamp near College and Main. The other two signs pointed to the nonprofit SEEDS Nature Center and a Civil War–era cemetery, tourist attractions that are enough off the beaten path that I sometimes forget they exist.

As we finished putting up the last one, I said, "Well, we didn't get arrested," in what I hoped was a voice of triumph. Yet all afternoon I braced myself — for what, I wasn't sure. An official city reprimand? I heard nothing at all until Ella came home from walking to the frozen yogurt shop with some friends after school. "Mom, we totally saw your sign," she exclaimed, "the one by the Huckleberry Trail! I was like, 'Hey, my mom put that sign up,' but no one believed me." I realized, with relief, that even if people wanted to complain, it would be tough to trace the Walk [Your City] signs to me. I was used to being anonymous in my town. Placemaking called a bit too much attention for comfort.

Still, every few days I skulked, stalkerlike, to check on them. The signs were my $125 investment in Blacksburg. I was worried that they'd be noticed and torn down, and equally worried that they wouldn't be noticed at all. After a week, the latter seemed more likely. Over lunch with Quinn at Souvlaki, I pointed at the duck pond sign and said, "I have no idea if anyone's even looked at it."

"Well, you should take pictures of all of your signs," he suggested, "before they come down."

Coming down would be, I knew, the inevitable conclusion to all this. Even under the best of circumstances, Walk [Your City] signs are meant to be a temporary urban intervention, not a permanent addition to the landscape. Since it was a warm day, maybe one of the last of the season, after lunch I began walking through downtown, snapping photos of the signs on my iPhone until I reached the one that said "It's a 10 Minute Walk to a Civil War–Era Cemetery."

Including Westview Cemetery in the mix of walking destinations was mostly about assuaging my vague sense of guilt that we had a Civil War–era anything in town — a miracle for a California girl! — and that I had never once stopped to see it. Confession: I still hadn't stopped, even after Laura and I had zip-tied the sign for it on a lamppost across from a fancy nail salon. I liked the *idea* of a historic cemetery. It just wasn't someplace I would normally visit. For fun. You know.

Looking at the sign now, it hit me: If I couldn't be bothered to follow my own Walk [Your City] directions, how could I expect that anyone else would?

Right that minute I rerouted myself up Roanoke Street. On foot, it took me nine minutes and thirty-eight seconds to reach Westview Cemetery, where I was the only visitor other than the man mowing the grass. The air smelled loamy; the oak trees burned in brilliant autumn colors. Inside the gates, everything felt hushed and reverent.

Cemeteries can tell you a considerable amount about the city where you live. Here, a marble obelisk dedicated "To the memory of the Confederate Dead of Blacksburg and Vicinity, 1861–1865" reminded me that my town, founded in 1798, was solidly gray during the Civil War. Maybe parts of it still were. The hump of earth under the memorial had been worn bald by pilgrimages.

Among the gravestones eroded by wetness and weather, I made out birthplaces in West Virginia and England. Like every town in America, Blacksburg's origin story includes a motley cast of outsiders — primarily immigrants from Scotland, Ireland, England, and Germany, intent on pushing the boundaries of civilization steadily south and west. In 1850, when the town had 330 residents, was anyone worried about liking where they lived? Or was sleeping under a warm roof and not starving enough?

Even in circumstances where survival is the best that can be hoped for, the idea of home exerts a pull. One of the area's most famous historical figures is Mary Draper Ingles, a settler who was taken captive in 1755 by Shawnee warriors. Two and a half months later she escaped. The eight hundred miles of wilderness that separated her from her home couldn't keep her from making the journey, alone and on foot. Walking was her only option.

Not long after that day at the cemetery, my Love Where You Live experiment began to unravel. Matt Tomasulo had warned me that the Walk [Your City] signs had a naturally limited life span — they were printed on cardboard, after all — but mine appeared to be mostly accident victims. The sign by Souvlaki was karate-chopped in half, presumably by a drunken college student. A couple more mysteriously disappeared. The director of the nature center tracked my e-mail address down through Matt to let me know that my sign had pointed someone in exactly the wrong direction. I explained that the zip ties must have come loose, allowing the sign to twist on the pole, but he seemed unconvinced. "I'm just curious," he responded. "Did you have town permission to put up those signs? I don't think anyone has complained, but I would think that some kind of permission would be needed."

I'll never know for certain if my Walk Blacksburg signs inspired anyone to walk more or to discover the sites I flagged. But in the days and weeks that followed, my perspective on Blacksburg was changed. I kept thinking about the day I walked up Roanoke Street toward the cemetery. On foot, going slow, I saw its details. Attic windows made of old-fashioned wavy glass. Gold stone lions keeping vigil outside the Sigma Alpha Epsilon house. I entered a narrow alleyway I'd never seen before, which revealed, *Secret Garden* style, a tiny church across from a minuscule park.

As many times as I'd driven on Roanoke Street, I'd never noticed the alley, the church, or the park, let alone the wavy glass or the gold stone lions. Had I stayed in my car, I probably never would have.

There's something about being on foot or on a bike that makes us explorers of where we live. Walking and biking in Blacksburg, I developed an intimacy with the town that made me find the hidden gems and appreciate where I was. I suspect that anyone, in any town, could have the same experience. Like Lewis and Clark, we plunge into the undiscovered country, and in so doing, we master it. One bike shop owner told me that, for him, cycling through an area effectively made it his. Sure, he could drive through a town, figure out how to get around. But once he'd ridden the streets on his bicycle, he owned the place.

LOVE YOUR CITY CHECKLIST

☐ Follow the "1-Mile Solution": On a map, draw a circle with a one-mile radius around your home. Figure out which tasks you can complete inside the circle (the grocery run? school pickup?), and try to replace one car trip per week by biking or walking instead. Eventually you can work up to walking or biking all your errands under a mile.

☐ Explore unfamiliar parts of your town without a GPS. Wandering, then finding your way back to where you started helps you establish and maintain strong mental maps.

☐ Draw a map of your part of town. How many details can you fill in? Houses? Trees? Store names? Dogs? Flower beds? If your map isn't very detailed, take a nice, slow walk with your eyes wide open, then try again.

☐ Sign up for a local walking tour — of a historic district or a neighborhood, a park, or restaurant row. (Google "walking tour" and the name of your town to find one.) If it goes well, consider leading a walk yourself as a stellar way to get attached to your town. Jane's Walk offers free, citizen-led walking tours in cities across the country; see JanesWalk.org.

☐ If possible, switch to a walking or biking commute. Virtually nothing else you do will make you happier, and the effects will trickle down to how you feel about where you live.

☐ If you're moving soon, aim for a neighborhood with a high Walk Score.

☐ Make your own Walk [Your City] signs at WalkYourCity.org. Maybe ask for permission first.

CHAPTER THREE:
BUY LOCAL

In 2008, just as the recession was steam-rolling the economy, the portion of Americans who moved dropped half a percentage point, to 11.6 percent of the population. That's not terribly surprising. Both the housing market and the job market had gone haywire. Hunkering down seemed like the sane thing to do.

But mobility was at an all-time low for the country, and it had economists panicked, for two reasons. First, it suggested that Americans weren't willing or able to move around after job opportunities. Second, reported the *New York Times*, "The lack of movement itself . . . could have an impact on the economy, reducing the economic activity generated by moves."

What keeps our economy humming? All those U-Haul trucks fanning out across the country! All the homes bought and sold! All the bottles of ketchup and jars of mayo that must be tossed and then repurchased in the next city! Moving itself stimulates the national GDP because it involves so much buying and spending. Simply hiring people to box and haul your belongings can be incredibly expensive; in 2010, the average professional household move cost $12,230. Then there are the costs of kitting out a new residence. The vacant rooms need furnishing. The empty fridge demands filling.

Each time I moved, I headed to Target. Over the years and through all my place doovers, the store had become an old friend, not least because its rows of lightbulbs and laundry detergent were nearly identical in Maryland, Utah, Iowa, Texas, and Virginia. I didn't have to create a mental map from scratch! I already had one in place, guiding me like a cruise missile through the aisles as I speed-shopped for sponges and dryer sheets. No matter where in the country I was, the entire experience stayed uniform, down to the endorphin rush I got from scouting clearance stickers on the store's well-groomed end caps.

Such soothing consistency is the genius of the big-box store. When my friend Erika told me she was moving to a small town in Wisconsin, my first question was "Is there a

Target?" Yes, of course there was, she told me. I should have known, because (a) there aren't many towns left in America without a Target within thirty miles and (b) Erika would never move to one of those towns. "As long as I have a Target," she said, "everything will be okay."

Even fewer Americans, if any, are beyond the geographical reach of Amazon and the online shopping behemoth's near-mythical abundance of stuff. As I moved from town to town, I'd come to rely on Amazon as a no-hassle source of anything from books to baking pans, DVDs to Dansko sandals. Amazon required no parking lot battles. It never tried to engage me with chirpy salesperson chatter or flashed me a look of naked disappointment when I returned the shoes that didn't fit.

Online shopping worked so well for me because I was simultaneously lazy and pressed for time, and the Internet was always where I was, which was (usually) on my couch. Despite having happily walked my way around Blacksburg for my first Love Where You Live experiment, staying indoors and alone still seemed a preferable state of affairs some days. How fantastic that I could, with one click, buy almost anything I wanted, without leaving my house or having human contact of any kind.

The more I looked into the sources and nature of place attachment, however, the more I knew that I, and Amazon/Target devotees like me, were pretty much responsible for the downfall of Main Street America. My shopping habits might be killing both my new hometown and my prospects of connecting with it, and that had me worried.

One hundred years ago, you bought most of what you needed from a store in your community that was owned and operated by someone who lived there. Prescriptions came from the corner drugstore, whose pharmacist knew your kids and your ailments by name. Books were purchased from a local bookseller, who recommended a few new novels you'd like. With Main Street acting as both substitute town hall and open-air living room, you could chat with your neighbors, debate the problems of the day, and still cross milk and socks off your shopping list. Perhaps there are towns where this kind of close-knit shopping still occurs.

But as early as 1914 the chain store — one store with multiple locations — was taking over. Five-and-dime chains like Woolworth's and Ben Franklin could be found on hundreds of small-town street corners, and the Sears, Roebuck catalog — the Amazon of its day — sat in every living room. Small-town shopkeepers wrung their hands, and an anti-chain backlash began in earnest in the 1920s, when the *Nation* and the *New Republic* magazines ran stories called "Chains Versus Independents" and "Chain Stores: Menace or Promise?" In 1929, Indiana enacted the first anti-chain tax law upheld by the U.S. Supreme Court. Trying to galvanize small-town residents to save local retail, bombastic radio personality W. K. Henderson recruited twenty-five thousand "Merchants' Minute Men," promising "we can drive [chains] out in thirty days if you people will stay out of their stores."

For a while after World War II, inexpensive goods and pent-up demand allowed both the local stores and the large chains to prosper. It was the advent of malls and big-box stores in the 1950s and '60s, with their convenient, climate-controlled shopping, that made cheap toasters seem more valuable than the neighborly chatter that customers could get in independent stores. Once-thriving Main Streets across America slowly withered. Now, in half of America's zip codes, 80 percent of the available retail options are national chains like Walmart,

Dollar General, Target, Family Dollar, Kmart, JCPenney, and Sears. Downtown, boarded-up storefronts and empty streets are the battle scars from sparring matches with bigger, beefier competitors.

Financially, having a discount store on the corner instead of a locally owned drugstore seems like a win for local shoppers. (Hair gel and oven mitts for a buck? Hooray!) At best, low-price chain stores offer a short-term victory. One study suggests that for every new job a Walmart creates in a town, it eliminates 1.4 jobs locally as others stores are driven out of business, and it drives down wages citywide. The new retail that once seemed like a boon for a small town can eventually erode a community's tax base and drive its Main Street business district into ruin.

A dollar spent at Dollar General is not the same as a dollar spent at a locally owned variety store. In a study of businesses in Salt Lake City, researchers found that big-box retailers like Barnes & Noble, Home Depot, Office Max, and Target returned just 14 percent of their revenue to the local economy, while the rest filtered into faraway corporate coffers. Contrast that percentage with independent stores like the King's English Bookshop, Guthrie Bicycle, and the locally owned Harmon's grocery store chain, where 52 percent of revenue continued to circulate locally. If you spent $25 at a local Salt Lake City retailer, $14 of it stayed in Salt Lake. At a big chain, only $3.50 did.

Economists call this the "local multiplier effect," and the most obvious reason for it is that the people making money from an independent business aren't out-of-state megacorporations but entrepreneurs who live (and spend and pay taxes) in the same communities where they work. If you own a local store, you usually employ more people locally than a comparable chain would, because everyone works in town, not at headquarters — so a neighbor who's a CPA does the books, not the accounting department in Omaha. At an independent restaurant like Salt Lake's Red Iguana, about $28 of the $100 you might spend on dinner is paid out in wages to employees who live nearby. At chains, it's $19, about a third less.

Plus, people who own community businesses often reciprocally support other local business owners. They stock the bookshop with cards drawn by local artists. They source the pork loin for the restaurant from a nearby farmer. A town where locally owned shops and restaurants are doing well generally has a thriving job market, not just in retail, but overall.

The local multiplier effect is so substantial that the researchers in Salt Lake made a remarkable prediction: If residents started to make 10 percent more of their purchases at locally owned restaurants and shops instead of national chains, the city would be awash in an extra $500 million in revenue. "A dollar spent in a local business means a huge amount to all of us in economic terms," said Betsy Burton, who co-owns Salt Lake City's thirty-seven-year-old King's English Bookshop.

All the research adds up to this: Shopping locally is a concrete way to help your town thrive economically and to improve your own quality of life where you live. You start buying stuff in your town, particularly from small independent stores owned by people who live there, and all of a sudden more local people have jobs. So the city collects more taxes. Then the schools have more money for improvements. The streets get repaved, the parks department builds a new baseball diamond, and so on. With millions of dollars at stake, you'd think we'd all jump on board.

I know firsthand that the local multiplier

effect can be too abstract to make the shift to buying local easy. So does a man named Jeff Milchen, who in 1997 was warily watching the influx of big-box stores in Boulder, Colorado. "I really was just a concerned citizen," says Milchen, then a teacher. "I wasn't operating a business at the time. But I was seeing the loss of independent businesses and weakened downtowns and wanted to figure out something we could do differently in Boulder to prevent that from happening." To pool the marketing dollars and know-how of local shopkeepers and spread the word about the benefits of buying local, he created the Boulder Independent Business Alliance. The group was so successful that a few years later, Milchen founded the American Independent Business Alliance, a national umbrella organization that helps over eighty local IBAs do for their towns what Milchen did in Boulder.

Milchen is good at convincing people that buying local is smart. When I asked him why I should, he told me that, for starters, the products are often better quality, and the customer service virtually always is. Shopping where you live creates a smaller carbon footprint; it's better for the environment when you and your stuff don't travel as far. A locally based economy is more secure and resilient, less affected by global trade issues or terrorism. One study by a team of Penn State University researchers found that a high density of locally owned small businesses correlates with a higher regional GDP.

Importantly for place attachment, it's also more social. At a Gap in the mall, "the chances that the person you're walking past in that store is someone you recognize are fairly low," Milchen told me, because malls and big-box stores usually serve a broader regional clientele. "But if you're patronizing neighborhood businesses, a lot of those people are likely to live near you. You're likely to become familiar with them by face if not by name, and that's part of what builds a feeling of connection in a community, a feeling of trust and cohesiveness. Those casual conversations you have with folks that may not be your close friends are a key part of what creates community fabric."

National chains and big-box stores are cheap, quick, and comforting — the retail equivalent of a fast-food cheeseburger — and their spread has turned much of America into a string of bland Anyplaces. From sea to shining sea, generic strip malls and shopping plazas jammed with big-box stores ensure that Denver is no different from Dallas is no different from Delray Beach. On family vacations when I was a kid, my mom always made a point of checking out the nearest mall. It took me a few years, but eventually I realized that no matter what city we were in, malls were 95 percent identical. Drifting between Sears, Claire's, and Charlotte Russe, we could have been anywhere. How can you fall in love with a city if it's no different from the last five you've been in?

Districts of local, independent stores — Melrose Avenue in Los Angeles, the Pearl District in Portland, the West Village in New York — use architecture, streetscapes, and storefronts to give a town its distinct character. You could be kidnapped, blindfolded, and thrown in the trunk of a car, but if they let you out in San Diego's Gaslamp Quarter, you'd figure out where you were in short order. (Good luck, on the other hand, if you land in a Target parking lot.) Cities that support local businesses have stronger personalities, and it's easier to become attached to our city when we know exactly who and what it is.

Preserving quirky independent businesses in the face of the chainification of America is tricky, even for cities that understand how vital they are. The blog *Jeremiah's Vanishing New York* is the obituary page for independent businesses in New York City, and it has chronicled the closure of hundreds of pizza joints, greasy spoons, bakeries, bars, laundromats, shoe repair shops, and record stores. Gone the way of the dodo is the Hair Box barbershop, whose Soho storefront — home to various incarnations of barbershops for a hundred years — is now a frozen yogurt shop. Shakespeare & Co. Bookstore, near NYU, suffered "death by massive rent hike" in 2014. It's now a Foot Locker. That same year, an average of 491 small businesses closed each month in New York City.

Thus the cookie crumbles for businesses that can't compete, one might sniff. But what happens to a city's sense of place when we allow gentrification, rising rents, or shifting values to drive out local businesses? When even a city as famously iconoclastic as New York becomes awash in Paylesses and Family Dollars? As one anonymous commenter wrote on the *Vanishing New York* blog, "Doesn't NYC know that if you take the essence of NYC out of NYC, people won't want to go there anymore?"

In cities where the dying-off of small businesses has reached pandemic levels, large-scale solutions are required. Advocacy groups in New York are lobbying for the Small Business Jobs Survival Act, which would require landlords to negotiate with current tenants before imposing outrageous rent hikes or refusing to renew a lease. Others are suggesting new zoning — a cultural heritage district, say — that could prevent an influx of chains in certain parts of the city. As Jeremiah Moss, the creator of *Vanishing New York,* points out, "Clearly, we need strong protections for the city's small businesses."

Sometimes the enemy is us. The many benefits of buying local have to compete with Americans' overriding preference for cheap, convenient, abundant stuff — exactly what the big chains excel at. Asking people to buy a fly swatter at a locally owned variety store, where it probably costs a couple bucks more than at Lowe's, is like asking them to sacrifice their fundamental human need for a wicked bargain. We demand Bluelight Specials, even if it kills us, or, more to the point, our hometown.

Soulless Amazon addicts and big-box regulars like me need a reprogramming of sorts. We have to be trained to believe that supporting local business is altruistic, ethical, seriously cool — and worth it. That's the goal of a spreading movement of creative

"Buy Local" (or "Live Local") marketing campaigns, some modeled on the ones Jeff Milchen, of the American Independent Business Alliance, introduced in Boulder in 1997.

In Florida, for instance, the nonprofit group Keep Saint Petersburg Local debuted "The Shop Dogs of St. Pete," a fund-raising pinup calendar featuring the likes of a shih tzu–poodle mix named Oscar (Mr. October), whose owner runs the Strands of Sunshine jewelry shop. In the Mission District of San Francisco, $20 buys a Live Local card and accompanying iPhone app that offer discounts at independent businesses like Dynamo Donut (home of a raved-about maple-glazed apple bacon donut). At the nine-hour street party that the Grand Rapids, Michigan, Local First group throws each spring, ten thousand attendees rock out to indie bands and nurse bottles of locally brewed Dirty Bastard beer. Rather than just lament the fall of independent businesses in New York City, Jeremiah Moss started pushing the #SaveNYC hashtag and encouraging supporters to upload videos lauding their favorite endangered retailers.

Efforts like these have had measurable effects. In 2012, independent businesses in communities with a Buy Local campaign saw average revenue grow by 8.6 percent, compared to 3.4 percent elsewhere. Three out of four small-business owners in those places agreed that the campaign boosted their business.

That happens in a couple ways. First, the discount cards and calendars spell out to residents who've never looked past the Bed Bath & Beyond mailer that local options exist, right where they live. Your town does indeed have a locally owned hardware store, jewelry shop, and fifty-year-old stationery store, and they're all much better options than Amazon. Even in cities without a walkable, retail-lined downtown, small-scale entrepreneurs are usually alive and well in the old-school yellow pages. Just look under Plumber, Dry Cleaner, House Painter, and Hair Salon.

Second, Live Local campaigns slowly move the needle on a town's culture by inculcating the idea that our shopping habits are largely responsible for creating the place we live. "It begins with getting people to recognize that every time they spend a dollar, they're in some form casting a vote for the kind of community they want to see," says Jeff Milchen. "Creating that kind of shift in individual thinking and in community culture takes time. It's not going to happen overnight. It takes sustained effort and it takes grassroots engagement."

I could see the effects of that long-term cultural shift in Austin, where even the airport sports homegrown favorites like Amy's Ice Creams and Ruta Maya Coffee, and prizing local businesses feels as much a part of the city's bespoke quirkiness as its "Keep Austin Weird" bumper stickers. The Austin Independent Business Alliance, a collective of hundreds of local business owners, lobbies city council to make property more affordable for small-business owners. Residents self-identify as people who care about indies.

The feeling was contagious. When we lived there, Quinn and I regularly bypassed a Barnes & Noble or two to get to BookPeople, the two-story independent bookstore downtown whose honeyed shelves and high ceilings made me want to sink into a tattered armchair and never come out. The store hosted souped-up author readings and story times. In 2011, when Rick Riordan released one of his megabestselling mythology-themed Percy Jackson novels, BookPeople transformed its asphalt parking lot into an ancient Roman streetscape. The arena for faux sword fights and the quarter-scale rotunda guarded by men in breast-plates made Ella and Ruby giddy with literary enchantment. This was what a bookstore was meant to be. It's hard to imagine a chain bookstore pulling out all the stops like that.

Strong indie businesses like BookPeople funnel money back into the city in a feedback loop of spending and earning that keeps the economy vibrant. But I didn't go there because of the local multiplier effect. I went because I loved BookPeople and because BookPeople made me like living in Austin.

Here's my shameful confession: For all my admiration, I didn't always buy my books at BookPeople. Sometimes I made mental notes of titles to check out later from the library. (I know, I know.) Showrooming, which is when shoppers browse in brick-and-mortar stores then buy the same item cheaper online? I may have been guilty of that once or twice, too. The pull of my frugality was too powerful to overcome.

The first step in any long-term recovery is recognizing you have a problem. I now had a new Love Where You Live experiment: wean myself off Target and Amazon and start spreading more of my cash around Blacksburg. It was time for a big-box detox.

Among the fifteen people waiting for the cash mob to start, I was the only one who came alone. Everyone else clustered on the sun-warmed sidewalk in downtown Blacksburg in twos and threes: a few well-heeled older couples in Lands' End jackets; a husband and wife gripping a stroller; a toddler in a pink tutu, her parents trailing after her like streamers. Someone started passing around a stack of free "Buy/Eat/Live Local Blacksburg" bumper stickers. The man next to me pressed them into my hands without taking one, explaining, "I have a few of these already." I suspect that in the Venn diagram of people with "Live Local" bumper stickers and people who participate in cash mobs, there is some significant overlap.

Cash mobs are the brainchild of Andrew Samtoy, who, as a thirty-three-year-old lawyer in Cleveland, was meeting with a group of community leaders in 2011 when the discussion turned to flash mobs — not the surprise-dance-routine-in-a-public-place kind, but the ugly ones where 150 teenagers converge at a store simultaneously and loot it en masse. "What would happen," Andrew wondered, "if someone organized the opposite kind of flash mob? Where instead of pulling things off the shelf and stealing them, you're spending money?"

"Yeah," his friend Marty said, "we could call it a cash mob."

Excellent name in place, that November, Andrew and his friends set up the first cash mob at Cleveland's local indie bookstore, Visible Voice. With no more publicity than social media word of mouth, the event attracted forty-five people and made Visible Voice at least $900 in sales. The idea was so doable, concrete, and simple that it went viral.

Since then, hundreds of cash mobs have invaded locally owned businesses with their own kind of guerrilla economic stimulus. At a cash mob at FCA Country Store in Gillette, Wyoming, close to fifty people spent $4,600 in under an hour. In Knoxville, Tennessee, nearly eight hundred people formed lines down the block for a cash mob at Emery's 5&10, the country's oldest five-and-dime store. The idea turned into a bona fide phenomenon. By 2015, there had been a cash mob in every state and on six continents.

Downtown Blacksburg, the local business alliance, jumped on the bandwagon in early 2012. Since then, monthly downtown cash mobs here have drawn a crowd of up to fifty people, who each cheerfully submit to the following rules:

1. Spend up to $20 at a downtown store.
2. Meet three new people.
3. Have fun!!!

The three exclamation points on "Have fun!!!" appeared on all the event flyers, and when Laureen Blakemore, the director of Downtown Blacksburg, explained the rules to the gathered crowd, she did her best to insert them, drawing her words out in a singsong while the old-timers around the circle chimed in with her.

The trick to Blacksburg's cash mobs is that you commit to spend money before you know where you're spending it. The identity of the store is kept a secret until the last minute, so it's like a weird surprise party for retailers — and for customers, too. (*Surprise! You're spending $20 at John's Camera Corner!*) I waited, antsy, until Laureen finally revealed the evening's mob target. "Tonight," she said, "our cash mob is going to Greenhouse Boardshop."

It took me a second to realize that she was talking about the dark little skateboard shop sandwiched between a bar and Souvlaki, the Greek restaurant where I had put my duck pond sign for my Walk [Your City] experiment. The old people looked at one another warily. *Really? Us? There?* A few people guffawed. "Don't worry," Laureen said quickly, "they have a lot more than skateboards."

Five minutes earlier I had been pretty eager to "have fun!!!" Now, the cash mob felt disturbingly like I was at a friend's Mary Kay party, being guilted into buying blue eyeshadow because *Well, they went to all this trouble and I ate their food.* I'd mustered up the courage to throw frugality to the wind; now I was going to have to buy skating paraphernalia? Was there any chance Greenhouse would actually have something I wanted? Conversely, was it possible to slink away from a cash mob with dignity intact? Guessing no on both counts, I dutifully fell in line behind Laureen as she led the way down the street.

Inside Greenhouse, the walls were lined with skateboarding paraphernalia — helmets, wheels, Black Magic Griptape, boards with cartoony renderings of skeletons. As Laureen promised, there were also racks of knit hats and sunglasses, things that one could conceivably wear without knowing how to ollie. I fingered some $8.95 socks, then considered a T-shirt with the slogan

"Avoid Hangovers, Stay Stoned." I briefly thought about Instagramming it but wasn't sure what kind of message it would send.

I wanted to spend freely; I really did. But I was used to saying no to myself; my default mode in stores like this was "Don't touch." There was nothing here that I really needed, no household necessities to stock up on, and the things that looked cool were well out of my price range. *What am I doing here?* I wondered. *Why am I wasting my money like this?* People in the cash mob began shuffling out the door with shopping bags; I looked around and realized I was one of the last ones left to make a purchase.

In a rush, I finally settled on a (not quite) $20 Virginia Tech T-shirt and slid it across the counter to Daniel Johnson, one of two brothers who have co-owned the shop for the last twenty-five years. He swiped my credit card, dropped my shirt into a plastic bag, and said, "Thanks for coming in tonight. It's awesome what you're doing. We really appreciate it."

That moment was when it clicked for me that this store was owned by an actual human being. It sounds crazy, but most of the time I never thought about the cause-and-effect line between the money I spent and other people's lives. Shopping online divorced my buying habits from human inter-action, which made them seem like they carried no consequences. In Greenhouse, I understood what Jeff Milchen had said about how what I buy affects my local community.

A cash mob isn't just an excuse to toss money pell-mell into the gaping maw of capitalism. By introducing me to the people who have pegged their livelihoods to my city, people whose financial fortunes rise and fall along with my town's, it made me care about a local business and the people who run it. It made me want to help. Maybe Daniel Johnson was doing just fine, or maybe the cash mob made it easier for him to pay that month's electric bill. I don't really know. What I do know is that, having met Daniel Johnson, I'm 100 percent more likely to send all the skaters and fashion-forward high-schoolers I know his way.

PRACTICE NEIGHBORLY ECONOMICS

Stacy Mitchell, the codirector of the Institute for Local Self-Reliance and the author of *Big-Box Swindle: The True Cost of Mega-Retailers and the Fight for America's Independent Businesses,* tells a story about her brother's quest to buy her a book for Christmas. He placed the order on the website of

Mitchell's favorite local bookstore, Longfellow Books in Portland, Maine, and had it shipped to her at their father's house in South Carolina, where Mitchell would be spending the holidays. "So here's this order," Mitchell says. "It's coming from Maine. It's going to South Carolina. It doesn't have my name on it, except my brother asked that it be gift wrapped and the card says, 'Merry Christmas, Stacy.' "

A few minutes after he placed the online order, her brother's phone rings. The person says, "Hi, this is Stuart at Longfellow Books. Thank you for your order. I just had a question about it. Is this book for Stacy Mitchell?"

Surprised, her brother says, "Yeah, it is. She's my sister."

And Stuart says, "Well, I thought I should let you know that she's already read it."

It's hard to imagine anywhere else this exchange could occur besides an indie bookstore. "Communities that have a lot of locally owned businesses do in fact have stronger social networks," explains Mitchell, "and those social networks in turn give them an edge when it comes to solving problems and innovating." Because small businesses are, well, small, and because they're rooted in their communities, their owners and employees cultivate relationships with customers more energetically than a big-box store might. When you frequent a local business, you start to feel recognized. Someone knows you — no small thing these days.

My friend Kristy, who works at a clothing boutique in downtown Blacksburg called Fringe Benefit, describes the owner, Nancy, as an "iron vault. She remembers everything. We have customers go, 'I don't know if you remember me . . . ,' and we're normally, like, 'Yeah, we totally do.' "

Relationships like these are reciprocal; they work best if the customer pays attention to the employee, too. Kristy's a good example of how it works. She went to college here in Blacksburg and fantasized for years about moving back. By the time she and her husband did in 2012, all their college buddies had moved on. Faced with developing a brand-new social network, her approach was: *Show up to everything; talk to everyone.*

At the farmers' market and in stores, she'd chat up the sellers, saying, "I just moved here. Where should I shop? Where's a good place to eat?" She went to a few downtown cash mobs by herself, forcing herself to start conversations. When the local toy store,

Imaginations, had a summer scavenger hunt, she took her kids every single day. Soon everyone who worked there knew her name, and she knew theirs.

Some experts say that these kinds of "commercial friendships" are symptomatic of a pervasive modern loneliness. Lacking real friends, we seek social connection with shopkeepers and baristas — something that one woman I talked to described as being akin to a prison friendship, a relationship you fall into only because you have no choice. Knowing the names of your dry cleaner's kids or sharing LOLCats videos with the lady who runs the pet store feels somehow like cheating. These people have to be nice to us! They're selling something!

Except that even commercial friendships build our network of weak ties, the casual social relationships that make us feel woven into the mesh of our city's daily life. Talking to the same employee week after week at the hardware store builds a sense of familiarity and loyalty that makes you like where you live more. And it seems to happen more easily at the Fringe Benefits and Book-Peoples of the world, where local shopkeepers, less anxious to push you along the consumer conveyor belt or maintain a monolithic corporate facade, look you in the eye and remember you. Small, locally owned businesses feel friendlier. Generally they contribute more to their communities. They're worth preserving, most effectively by spending money at them.

Not long after he moved to Wilmore, Kentucky, a thirty-five-year-old named Jay Leeson went to buy groceries at the local grocery store, Fitch's IGA. He hated how dingy the market looked — the worn concrete floors, the dusty shelves, and the too-bright lighting showing every bit of the place's fifty-five years — but it was the only grocery store in the town of 3,700. That day, Leonard Fitch, the seventy-two-year-old owner, was working the cash register. *Why is he checking people out?* Jay grumbled to himself. *Look at this place! He's got a lot of things to address.*

As Jay piled his groceries onto the counter, Leonard asked, "How are you doing?"

"I'm okay," Jay replied.

Leonard ducked his chin so Jay would make eye contact with him. "No," he said. *"How are you doing?"*

Jay blinked. The reality was, he was feeling a little broken. He and his wife had twins and a twenty-month-old at home, and he'd just moved the whole family from Texas to Kentucky to start a graduate program at Asbury Seminary. He was barely treading water, and the little old man at the grocery store seemed to be the only one who could tell. "There I was, a grown man standing in line behind the celery and the carrots and the eggs, and I almost cried because he meant what he said," remembers Jay. "He was saying, 'I want to know how you are.' You're not used to that at a grocery store."

The more Jay asked around about Leonard, the more stories he heard. Leonard had been elected to city council twenty-four times in a row and he'd never put out a sign. He'd led more funerals than any preacher — six one dismal February alone. In a poor town on the edge of the Kentucky River, when widows heard a rustling on the porch, they'd look out and see Leonard shuffling down the sidewalk and a line of grocery sacks left in front of the door. "He believes with his whole heart that he was put on this planet to run that grocery store," Jay says. "Not in a market economy sense but in the sense of providing that town a true service."

Jay started going to the store after class and helping out a little, organizing the shelves, sweeping, dusting. One day, he said, "Leonard, tell me how business is doing."

"Well, it's doing okay."

"What kind of profits do you have?"

Leonard laughed. "Well, I've not drawn a profit since 1996."

That was the year Walmart and Kroger expanded to nearby Nicholasville, and the Dollar General started selling bread and milk. Since then, Leonard and his wife, Emily, had poured their monthly social security checks and $700,000 in personal savings into keeping the market afloat. As Emily battled stage four lung cancer and Leonard recovered from a hip replacement, both store and family were barely hanging on.

People in Wilmore loved Leonard Fitch, that was clear, but they still went to Walmart because it was cheaper. And then they started to get their tires fixed and their prescriptions refilled there, too. Jay thought that had to change. "I began to make that pitch to people, to say, 'You know, there's a cost to these bargains,' " Jay says. Every dollar spent in a local business like Fitch's would change hands six more times in Wilmore; that money didn't circulate locally when people shopped at a big chain.

The most significant cost was unquantifiable. If Fitch's IGA closed, Jay would tell people, "you'll lose this man in the community. And there is no amount of money that could replace that." In a pleading newspaper editorial, Jay wrote, "Our economic practice of bargain over neighbor isn't only incompatible with what we say we believe — it's incompatible with the survival of our community. Fitch's can't offer the selection or prices of the discount stores. But somehow he's still offering neighborliness."

In March 2011 Jay organized a group called Fitch's Neighbors, to give the aging grocery store a modern makeover, with spruced-up shelves, new signage, and a paint job inside and out. The local water company donated a mechanical lift for unloading delivery trucks. Volunteer businesspeople overhauled the store's operations and pricing. Someone installed a new security camera. In a single month, students, Boy Scouts, and neighbors gave four hundred hours of service to Fitch's.

An ongoing Buy Local campaign encouraged townspeople to get the fixings for at least three family meals a week at Fitch's, even if it cost 40 percent more than Walmart prices. "We all buy enough food that if we spent part of those dollars here, we could save this store," explained Mayor Harold Rainwater. "And to lose this grocery store, it'll change this town forever." So far it's working. Fitch's IGA is still chugging along.

A couple years ago, Jay graduated from

Asbury and moved his family back to his hometown of Lubbock, Texas. But he's thought a lot about the power of what he calls "neighborly economics." It's a whole new way of buying things — or rather, an old-fashioned way, closer to how Americans shopped before the second half of the twentieth century. Practicing neighborly economics means you don't go for what's cheapest and easiest. You think about which relationships and stores you want to preserve in your town, and you shop there. Sometimes it's a financial sacrifice, but "you need to sacrifice for where you live," Jay says. "Sacrifice is going to make your town stronger."

SPEND $50 AT THREE LOCALLY OWNED STORES EVERY MONTH

Preserving local businesses — and fending off the big guys — is not simple. A few years before we moved to Blacksburg, an epic David-and-Goliath battle erupted when the Blacksburg Town Council passed an ordinance requiring a special permit for stores above eighty thousand square feet. It was a deliberate move to prevent a Walmart from setting up shop in the new First & Main shopping center on the south end of town. The Ohio-based developer, Fairmount

Properties, fought it all the way to the Virginia Supreme Court, but in 2009, the court ruled in favor of the town. Walmart slunk away. Proponents of small business rejoiced.

My friend Jane, who was one of twenty-two plaintiffs on the Supreme Court case, told me that her main objection was how close the proposed Walmart would be to her children's elementary school. Traffic would have increased substantially, putting her kids in dangerous proximity to cars and outsiders. A big-box store could be planned elsewhere for Blacksburg and she might not fight it, she said.

Then again, Jane understands how important independent businesses are to the identity of a place and how difficult a Walmart makes it for people like her friend Nancy, the owner of Fringe Benefit. "There's reams of stories of Walmarts coming into communities and the whole downtown goes out of business. The hardware store goes out of business, the paint store goes out of business. People work really hard to keep the independent stores going." Jane makes a point of going to Heavener Hardware in town instead of Lowe's when she needs a couple of screws, or to Mish Mish instead of Michaels when she runs out of paintbrushes.

The victory against Walmart in Blacksburg was not without fallout. According to First & Main's manager, Nate Kiser, the Walmart debacle stigmatized Blacksburg as a place unfriendly to business. Lacking an anchor store, First & Main slowly leaked away clients. In 2014, 40 percent of its 130,000 square feet of retail space stood empty, the dark storefronts bracketing an Italian restaurant, a jewelry store, and a Blue Ridge Mountain Sports. Recently the development was sold to a new owner, and an IMAX movie theater was built, which looks like it may revitalize the shopping center. (Fingers crossed; First & Main is within a half mile of my house, perfect for walking errands.)

As in many towns, there is a tension in Blacksburg between the national chains and the locally owned stores, between residents who want to roll out the welcome mat to all retail comers, and others who'd rather bar interlopers to give indie businesses a fighting chance. How these choices affect cities depends on who you ask. Do they preserve the kind of idiosyncratic identity that makes cities attractive to Movers? Or do they harm towns economically by depriving them of much-needed tax revenue? That all the big-box stores that Blacksburg kept out simply moved one town over to Christiansburg didn't necessarily mean we didn't shop there. We just drove a little farther. And by "we" I mean me.

I suppose everyone has to create their own hierarchy of purchasing values, and for years, "cheap" headed up mine. Anyway, I didn't think it would be possible to shop entirely from small, independent businesses in Blacksburg. Where would I get the light-bulbs? The Band-Aids? The local five-and-dimes that sold them went out of business long ago. I could, though, nudge out "cheap" for "local," at least some of the time.

Early in the recession, a retail consultant named Cinda Baxter realized that the best way to help the faltering American economy was to shop in small businesses owned by people in your town. The dollars you spent would boomerang back to you in the form of better schools, new roads, and all the comforts increased tax revenue can buy. You'd keep hardworking neighbors afloat in tough times. You'd make your city the kind of place other businesses wanted to move to. The effect could be enormous.

To make local shopping seem more do-able, Baxter came up with an easy formula:

Spend a total of $50 at three businesses in your town each month. The 3/50 Project was born. "What three independently owned businesses would you miss if they disappeared?" Baxter asked on The350Project.net. "Stop in. Say hello. Pick up something that brings a smile. Your purchases are what keeps those businesses around." She offered convincing statistics, too, like this: If half of employed Americans spent $50 a month at locally owned businesses, it would generate $42.6 billion in revenue.

I wanted to see what my $50 could do for me in one of the independent stores that made Blacksburg special. Immediately, I thought of Imaginations, the toy store on Main Street.

For a few weeks last fall, Ella took a sewing class in a room above the store. While we waited to walk her home, Ruby and I wandered among the displays of cunningly designed puzzles and child-size umbrellas. Every few minutes Ruby would clutch at a felt doll with yarn hair or a papier-mâché kit and squeal, "Can I have this? Please?"

No. That was always my answer. *No, no, and no.* "It's expensive," I told her. "And if we buy one more toy your room is going to explode." (That part, at least, rang true.

What six-year-old needs more toys?) Sometimes I'd pick up a game, glance at the price tag, and set it firmly back down, thinking to myself that I could find the same thing online way cheaper. After a few weeks of browsing and never buying, I guiltily caved on a $2 yo-yo, the absolute cheapest item in the store.

The toy store held book readings and parties. Its front windows were always decorated for holidays. A mammoth stuffed bear was usually dressed up and posed in ridiculous fashion behind the glass. The idea of those windows turning dark and bereft of bears struck me as desperately sad. In ways I could barely explain, Imaginations created joy in Blacksburg, even when I wasn't buying things there.

Paying full price made my bargain-hunting spidey sense tingle like mad, but simply basking in the free ambience of stores — a practice I ignominiously fell into at Book-People — didn't pay their electric bills. If we want businesses that contribute character and vibrancy to our towns to stick around long term, we have to spend some cash there.

The good news is, it doesn't take a lot of money to make an impact on your local economy. Once he crunched the numbers,

Jay Leeson realized that residents of Wilmore didn't have to buy *all* their groceries at Fitch's IGA to keep it afloat, just three meals a week, or less than 15 percent of their total budget. In the Salt Lake City study, a 10 percent shift was enough to make a multimillion-dollar impact. That meant pushing one in ten shopping trips from a big-box store to a little guy. That was totally doable.

So with the 3/50 Project in mind, one afternoon I walked over to Imaginations to buy a birthday present for a friend of Ruby's. A Putumayo soundtrack played gently in the background as I wandered the store's carefully curated collection of playthings — beautiful board games, exquisitely soft hand puppets, science books, inflatable planets. Among the racks of kits for making your own Russian nesting dolls and chalks that turn your hair different colors, I found a $9.99 fashion plate coloring set. Perfect. A friendly shopgirl wrapped my gift in multicolored paper, for free. The $10.50 I spent was maybe more than I would have paid for a similar item at Target, but it felt like a better bargain for where I live. (Should I mention that I passed up the $7 box of colored pencils to go with it? These things take time.)

A few months later I went back to Imaginations for Small Business Saturday, a made-up marketing holiday sandwiched between the also made-up but more established consumer orgies of Black Friday and Cyber Monday. American Express launched Small Business Saturday in 2010, promising a $25 statement credit to cardholders who patronized participating local businesses; by 2012, consumers were spending an estimated $5.5 billion at local businesses on that day alone. It seemed like a good million of those purchases were happening at Imaginations, which was packed with moms and dads and grandparents in a holiday weekend frenzy.

Outside, blue and white balloons bobbed next to a banner that read, "Shop Small" and "Celebrate Your Neighborhood." Clutching a free cup of hot apple cider from a table at the front of the store, I collected an armful of presents, including a ladybug watch that Ruby had begged for on multiple occasions and a Christmas-themed puzzle for my niece and nephew in Arizona. Paula, the store owner, stood behind the counter in her candy-cane-striped apron, wrapping gifts in record time. Unlike the well-trained but generically pleasant big-box store employees, Paula seemed authentically grateful for my business. My purchases made a difference for her.

Fifty dollars a month sounds like a lot of money, and when you're spending it on yo-yos and fashion plate coloring sets, maybe it is. But I decided to turn my effort into a long-term Love Where You Live experiment that could stay with me (and my new town) for a while: Whenever the kids needed a birthday present for someone, we'd buy it at Imaginations. Once or twice a month I was back in there, buying a foam rocket launcher for Ruby's classmate or a stuffed panda for a friend who'd had a baby. Each time, the women at the counter small-talked me a little, asking who the present was for, saying how much they loved this or that toy. I didn't kid myself that they recognized me, but I started to recognize them.

Laureen Blakemore, the woman who'd orchestrated the cash mob, opened her own shop, Uncommonly Gifted, in Blacksburg in 2013. (I bought my "Blacksburg Is for Lovers" T-shirt there on Small Business Saturday.) She knows how hard it is for the little guys to compete with big-box stores. "We simply cannot match the low prices of a chain store. We have the constant concern that people complain about parking and convenience. Being a business owner as well

129

as director of Downtown Blacksburg really has brought home to me that our businesses are owned and operated by our friends and neighbors, and that we rely on our community to support us."

So this is how it works. You buy stuff. Your local thing might not be birthday presents. It could be bicycles, running shoes, books, lamps, camera gear, art prints, oil changes, carpet cleaning, piano tuning, or picture framing. Pick something to buy, pick a store or a person to buy it from, and then stick with it. As Andrew Samtoy, the man who came up with the idea for cash mobs, says, buying local in this way makes you feel more attached to where you live simply because it's an investment. "If you're going to spend time with someone, you'll be more connected to them. If you're going to spend money in your community, you'll be more connected to your community."

Sometimes when I go into a shop on Main Street in Blacksburg, I tell myself that I'm a cash mob of one. *You have $20 to spend,* I think. *Go.* In no other capacity does buying stuff feel so noble.

LOVE YOUR CITY CHECKLIST

☐ Find the one item that you can commit to buying from a locally owned business, then stick with it.

☐ Every month, spend a total of $50 among three locally owned businesses. Your town's Independent Business Alliance can point you in the direction of qualifying shops — or ask locals for their recommendations.

☐ Before you decide that buying local costs too much, consider the unexpected benefits, like advice, free gift wrapping, or tie-in promos that support other local organizations. At RunAbout Sports, a shoe store a half mile from my house, a trained salesperson helped fit Ella with new Nikes for her track season, and I received a gift card worth 15 percent of the purchase price because the store sponsors Blacksburg school sports.

☐ Shop at an indie business in your town on the Tuesday night it's giving 10 percent back to the animal shelter. Because local businesses are for more likely to give to place-based charities than chain stores, it's a two-fer.

☐ Attend a cash mob or start one in your own town. Andrew Samtoy's website

Cash-mobs.com has details about how to do it.

☐ Don't showroom. If you find a product you love at a local business, buy it in the store, not on the Internet. It can be more expensive, but you get the benefit of turning weak ties into strong connections, especially if you attend store-sponsored events, like wine and cheese night at the art gallery or Ticket to Ride night at the game store.

☐ Invest locally. Amy Cortese, author of *Locavesting: The Revolution in Local Investing and How to Profit from It,* suggests a simple step to get started: Open a savings account at a community-owned bank or credit union. Or join a Local Investing Opportunities Network, whose members pool their money to bankroll hand-chosen local businesses. Since the 2006 organization of the first LION in Port Townsend, Washington, a half dozen others have formed in cities like Portland, Oregon, and Madison, Wisconsin.

CHAPTER FOUR:
SAY HI TO YOUR NEIGHBORS

The first time Sloan Mandler saw Ridgefield, Connecticut, it was by accident. She and her husband were driving to visit friends in another town, and they stumbled into the middle of Ridgefield's Halloween Walk. Streams of costumed kids were trick-or-treating among the old-fashioned storefronts and white-steepled churches of Main Street. Beguiled, she and her husband soon bought a big house in town, and for seventeen years they lived in this New England version of Lake Wobegon, full of polite men, well-dressed women, and above-average children.

Everyone was friendly. People left their doors unlocked. The local schools the Mandlers' two children attended were stellar. It was in all respects "a really beautiful place to raise a family," Sloan says. Except for one thing: It never quite felt like home.

Home for Sloan, at least psychologically,

was Marlboro Township, New Jersey, where she grew up and where her parents, her brother, her sister, and her five nieces and nephews all lived. It wasn't far — just two hours south, across the George Washington Bridge and down the New Jersey Turnpike — but eventually, no matter how much they visited, she never felt ready to leave. Her parents were getting older. Every time he saw her, her dad would say, "So when are you moving to Jersey?"

Back in Ridgefield, Sloan started to feel a mysterious malaise. For a long time she wasn't sure why. "I was blaming a million other things, like the layout of the house. Literally, we were putting our house on the market because I was convinced that it was the house that wasn't working." Then one day her husband announced that if they were going to move, they might as well move to New Jersey. (He'd refused for years; the lower cost of living finally swayed him.) Sloan was giddy. So were her parents, when she told them the news on April Fool's Day in 2014. "You're really not kidding?" her mother said.

Her entire immediate family, plus her childhood friends, live within a couple miles of her new home. Sloan sees her sister almost every day. She has leisurely coffee dates with her younger brother and regular lunches with her oldest friend, a woman she's known since 1971.

There are tradeoffs. The home they bought in Marlboro is a 1980s time warp, and the schools her kids attend are unquestionably worse, Sloan admits. Marlboro itself isn't a particularly beautiful town, not the way Ridgefield is. "I hate the area," Sloan told me. "It's congested, it's obnoxious, the houses are all the same. There is nothing appealing whatsoever about this part of New Jersey, except that all my people are here."

When we talk about finding the place where we belong in the world, we have to talk about families. For many people, a situation like Sloan's is the end game of geographic mobility. Almost a third of Americans who moved in 2012 cited "family" as their main reason for doing so, a nebulous category that could, I suppose, mean anything from "I moved back to Peoria to take care of my ninety-year-old father" to "We jumped to the better school district because our son was about to start kindergarten." My guess, however, is that often it means a story a lot like Sloan Mandler's.

Once I started asking around, everyone knew someone who'd sacrificed to live near relatives. There's my friend Tracey, whose parents sold their house in Rohnert Park, California, and built a new one next door to Tracey's family in Burlington, North Carolina. A stone path connects their back doors, and Tracey's kids run across for movie nights and sleepovers at Grandma and Grandpa's house. "Both my parents have said they are less depressed and have more joy in their lives being able to share life with us," she tells me.

My childhood friend Dantes moved into a house a block away from the one where he grew up and where his parents still live in Fullerton, California. His older sister lives around the corner, and his younger sister and her family live at home with his parents. Why? "Maybe it's the Filipino 'extended family' culture," he says. "Or maybe that finding trust can be difficult nowadays."

Laura Delaney Roessler and her husband built a home on the 850-acre corn and soybean farm where she grew up in Trempealeau, Wisconsin, a quarter mile from her parents' house. When she goes to the bathroom in the middle of the night, her mom, Lynita, texts her: "Are you up? I saw a light on." Lynita thinks they might be weird. "Near is one thing, but a quarter mile away is something else. I know in other parts of

136

the world that it's quite normal to have grandparents and parents and children close, but in the United States it's not that normal, even in a farming community."

It's not normal because it's not always desirable. For some, this kind of familial proximity is the stuff of nightmares. Middle-of-the-night texts from Mom? Is it worth the free child care? Even when we crave connection with our family, we may be reluctant to exchange our privacy and freedom to be close to them, or doing so may simply feel untenable. We've built our lives elsewhere. There's nothing for us in our hometown anymore.

Yet overwhelmingly, the people who are the most rooted in their towns are the ones who live within an hour's drive of at least a half dozen members of their extended family. They're the most likely to be Stayers, not Movers. That's because their life satisfaction where they live goes up, and they lose a major reason why many Americans feel restless in their cities. As my friend Sarah, who was raised near Chicago but lives in Austin, told me, "We live in a great town, our home is in a great location, and Matt has a great job. And yet I am often quite unhappy to be so far away from my parents and siblings. My town has a million quality of life pros, but on many days, they don't outweigh the biggest con."

In Blacksburg, my husband and I live almost as far away as it's physically possible to be from both sets of parents. The whole substantial girth of the United States separates East Coast us and West Coast them. In the past this wouldn't have made me bat an eye. For many years, I'd considered distance a sort of get-out-of-jail-free card that prevented relatives from dropping in unannounced with "helpful" suggestions about our kids' behavior. As a lot of our friends angled to get closer to their relatives, I'd think in a self-congratulatory way, "We don't have to live near family. We can go anywhere we want."

Sometimes, though, I wondered: How would life be different if we were just *there* more often? Would we feel tighter with our faraway siblings? Would we have more fun on family vacations if there weren't so much pressure to cram twenty-four months of connection into five days? Would our presence help our parents, now in their seventies, age more successfully? Recently, Quinn's mother had taken up the refrain of Sloan Mandler's parents: "When are you guys going to move to Utah?"

In the summer of 2014, for the first time,

I was seriously tempted. My college roommate Adrienne lives in Orem, Utah, between the town where Quinn graduated from high school and the one where all three of us went to college. Laughing at twenty-year-old inside jokes around her kitchen table felt like slipping through time to the very best days of my adolescence, when we giggled ourselves breathless in our shared dorm bedroom.

Because ours was a familiarity that can only be achieved with time, intensity, and late nights, I doubted I could ever replicate it with anyone else. Why, I began to ask myself, wouldn't I want that kind of friend in my life more than once every five years? Living near Quinn's parents might be the initial draw, but the thought of Adrienne in my daily social network considerably bumped up Utah's spot on my list of forever places.

One of German-born geographer Ernest George Ravenstein's original laws of migration posits that people are motivated to move by economic opportunity. Broadly speaking, we go where the jobs are. Real-life experience, however, confirms that when your family lives in your town, you're less likely to go after a new job out of state, even when it's better for you financially. One

Danish study put a dollar figure on it, showing that if a job seeker who lived next door to his sister was offered a position far away from home, he'd have to be paid an extra $12,475 a year to make the move worthwhile. If a person goes from seeing friends or relatives less than once a month to seeing them most days, a British study conjectured, the resultant life satisfaction bump would be the equivalent of getting an £85,000 raise, about $130,000. Friends and family are intrinsically valuable, it seems.

The appeal of living near people like Adrienne who already knew everything about me increased in equal and opposite measure to the difficulty of cobbling together a brand-new social circle every time I moved. The fact was, Quinn and I didn't have any old friends or family in Blacksburg. It was unlikely we ever would.

Place attachment research shows that many of the good feelings we have about the cities where we live stem from the sense that we have relationships there. Here was my chance to craft a Love Where You Live experiment that could, potentially, make me happier in my town immediately. I would make an effort to get to know the locals.

SAY HI TO YOUR NEIGHBORS

How, precisely, I was going to make friends was what I wasn't sure about. Mostly I met new people at church, where fellow congregants were morally obligated to be nice to me. Sometimes I chatted with other moms at school pickup. Quinn waited for new colleagues to invite him to lunch. In the first lonely days after moving to a new town, finding the right balance between "Want to be my friend?" and "Please don't notice how desperate I am for social interaction" can be harrowing.

How do adults meet people, anyway? Googling "how to make friends in a new city" produced 585 million hits, with suggestions like: Join a club. Join a church. Sign up for a sports league or a running group. Take a class. Volunteer. Go to a meeting of your local Newcomers Club. Walk a dog (it's a great icebreaker). Have kids (same reason).

Half a century ago, neighbors would have been the most obvious line of defense for forming social connections in a new town, long before joining a rec league soccer team. In the 1950s, 44 percent of neighbors socialized with each other at least once a week. Neighborhood cocktail parties and poker games, picnics, and potlucks dominated a person's social life. By 1971, that number had fallen to only 24 percent, and it continues to plummet. By the end of the twentieth century, Americans spent 30 percent less social time with their neighbors than they had just fourteen years earlier.

We could blame that on the Internet, the most perfectly calibrated time suck known to man, or on the average American's frenzied schedule. Most of us are working more hours each week than our parents did (and are ironically too occupied for extracurricular socializing with coworkers).

When chronic stress and busyness haven't quashed the desire to interact with our neighbors, changing neighborhood mores may make it difficult anyway. Marc Dunkelman, author of *The Vanishing Neighbor,* points out that in the wake of World War II, "being neighborly meant reaching out to the people who lived next door — taking a homemade cake to the family moving into the house across the street, offering to watch the kids in a pinch, saying hello at an annual block party, or inviting acquaintances to join a Wednesday night bowling league. Over the years, however, the term came to denote almost exactly the opposite. Today, being 'neighborly' means leaving those around you in peace. . . . The sense of warmth once suggested by the term . . . has been replaced by a kind of detachment."

As a result, most American adults know only a handful of their neighbors by name, and 28 percent know no one at all. Almost a third of Canadians feel disconnected from the people who live around them, leading the Canadian magazine *Maclean's* to declare "The End of Neighbours" in 2014. Meanwhile, according to a poll in the United Kingdom, one in six Brits is actively feuding with a neighbor over crimes like blocking their driveway or allowing their cats to "do their business in my garden." Some of those surveyed admitted that they ignored or avoided their neighbors simply because "I just can't be bothered to speak to them."

The truth is, having neighbors is a scary business. With no prescreening mechanisms beyond checking the Sex Offender Registry — always a cheery part of any house search — most of us choose where to live without having any idea at all about what kind of hard-bitten souls will flank us. In a neighborhood, we sometimes end up wall to wall with people whose irritating behaviors become our daily personal catastrophes. Screaming neighbors. Drunk neighbors. Nosy neighbors. Neighbors whose wiener dogs yap all night.

On Twitter, one man used the #MyWeird-Neighbor hashtag to share that "my neighbor used to steal my paper, read it, then knock on my door to distract me while his wife put the paper back." A woman tweeted, "If we threw our Frisbee or ball over the fence by accident, we would get it back with a note attached saying 'I hate kids.'" The potential for discomfort, not to mention true drama, is epic.

It's gotten to the point where trying to get to know your neighbors is seen as an affront to privacy. In a thread on City-Data.com, one poster wrote, "I'm friendly but I don't really need you knocking on my door trying to get me to come to your house for a BBQ on the weekend. . . . Sorry, that's just not for everybody." Another added that he prefers not to talk to the people who live around him because, in a dangerous world, "I don't want strangers knowing my name anyway." There's no comfort to be had in realizing that all of the truly awful people in the world were once somebody's neighbor. (Although serial killers reputedly make admirably quiet neighbors.)

So why am I convinced that falling in love with your town needs to involve knowing (and at least sort of liking) your neighbors? Because of this little thing called "neighborhood cohesion," a term that social scientists use to describe the level of closeness and connection neighbors feel toward each other. In studies, it's measured by asking people whether they can agree with statements like these:

- This is a close-knit neighborhood.
- People around here are willing to help their neighbors.
- People in this neighborhood generally get along with each other.
- People in this neighborhood share the same values.
- My neighbors can be trusted.

When people answer yes, it portends positive outcomes for both physical and emotional health. For instance, a recent University of Michigan study found that those who trusted, liked, or spent time with their neighbors were 67 percent less likely to suffer a heart attack and 48 percent less likely to suffer a stroke. If they did have a stroke, their survival chances went up significantly. Other studies have found that stress, depression, and anxiety go down for people in tight-knit neighborhoods and that the effects of poverty are mitigated. In a low-income but socially cohesive neighborhood in Adelaide, Australia, where neighbors fed each other's pets when someone went on vacation, residents were as healthy as people living in a far wealthier but less connected part of the city.

Highly connected neighborhoods can even make us better parents. In a landmark 1980 study conducted at the Center for the Study of Youth Development in Boys Town, Nebraska, it emerged that one major difference between parents who were likely to abuse or neglect their children and parents who weren't was how social their neighborhood was — particularly how willing parents were to ask neighbors for help or to allow their children to play with neighbor kids. For first and second graders with rough home lives, living in a socially cohesive neighborhood offers a protective effect that makes them less likely to act out in class.

Why is neighborhood cohesion a wonder drug for so many ills? To find out, researchers from the University of California, Irvine, and Penn State University examined data from two thousand Americans who were surveyed about their well-being. For eight days, participants reported in telephone interviews whether they had experienced a stressor like an argument, a work deadline, or a family crisis. They also described their emotional state and any physical symptoms like headache, nausea, chest pain, or shortness of breath. Researchers correlated participants' responses to their agreement with two statements about neighborhood cohesion: *I could call on a neighbor for help if I needed it* and *People in my neighborhood trust one another.*

The study found that when participants reported more neighborhood cohesion, they had more positive emotions and fewer physical ailments. They even reported experiencing fewer daily stressors. It's not quite clear whether the happy, close-knit neighborhood caused their lives to be substantially less stressful (perhaps because there was no cat business in the yard to worry about), but the upshot of the study was that neighborhood cohesion offered a protective buffer against stress. Even when people endured stressful events in their lives, they reacted less negatively to them.

Living near family or good friends doesn't inoculate you against the need to befriend your neighbors. The same daily diary study found that strong relationships with neighbors make you healthier and happier independently of other forms of social support, like a spouse or a good friend.

One of my ideas about place attachment

is that whatever makes you healthier and happier in general also makes you healthier and happier *where you live.* Strong neighborhood relationships do that on two levels, since they boost your well-being and make you attached to your immediate neighborhood. That's not exactly the same as loving your city, but close.

Despite so many appealing reasons to befriend your neighbors, neighborhood cohesion isn't easy to achieve. Relationships in general are tough; trying to strike up a friendship with someone who throws late-night Metallica sing-alongs in their backyard, tougher still. In various cities we've had neighbors who kept us up past midnight, neighbors who allowed a wolf pack of feral children to roam the streets unsupervised, and neighbors who refused to acknowledge our existence. In one city that will not be named, we shared half a duplex with a fifty-something single woman who was so eager to fend off human contact that she grabbed her mail through the car window, then sealed the garage door behind her before she exited her sedan. (What, I wondered, could she hear through that wall of ours?)

On the other hand, let's just come out and say it: I'm no great shakes as a neighbor myself. I won't hug you after the school bus pulls away or gossip in your kitchen over coffee. I'll let the lawn grow too long. My leaves will blow into your yard in the fall. Chances are I'll learn your name, promptly forget it, then wave sheepishly from a distance for months. Nothing personal; it's just my subconscious mind's way of saying, *Hello, nice to meet you. We'll probably be moving again soon, so why bother?*

My friend Faith told me that as she approached her across-the-street neighbors one day to say hello, she could see them worriedly conversing with each other. "Oh no, not the crazy lady again," they seemed to be saying. When she tried to strike up a conversation, they were awkwardly nonresponsive. "Talking to them was like talking to a wall," she said. "And I'm a talker."

I knew that in the universe there existed neighborhoods like my friends Katie and Mike's in Reston, Virginia, where within twenty-four hours of their arrival, five neighbors dropped by with food to welcome them. Six years later, Katie told me that "we have a neighborhood book club, a neighborhood e-mail group, summer parties, Christmas parties, and everyone is just really looking out for one another. We had two women go through breast cancer in the last few years, and for months the neighborhood provided dinners and rides."

Why the fond feeling there? Katie attributed it to one or two neighbors who organized events that allowed people to get to know each other. Conversations struck up at a backyard cocktail party continued at the bus stop pickup and on the sidewalk. Such is the reputation of the neighborhood's social cohesion that it regularly attracts new residents who want to be part of it. Katie's sister Kara eventually bought the house next door to hers, achieving mobility's holy grail for both families, but Katie says that even if her sister moves away, she'll stay put. "It's a model of how a good neighborhood should be."

If I was going to use a Love Where You Live experiment to challenge my default settings on behaviors that were making it difficult for me to become attached to my town, I knew I had to be a better neighbor. My first simple goal: find out who my neighbors were.

Right after moving to Blacksburg I found myself yoga-chanting the name of everyone I met as a memorization device. Next door, Jenny: roundly pregnant, lilting Scottish accent. Kirk: her goateed husband. Marhaid: their teenage daughter. ("Her name rhymes with 'parade,' " said Jenny. "Parade, parade, parade," I muttered to myself.)

In the house on the other side of us was a Sri Lankan family, with their taxing monikers. "Her name is *Sha*-nee-ka," said the chemistry professor mother, pointing to her four-year-old daughter. "And I'm Shami."

And . . . that was it. All I managed to lock into memory. The rest of the neighbors, whose names I heard but forgot, were consigned to nicknames: Elderly Man Across the Street, Dude with Dreadlocks, Shami's Husband, Shami's Parents. Occasionally Dude with Dreadlocks and I would chat about the weather as we checked our mail, but there was never a good time to say, "Listen, I can't remember who you are." Two years later, Dude with Dreadlocks was still Dude with Dreadlocks.

Unlike other neighborhoods in Blacksburg, the area where I lived had no community center or neighborhood coffee shop, no sidewalks, pocket parks, or places for Ruby to ride her bike. We'd only moved there because the rental house was well priced and its windowsills weren't lined with beer cans. Most of our neighbors were renters, too, which made the place feel transient, as if any of us could pick up and move at any time. Was it worth investing the effort in a nothing neighborhood like this? In getting to know people who might not be here six months from now? What if *we* moved six months from now?

No matter where you live (besides a remote rural acreage, and even then . . .), your neighbors provide your first intimate contact with your city. It's where you make judgments about where you've landed and what people are like. Are they friendly? Do they want to get to know you? Are they the kind of people who let their cats do their business in your yard? A neighborhood of boorish driveway-blockers doesn't have to keep you from liking your city, but it can certainly give you second thoughts. On the other hand, an enthusiastic neighborhood welcome can, by extension, make a whole city feel welcoming.

The "place" in place attachment isn't an abstract concept. Place is physical proximity. The process of putting down roots naturally begins close to home, with the people who live right around us. Unfortunately, on my street they acted like strangers who happened to have stepped into the same elevator together. Except the ride had been going for several years now. Eventually someone had to break the silence.

So there was my Love Where You Live

experiment: Rather than accept the awkward status quo, I would get to know my neighbors. Not just know them. Like them. Trust them. Find a well of common interest, or at least common humanity.

Thankfully, that was when I heard about Good Neighbor Day.

THROW A BLOCK PARTY

Few people know Good Neighbor Day exists. Fewer still celebrate it. At least on national Talk Like a Pirate Day you get a free donut at Krispy Kreme. On Good Neighbor Day, you get blank stares.

Anyone can make up a wacky holiday and post it on the Internet, but this particular wacky holiday was conceived by Congress and made official by Jimmy Carter in a 1978 presidential proclamation. A week after talks at Camp David led to a peace treaty between Egypt and Israel, Proclamation 4601 movingly exhorted Americans to remember "that the noblest human concern is concern for others. . . . For most of us, this sense of community is nurtured and expressed in our neighborhoods where we give each other an opportunity to share and feel part of a larger family." The document ends with a call to observe September 28 as National Good Neighbor Day, with "appropriate ceremonies and activities."

"Appropriate activities" sounded to me like: banana bread.

When Good Neighbor Day rolled around, the kids loitered hopefully as Quinn mixed up a double batch of banana crumb muffins. "Do we get to eat these?" asked Ella.

"They're for the neighbors," I said. "It's Good Neighbor Day. We're going to take them around and drop them off."

"Do I have to go with you?"

"What, it's embarrassing to take treats to your neighbors?"

Ella cast a cold look my way. At nearly thirteen, she had entered the biological stage where embarrassment was her default emotion. "It's kind of weird," she said finally. So much for Jimmy Carter's vision of a world where seething issues of race and class find a healing balm in the communal backyard barbecue.

Ultimately Ella deigned to tag along as we made the rounds to the nearest neighbors — Kirk and Jenny, Mr. Smith (formerly known as Elderly Man Across the Street), and Shami and her family. At each door we exclaimed, "It's Good Neighbor Day!" and handed over a plate of muffins, like we were reenacting a strange 1950s greeting ritual. If they thought we were crazy, they hid it pretty well. "I didn't know it was Good Neighbor Day," Shami exclaimed.

I laughed. "I don't think anyone knows that it's Good Neighbor Day."

Last, we headed to the tiny brick bungalow where Dude with Dreadlocks lived. Though I still didn't know his name, I had identified a few other salient facts about him: (1) He had many cats. (2) He had a beard like King Tut. (3) He drove a yellow SUV like the one that Logan Echolls owned in *Veronica Mars.* Beyond that, he was a bit of a blank slate, and it was unclear how a guy with enormous ear gauges would respond to something as after-school special as banana muffins from the people across the street.

Here's how: like Good Neighbor Day was Christmas morning, and our proffered banana muffins were the present he'd always wanted. "No way," he said. "I can't believe it! This is so great!" His pleasure was so genuine that soon we were all laughing and beaming at each other.

After a minute, I said, "I know this is really sad, but remind us of your name." That easily, Dude with Dreadlocks became Jeff.

There are things about your town you can only learn by having conversations with other humans, and I realized that in my neighborhood, Jeff was the guy to ask. He told us, for instance, that the lot on which our house stood once had a tiny brick ranch like his, until it was razed to make room for our prefab vinyl-clad colonial. "Tyler told me it went up in one day," Jeff said. (Tyler was the professional disc golfer next door. *Tyler, Tyler, Tyler.*) "He went to work in the morning and there was a crew messing around, and when he came home that night the house was done." Five hours of the finest Googling would never have turned that dirt up.

Also: Jeff sold Jack Daniel's for a living. Also: He really liked banana muffins. Even as we walked away, we could hear Jeff repeating, "That is *so* awesome."

I was beginning to understand the value of meeting our neighbors face-to-face, even when — *especially* when — they're not like us. In many cities, neighborhoods are self-segregating, often by income, race, and culture, and sometimes by age, profession, or religion as well. According to University of Washington sociologist Kyle Crowder, migration patterns show that blacks and whites rarely move to neighborhoods dominated by another race or ethnicity. We tend to want to live among people who are like us.

Happily, diverse neighborhoods are on the rise in America, and one of the simplest things we can do to ensure they're comfortable places to live is to talk to people. In person. Jay Walljasper, author of *The Great Neighborhood Book,* sums it up: "You simply aren't going to develop strong bonds with someone that you wave to through the window and honk at. You need a face-to-face encounter where you say, 'Hey. Pretty warm for May.' "

Walljasper points to a few design features that can promote interaction in neighborhoods, like wide sidewalks, front porches, local parks, and community gathering places. Walking is important, because it leads neighbors to spontaneously bump into each other, which can spur conversations and friendships.

Even on streets like mine, with no sidewalk and lots of cars, neighbors can connect. It just takes more planning. "Potlucks are a great tradition to bring people together," Walljasper says. So are seasonal festivals, like a Halloween party or a Christmas caroling get-together. One neighborhood he knows of in Milwaukee created several clubs — a mother-daughter club, a breakfast club, a board game club — so that everyone would have a way to get to know their neighbors. Others have tried seed exchanges and yard sales.

The Harvard political scientist Robert Putnam posits that traditional markers of social capital, like neighborhood picnics and potlucks, are fading fast from the American psyche, and indeed some of these neighborhood get-togethers struck me as painfully old-fashioned. A neighborhood board game club? Even a block party, which Walljasper gushed about as "a wonderful American tradition," seemed like a relic from *Leave It to Beaver*.

In truth, a block party's broadness and blandness are what make it so perfect under the circumstances. Neighborhoods aren't the Internet, where you can search out a superspecialized interest group (female World of Warcraft players, vegan ultrarunners) to ensure you hang out with only people precisely like you. Neighborhoods are — or should be — catchalls for all kinds, including people from other countries, people from other states, people who don't make as much money as you, and people with dreadlocks and enormous ear gauges. Block parties and potlucks speak everyone's language.

Surprise, Arizona, is a suburb forty minutes north of Phoenix whose population (now 120,000) grew by 300 percent between 2000 and 2013. Out-of-towners bought up cheap housing in developments with faux-western names like Asante and Greer Ranch. When the recession hit the area, many of the newly paved streets were pockmarked with foreclosure notices. These expansions and contractions haven't been easy for the city economically, so it says something that one city program Surprise has faithfully funded for nine years is its Block Party Trailer.

The trailer is a two-wheeled pull-behind loaded with all the accoutrements of a good party: footballs, soccer balls, tables and chairs, lawn games, a PA system with some music. Rental is free. The city provides a $125 credit for a bounce house or a snow cone machine, along with a $75 supermarket gift card for snacks.

What residents build around that basic scaffolding varies. A couple moms in the Desert Oasis neighborhood put together a family-friendly fall festival for 225 neighbors, complete with a bounce house, a cake walk, face painting, a chili cook-off, and grilled hot dogs. Other neighborhoods have organized bike parades or driven kids around on a flat-bed trailer to look at Christmas lights. One in six of Surprise's

120,000 residents attends a trailer-facilitated block party annually, where neighbors might work out their issues about a barking dog, or learn that the guy down the block is a rabid Packers fan, too, and hey, why don't you come over and watch the game next week?

Standing by the PA system, Jeff Martin, the Neighborhood Services Division technician who coordinates the program, overhears this kind of small-town chitchat with clear affection. A transplant from Huntington Beach, California, Jeff moved here for the affordable housing, but found the neighborliness refreshing. "When I was in California, I lived in the same place for five years, and I never met the guy living next to me. He came over one time looking for a FedEx package."

Now, as a father of small kids, he wants to know who's around, who he can rely on, and who will tell him he left his garage door up. "I think our city wants everyone to know each other," Jeff says. "That's what helps build community on the neighborhood level."

Cities that understand the importance of neighborhood social cohesion are the ones that pay for a block party trailer, like Surprise, or organize a citywide Council of

Neighborhoods, like Rock Hill, South Carolina. Some towns coordinate National Night Out programs, with ice cream socials or flashlight walks meant to ward off crime. Seattle's Department of Neighborhoods offers small grants for neighborhood-based community gardens, playgrounds, festivals, and tournaments.

These actions bear out a maxim from the Saguaro Seminar, a center at Harvard's Kennedy School of Government dedicated to studying civic engagement: "If you had to choose between 10 percent more cops on the beat or 10 percent more citizens knowing their neighbors' first names, the latter is a better crime prevention strategy." Even when things go terribly wrong in a city, small attempts to connect neighbors have outsize results.

HELP YOUR NEIGHBORS

In a 2013 report by NeighborhoodScout on the most dangerous neighborhoods in America — where you have a better than one in ten chance of getting assaulted, robbed, raped, or murdered — the #2, #3, and #7 spots on the list were all in Detroit. The following year, things had improved marginally; Detroit claimed only #8, #9, and #11.

One would guess that high-crime, low-income areas get that way precisely because nobody cares about where they live. In fact, the more troubled a community, the stronger the palliative effects of old-fashioned acts of neighborliness, like keeping an eye on a neighbor's house while they're away or borrowing some sugar. When your neighbors are neighborly, stressful events become less stressful and you're more likely to feel the place attachment that prompts you to spruce up your own property or pitch in on a block cleanup.

Indeed, residents of economically depressed neighborhoods often care *more* about their communities than people who live in wealthy neighborhoods. In one study, researchers surveyed low-income African Americans who lived in a large midwestern city about their "community care and vigilance" — a vocabulary stand-in for neighborhood cohesion — by having them rate their agreement with statements like these:

- If I witnessed a crime in my neighborhood, I would report it.
- People in my neighborhood care about the area.
- My neighborhood feels like a com-

munity.

- I feel good about living in my neighborhood.
- There is not a lot of crime in my neighborhood.

One of the study's lead researchers, Man-soo Yu, an associate professor of social work and public health at the University of Missouri, hypothesized that people with higher incomes would show higher levels of community care and vigilance. "But the opposite was true," he said. "Residents with lower incomes were more likely to care about their communities than their higher-earning neighbors." Though 66 percent of the study participants earned less than $20,000 a year, those who had the very lowest incomes were the most likely to care about and invest in their community. Maybe, suggests Yu, with fewer resources to move to better neighborhoods, they're *forced* to invest where they are.

Block parties and neighborhood watch seem like an underwhelming solution to the grandiose problems of a distressed city, and yet they may be the key to Detroit's resurrection. In 2013, Mayor Mike Duggan was elected in part by championing a ten-point plan for rebuilding Detroit's neighborhoods.

Item #1 on the agenda: create a Department of Neighborhoods to partner with the city's hundreds of existing neighborhood groups and block clubs to solve problems.

In another town, an HOA might be a collection of social matrons who bemoan falling property values. Here, block clubs keep neighborhoods from falling into ruin. Members board up vacant houses to deter squatters. They plant rain gardens in empty lots. They arrange piñata bustings and community yard sales — rebellious acts of normalcy that build social capital and trust. More than in most cities, neighbors in Detroit are the last bulwarks against despair.

In 2003, a woman named Belva Davis fell in love with the East English Village neighborhood of Detroit for its friendly streets — green, full of life, and less chaotic than other parts of Detroit. "A lot of people were there — older people, younger people, people with kids, people with little red wagons and little kids, baby strollers," Belva says. "It felt like a community, like when I was growing up."

She paid $110,000 to buy her first house there as a fiftieth birthday present to herself. Two years later, her contract as a teacher with the Detroit Empowerment Zone Coalition ended. Other job leads fell through.

For several years, she struggled to find steady work.

As Belva fell on hard times, so did East English Village. Once considered one of the best neighborhoods in Detroit, now one in ten homes were vacant at any given time. Because the city couldn't afford a robust police force or routine services like snow removal, the HOA in the seventy-two-block area raised money to pay for it themselves. Neighbors began watching out for crime, busting scavengers stripping copper wiring from air-conditioning units as fiercely as they scolded neighbors who left their trash cans on the curb too long.

From the beginning, Belva was active in her neighborhood. She attended neighborhood association meetings and helped with the community yard sale and the annual East English Village holiday dinner. No one would have guessed she was on the verge of losing everything. The substitute teaching jobs she cobbled together weren't enough. Eventually she took out a home equity loan to pay the bills.

By the time Belva found a good job with the U.S. Census in 2008, she was $18,000 in arrears, and the letters from her mortgage company had become increasingly alarming. "I received a notice that I would be evicted around Christmastime," she recalls. Every day, turning the corner onto her street after work, she braced herself. What if her belongings were piled in a Dumpster out front?

A few people told her to walk away, cut her losses. Belva wouldn't do that. "I didn't buy a house to leave it; I bought it as a long-term investment," she says. "I didn't buy it to just walk away from it, or walk away from the community." Leaving felt like giving up on both her home and East English Village. Desperate, in 2008 Belva stood up in a neighborhood association meeting and asked for help to save her home.

After that, the problem wasn't hers alone; it was the community's. Two neighbors she barely knew, husband and wife Nancy Brigham and Steve Bapps, helped Belva organize a grassroots campaign to fight the foreclosure. At a protest rally, East English Villagers milled with city council members in Belva's yard. They ate hot dogs that Nancy and Steve had persuaded a local market to donate. A few weeks later, they held a second protest in front of a Wachovia bank branch in the suburbs. Finally the mortgage lender agreed to a loan modification that allowed Belva to stay in her home.

What stands out to Belva about those

high-anxiety years of her life are the neighbors. Nancy and Steve planning protests
with her. The association president encouraging her to ask for help. One neighbor
handing her $125 out of the blue, which
made her cry. Neighbors she didn't even
know introducing themselves by saying, "I
was at your protest."

"It takes a community of people, a neighborhood," Belva says. "Not only in Detroit
but all over the nation, neighborhoods are
being devastated. If more people would
band together, people could stay in the
neighborhood, the houses would be intact,
you wouldn't have vandals coming in stripping houses, or houses deteriorating so
much that the city has to bulldoze them.
There's got to be a reversal of thinking here.
Because people make a community, and I
think your community is only as strong as
the people."

In the place attachment literature, band-
ing together to pursue a common purpose
— to fix problems and get stuff done,
whether it's saving someone from bank-
ruptcy or just demanding speedier trash collection — is called "collective efficacy," and
some experts think it may be the most
important sign of a healthy neighborhood.
"It's less whether you have real relation-

ships and more that if you have a problem you can solve it," explains Marc Dunkelman, the author of *The Vanishing Neighbor.* "You can get a streetlight fixed or get a new stoplight put in."

Again, the effects of collective efficacy in neighborhoods are far-reaching. In a 1997 study published in the journal *Science,* researchers from the University of Chicago and Harvard discovered that when neighbors in Chicago could count on each other to intervene when, say, neighborhood teenagers were skipping school or spray-painting graffiti on a building, violence in the neighborhood went down. In fact, collective efficacy accounted for 75 percent of the difference in levels of violence between neighborhoods. Other studies have shown that people who live in neighborhoods with high levels of collective efficacy are less likely to be depressed, use drugs, or be victimized by violence. They're also more likely to be attached to where they live.

Marc Dunkelman told me that after writing *The Vanishing Neighbor,* he and his wife, who have two small children, realized their jobs were flexible enough that they could move almost anywhere on the East Coast. Taking a lesson from his own book about the value of social relationships in a changing world, they settled on Providence, Rhode Island, specifically a neighborhood called Paterson Park that's famous for its annual block party. "People look at us funny when we tell them the story," Dunkelman says. "It's not that we came here for a job; it's not that we had family here. We just wanted to live in Providence, and once we settled on Providence we knew we wanted to live on this street."

The neighborhood block party, he says, is just what you'd expect — a potluck where someone drags out a grill and everyone contributes a pasta salad or a plate of brownies. The kids play at the pocket park, and you get to meet the vet from across the street and the computer software developer on the corner. All good, but Dunkelman didn't become truly connected to his neighbors until he helped organize them to lobby the city council to repave their street. He was the new guy, but he got it done. By being proactive about working with other people, he's not only developed good relationships with his neighbors: "I've become the unofficial mayor of the street."

EAT DINNER WITH YOUR NEIGHBORS

Part of me wanted to be the unofficial mayor of my street, too, or maybe the general, leading the troops into battle over sidewalk widths or setbacks or something. Except I couldn't think of a cause that would galvanize anyone, so I reminded myself that small acts of neighborliness strengthened community ties as effectively as grand gestures did. Belva Davis's first contact with her neighbors in East English Village wasn't organizing a protest; it was attending Christmas parties and hobnobbing on the sidewalk. My Love Where You Live experiment could be simple or complex. It just had to build a little more neighborhood cohesion on my block.

As I was thinking about how to do that, I talked to a woman named Tonya Beeler about a tradition in her Indianapolis neighborhood, something called Sunday Night Dinner. It started in 2006, not long after Tonya moved into the Fountain Square neighborhood near downtown. Her friend Carrie mentioned that she dreamed of everybody on the block getting together once a week and sharing a meal, and since Tonya's a doer, she immediately e-mailed five neighbors about it. Three weeks later, the families were having their first Sunday night meal together.

I asked Tonya how it worked, and she told me that when it's her turn to host, her family handles cooking, setup, and cleanup to feed as many as fifty neighbors who live within walking distance of Pleasant Street. If the weather's nice, they spread outside, but in winter, people find a perch inside the house and eat with plates of lasagna balanced on their laps. "It's kinda crazy," she admits.

After hosting, the Beelers get six or seven weeks to simply show up for Sunday dinner at someone else's home. "You don't have to worry about a thing. You don't even have to clean up after you are done. If you're not feeling like socializing, then you just take some Tupperware and get it to go."

Sunday Night Dinner has become such a Fountain Square institution that mayoral candidates and state legislators sometimes swing by during election season. But what Tonya likes best is having a time set aside "where we meet to take a breath, sit down, and eat together. It's my favorite day of the week," she tells me. "If we ever leave, it will make me very, very sad. I don't know if you are the religious sort, but it really is like a picture of what we believe Heaven will look like."

In eight years, Tonya could count on both hands the number of times she'd missed Sunday Night Dinner. Ironically, I could use the same metric to count the number of times I've eaten with a neighbor in my whole life. Even knowing all the benefits of close-knit neighborhoods, I still fought a tendency toward social misanthropy. I wanted strong relationships with my neighbors in theory, but it will tell you something that I occasionally put off getting the mail if I saw a neighbor outside, just so I wouldn't have to engage in conversation. Delivering banana bread was an arm's-length gift, the kind that said, "I want to know your name and *that's all.*" Inviting a neighbor to actually eat with us? At our house? That was commitment — particularly if I hoped that it would be more than a one-off experience.

I wasn't sure that Shami's family next door didn't feel the same way as I did about neighborhood socializing. They were among the 57 million people living in a multigenerational household — child, parents, and grandparents sharing a floor plan smaller than ours — and, perhaps because of that, I'd always considered them to be self-contained, beyond the need of neighborly advances. They had each other! Why would they want to spend time with us?

My Love Where You Live experiments, I reminded myself, were expressly about pushing myself to embrace my community in ways I hadn't before. Finally I e-mailed Shami: Would her family like to come over for dinner? "You're so nice!" she e-mailed back. "What can we bring?"

Shami and I had been talking off and on at the school bus pickup for a couple years. Her parents and I were inveterate wavers and smilers. And there had been those muffins. But the Monday night that they arrived promptly at 6:15 was the first they'd ever come inside our house, and none of us was quite sure how to proceed. After some discussion of everyone's names and how to pronounce them, we gathered at the table to eat pasta and chopped salad. The forks clinked against the plates. The ice cubes rattled noisily in their glasses. Everyone chewed in silence. I was killing myself to think up a good topic of conversation.

Eventually what I hit on was: them. Who they were. After about ten minutes, it was clear that I'd had absolutely no idea.

As with Dude with Dreadlocks, I knew a few basic facts, primarily that they had immigrated to the United States from Sri Lanka. I had no idea that Shami's father, Muni, had been a higher education official there or that his gently smiling wife, Anula, had worked as a stenographer in government offices. Quiet Sanje, Shami's husband, revealed that on a Saturday night at the 7-Eleven, drunk Virginia Tech students could tear through four hundred taquitos spinning on those little rollers. For a couple hours, we laughed and talked and ate the potato-stuffed Sri Lankan dumplings that Anula had brought.

Shedding loneliness, I realized, was the first office of place attachment. Each person that slipped into my social network in Blacksburg — by way of church, piano lessons, or work parties, as strong ties or loose ties — made me feel more known, which in turn made me more place attached. More than anything else, relationships with people are what make you feel at home in your town.

By creating neighborhood cohesion, those relationships can also make us happier. Two days after Shami's family came for dinner, I ran into a scheduling bind with a doctor's appointment. Knowing I wouldn't be home when Ruby got off her school bus, I walked next door and asked Anu and Muni if Ruby could come to their house for a few minutes. "Of course, of course!" they said, falling all over themselves in their eagerness to help me out.

It was, perhaps, not quite like having my

own family living nearby. But it made me feel like I belonged in my neighborhood.

Love Your City Checklist

☐ Celebrate national Good Neighbor Day on September 28. There's also Neighborday on the last Saturday in April, or Valentine's Day, or Christmas, or basically anytime you feel like saying hi to your neighbors.

☐ To make friends, join a Newcomers Club, a loose network of social clubs for recent move-ins (and anyone else who's interested in broadening their network where they live). In Blacksburg, regular meetings host local speakers, but the club also organizes walking groups, brunches, outings, wine tastings, and other gatherings to help locals make friends.

☐ GIS-based apps aren't just for hooking up! Try the app Wiith for finding friends who live around you. Meetup.com is less techy but still useful for making local social connections.

☐ Keep a spreadsheet of the people you meet on your block: names, where they're from, where they work, what their kids are into. You know you'll forget otherwise.

☐ Welcome anyone who moves into a house that you can see from your front porch. You don't have to wait till you've baked homemade brownies. Just go say hello, perhaps with a couple takeout menus from your favorite local restaurants. In an apartment building, make a point of chatting with people in your elevator. At least say hi.

☐ Eat a meal with your neighbors. If hosting dinner seems too daunting, try something simpler — a potluck, a dessert night, ice cream cones on the lawn. Or invite your neighbors to Front Yard Friday. No one has to host. You just take whatever meal you were going to eat on Friday night anyway and picnic together.

☐ Join your neighborhood association, your block club, or your HOA. Talk to neighbors to see what they like about the block and what could be better.

☐ Offer to house-sit or pet-sit when neighbors go out of town, as a way to build social cohesion. (Bonus: Play with a cute animal!)

☐ Throw a block party. If you rent a bounce house or a snow cone machine for an afternoon, you'll be the most popular person in the neighborhood.

CHAPTER FIVE:
DO SOMETHING FUN

In a map-lined meeting room in the city hall of Sierra Vista, Arizona, a young marketing consultant named Kelley Brackett kicked off the focus group by asking a simple question: "If you could describe Sierra Vista in one word, what would it be?" The nine men and women around the oak conference table — among them business owners, a former mayor, and the president of the local art association — sighed and shifted in their seats. How do you distill the town where you've lived for thirty-five years (or for that matter, a year and a half) to its fundamental essence? Is it even possible? "I know it's a hard question," Kelley said soothingly. "Just tell me the first thing that comes to mind."

"Beauty," said the curator of the city's Henry Hauser Museum. "Tourism," said the president of the Southwest Association of Buffalo Soldiers. The frame shop owner added "weather"; the gray-haired founder of the genealogy club, "opportunity." The guy from the VFW — who, like almost 40 percent of Sierra Vistans, moved here to work at Fort Huachuca, the hundred-year-old army base on the hill — fudged the one-word requirement. "Nice place," he said.

"That must be hyphenated," someone said, giggling.

"Those are all great answers," Kelley said, smooth as glass. "Next question."

In twenty-seven-year-old Kelley Brackett's three years as a brand supervisor for North Star Destination Strategies, a Nashville-based community branding company, she'd led focus groups like these in twenty-five cities all over the country. (Last month: Jacksonville, Florida, and Fairburn, Georgia. Next month: Fargo, North Dakota, and Holmes County, Ohio.) "We don't market shoes or shampoo or anything else," she learned to explain to bewildered locals and reluctant city council members. "We only work with places. Research and marketing for communities is all we do."

That shoes and shampoo require clever marketing campaigns is a given, but if you've never believed that towns might need them, too, consider the case of Las Vegas. Before the ad agency R&R Partners created the slogan "What happens in Vegas stays in Vegas," Las Vegas already enjoyed a reputation as a place to zone out in front of a slot machine. Its sexier selling point? "The freedom to be someone we couldn't be at home." As R&R notes in its case study of the campaign, "At that point the strategy became clear. Speak to that need. Make an indelible connection between Las Vegas and the freedom we all crave."

In 2003, the city attracted about 35 million visitors a year. In 2006, three years after the "What happens here stays here" campaign debuted, an additional 4 million visitors came to cut loose in this rules-free wonderland of excess and anonymity. By 2006, the tagline had been so thoroughly absorbed into America's cultural lexicon that Laura Bush got a huge laugh using it on the *Tonight Show*. As an ad slogan, "What happens here stays here" has entered the pantheon with "Got milk?" and "Where's the beef?"

Every city dreams of having a public image so appealing that visitors, business investors, and potential residents get caught in its tractor beam. The places with a spare $50,000 to $150,000 sometimes hire a community branding firm like North Star Destination Strategies to make it happen.

Take the case of Glendale, California, a suburb of Los Angeles with 196,000 residents. In 2011, Glendale learned in a survey that locals thought the city was boring — the vanilla to hipper neighbor Pasadena's chocolate. Without the ability to actually become Pasadena, the most Glendale could do was to pay North Star $139,000 to rebrand it by changing people's minds without changing the city itself.

North Star's nine-month branding process, which included resident surveys and interviews, city tours, and creative work, ended when a team of people like Kelley Brackett unveiled the slogan "Your Life. Animated," a nod to the DreamWorks and Walt Disney Imagineering studios in town. (One resident remarked on Twitter, "Inspired by Glendale's 'Your Life, Animated,' I'm trying out a new motto for my neighborhood. 'South Glendale: Less Ghetto Than You Think.' ")

Community brands are easy to mock, troublesome to create. How do you make a town stand out when it doesn't? To distinguish the tiny fishing village of Petersburg, Alaska (population: 3,000), from a dozen other tiny fishing villages just like it, North Star played up its unusual Norwegian heritage with the tagline "Little Norway.

Big Adventure" and a new hand-drawn logo of a fleet of fishing boats. Green County, Wisconsin, has more master cheese makers than anywhere else in the nation, but how do you recruit high-tech businesses with artisan cheddar? Eventually, North Star hit on the idea of turning cheese making into a symbol of elegant craftsmanship. Slogan: "There's an art to it."

Branding has its own branding problem, which is that people think it's all catchy slogans and pretty logos. North Star's founder, a Nashville native named Don McEachern, told me, "We do a lot of great logos and slogans, but that's not really our core deliverable. I really see our work as strengthening the emotional connection people have with a community."

North Star can't change anything about its client cities (although it does make recommendations). Rather, the consultants try to shift the way people think about the place — particularly people who already live there. A branding campaign's target demographic always includes current residents alongside potential tourists or investors, because when residents believe their city is wonderful, they become ambassadors for it, doing for free the kind of personal handselling that a large-scale ad campaign can't.

"The key," said McEachern, "is changing the way residents feel about the town."

In short, community branders want you to like where you live more. They want you to become more place attached.

Mayors and town managers don't usually hire North Star if they're happy with the status quo. In 2015, when North Star began to work with Sierra Vista, Arizona, a city of 45,000 that's closer to the Mexican border than to Tucson, the place was having a bit of a self-esteem crisis. Sierra Vista wasn't a bad town. But it had an image problem, something I learned on the plane to Tucson to follow the North Star team around for a few days, when the woman sitting next to me asked where I was headed. When I told her, she rolled her eyes. "Why are you going to Sierra Vista?" she said. "I think that has got to be one of the three most boring places in the world."

"Sierra Vista is boring" turned out to be a recurring theme. Part of North Star's research agenda is collecting anonymous "man on the street" commentary in client cities, so while Kelley Brackett and Rupa DeLoach, North Star's research manager, conducted meetings and interviews at city hall, I prowled the city in a rental car to ask random people how they liked living there.

183

At the mall, I told the dark-haired twenty-three-year-old working at the cell phone kiosk that I was thinking of taking a job in Sierra Vista (minor fibs being a recommended way to get strangers to open up). How did she think my teenage daughter would like it? "There's absolutely nothing to do here for teenagers," the young woman responded firmly. "I don't want to make you worried, seeing as how you're new here and all, but I hate Sierra Vista. I tried to get away. I moved to Tucson, but then I came back. Sierra Vista is like this black hole you can't escape."

I heard a similar refrain from a woman whose eight-year-old daughter was selling Girl Scout cookies at the farmers' market. "Teenagers don't like it here," she told me matter-of-factly. "There's nothing to do." And then again from Rachel Gray, a thirty-something city councilwoman. The city recently built a teen center for thirteen- to seventeen-year-olds, tricked out with old-fashioned arcade games and a recording studio, but still, Gray said, "I hear more complaints about 'there's nothing to do in Sierra Vista' than anything else." (For the record, she doesn't agree.)

Economically, Sierra Vista was barely skating by. Most people in town worked at the army base, and a spate of closures at other bases had everyone worried. All the eggs were in one basket. What would happen to the city if the fort went away? A new medical center was being built, but despite the best efforts of the local Chamber of Commerce and Economic Development Foundation, Sierra Vista's geographic remoteness deterred other industries. Strip malls sprawled at every turn, land being one asset the town wasn't short on, but the new Walmart and Hobby Lobby belied a stalled-out local economy.

Yet Sierra Vista was not the cactus-studded cow town I'd envisioned before my trip. Based on what I knew of Arizona, I'd imagined a flat expanse of desert shimmering with heat and dust. Sierra Vista surprised me by being cool and green. Set in a bowl surrounded by mountain ranges that some people called "sky islands" — the Huachucas, the Chiracahuas, the Mules, the Dragoons — Sierra Vista was high enough in elevation that its summer temperatures topped out at around eighty-nine. The sun felt more present here than it did in Virginia, but cheerfully so, not mercilessly.

Also — and I can say this as an outsider — Sierra Vista wasn't nearly as boring as some residents seemed to believe. On the official city tour, Kelley, Rupa, and I were escorted to a historic ranch in the foothills of the Huachucas ("I've never even been here!" exclaimed Mary Jacobs, the straight-talking city manager), then detoured to a Nature Conservancy preserve where blue-throated and black-chinned hummingbirds congregate during migrations. At Veterans Memorial Park, Kelley took photos of the pavilion where the community band plays summer concerts. Nearby, non-bored-looking teenagers swooped in and out of concrete whorls at the skate park.

One night Kelley and I visited the local observatory. Some of the darkest skies in the world, well protected by local ordinances, offered a clear telescopic view of Jupiter's moons. I was awed. And still, said Mary Jacobs, "We can't get tourists to come here from Tombstone and Bisbee." What did people expect, Six Flags? When a woman working at Hobby Lobby confided (after I lied that I'd just moved to town) that her friends thought Sierra Vista had terrible shopping, I fought the urge to say, "You have a Hobby Lobby! *We* don't have a Hobby Lobby!"

In the car, Kelley and Rupa and I discussed it. "Would you live here?" I asked them.

After a minute, Kelley said, "Yeah, I would. And I don't say that about every town I visit."

"I'd totally live here!" Rupa said. "I already have ideas for half a dozen businesses I could open."

A woman in one of the focus groups put my thoughts into words. "I find it irritating when people say there's nothing to do," she sighed. "The *Herald* lists a mega amount of things to do on page two! Have you looked around? There's a lot going on here. There's something for everyone."

Trying to change the way residents think about their town is tricky business, something that became obvious to me in Sierra Vista when the young woman at the cell phone kiosk in the mall declared how wild she was to get out of town a few hours after the owner of the German bakery praised the city's perfection. *And they live in the same place.* It was like trying to hold two opposing ideas in your head at the same time without going insane.

The truth is, there's no precise metric to indicate how many museums, restaurants, monuments, hiking trails, amusement parks, shopping malls, and nature preserves make a town entertaining enough. Everyone's personal boring-meters are differently calibrated, based on who we are and what we love to do. That's why there are people who are perfectly happy living in New York City, with its 8.4 million residents (slogan: "The City That Never Sleeps"), and others who are perfectly happy in Pinedale, Wyoming, with its 1,977 (slogan: "All the Civilization You Need"). There are as many different kinds of communities in the world as there are blog posts and top ten cities lists to chronicle them, and the reasons why Person A loves a town are the exact same reasons why Person B hates it. Sierra Vista's problems had underscored that.

Surely when North Star unveiled the new brand identity in Glendale, at least a few people groused, " 'Your Life. Animated'? What the heck?" Maybe some residents of Green County, Wisconsin, complained, "Cheese has absolutely nothing to do with anything here." Eight months after our visit, North Star revealed a slogan meant to highlight Sierra Vista's dark skies, hummingbirds, and mountainous sky islands: "Extraordinary Skies. Uncommon Ground." I loved it, but I'm guessing some residents shook their heads in horror and said, "That's not my town."

"Edmund Wilson once wrote that no two people ever read the same book, and I've come to believe that no two people ever live in the same city," notes the writer Emily St. John Mandel. Our experience of the place where we live depends entirely on who we are, how we interact with it, and how we interpret what's happening around us. We create our places every day by the way we choose to view them.

To some extent place attachment requires donning rose-colored glasses. We must forcefully insist on seeing a place's charms. Of course, after we've been in a town for a while, familiarity can have the opposite effect, blinding us to a town's objective advantages. In Sierra Vista, Kelley, Rupa, and I toured a massive indoor swimming pool, complete with wave machine and multilane water slide, that would make Blacksburg children weep with envy. (Our aquatic center has a diving board. The end.) Yet in all the interviews and focus groups, I didn't hear a single person mention it as a community point of pride.

How many times had I done that in Blacksburg? Like the seventeen-year-olds in Sierra Vista, I carped that our midwinter Saturdays stretched bleakly empty. I had forgotten Blacksburg's small pleasures. After a while, I didn't even see them anymore.

"A place is nothing in itself," Wallace

Stegner said. "It has no meaning, it can hardly be said to exist, except in terms of human perception, use and response." A town is what you think it is. It had become clear to me that Sierra Vistans were missing things in their town. What was I missing in mine? I needed to rebrand Blacksburg, I realized, if only in my own mind.

CHANGE YOUR PERCEPTION

Admitting that you want to live in a particular city because there's so much to do there is a bit like saying you chose your university because of its reputation as a top-ten party school. Much more grown-up to value "serious" quality-of-life factors, like the cost of the four-bedroom homes or the strength of the high school's AP program. And yet research shows that your town's entertainment value may be more important than you'd think.

Throughout the 2000s, researchers at the Gallup organization regularly polled people about something called "employee engagement." They asked workers how connected they felt to their company and how passionate they were about their jobs, and over time they noticed an interesting pattern: An uptick in employee engagement was always followed within a year or two by a swell in

190

the company's productivity. The more engaged a company's employees were, the more prosperous the company became. Gallup could map the change over time.

The effect was so constant and transformative that Gallup pollsters started wondering if the power of engagement applied to other things as well. They thought of cities. If engaged employees helped businesses do better financially, did engaged residents help a town prosper? And if so, what about a town made people passionate about it in the first place? Basic services like police and fire and education? The more ineffable qualities of leadership, social capital, and civic involvement? Would it turn out that all that mattered was a decent local economy? Jobs equal happiness, full stop?

To find out, in 2008 Gallup partnered with the nonprofit Knight Foundation on a study called "Soul of the Community." The setup was simple: Call a random sample of adults and ask questions to determine how emotionally attached they were to the city where they lived, and what made them feel that way. The polling would happen in the Knight Foundation's "Knight Communities," the twenty-six cities where brothers John and James Knight originally operated their newspaper empire and where the foundation promoted community engagement projects. These places were a mix of metropolises like San Jose, California (population: 1 million), and smaller towns like Milledgeville, Georgia (population: 19,400), scattered coast-to-coast across seventeen states, and they would make for a diverse test sample.

The Soul of the Community survey questions probed participants' most personal feelings about their lives and where they lived. Questioners asked subjects to imagine a ladder with steps numbered from zero at the bottom to ten at the top, then said, "If the top of the ladder represents the best possible life for you, and the bottom of the ladder represents the worst, on which step of the ladder are you standing right now?" They asked people to describe how satisfied they were with their city as a place to live, how likely they were to recommend it to other people, and whether they thought they would move away in the future. Some questions zeroed in on specific amenities. How do you rank the availability of parks and playgrounds? The physical setting? Job opportunities? The availability of affordable housing? The leadership of elected officials? The effectiveness of local police?

Respondents were also asked to weigh in

on whether they were proud to say they lived in their town, whether they thought it had a good reputation among outsiders, and whether it was the perfect place for people like them — questions like the ones Kelley Brackett asks in her focus groups and a lot like the ones from the place attachment scale.

At the end of the first year of the Soul of the Community study, the study's director, a longtime Knight Foundation employee named Katherine Loflin, examined the results. What she saw floored her — even more so two years later, after Gallup had polled forty-six thousand adults and the results had stayed consistent over time. "It was just a huge, nobody-saw-that-coming kind of explosion on a global scale," she told me.

Bombshell #1: The three qualities with the strongest correlation to place satisfaction and place attachment were social offerings, aesthetics, and openness. When residents felt like their city offered a lot to do, looked nice, and welcomed all kinds of people, they felt most attached to it. Serious factors like good schools, affordable housing, and local police — the kinds of things that every day guide Americans' decisions about where to live — didn't register nearly as strongly.

And these fuzziest of fuzzy qualities were important for all twenty-six cities in the study, no matter their size, geographic location, local economy, or culture. Big cities like Philadelphia and smaller cities like Gary, Indiana, coastal communities like Miami and landlocked midwestern towns like Aberdeen, South Dakota, all showed the same result.

Bombshell #2: The more emotionally attached residents were to their cities, the better their cities did economically. The same trend Gallup had noticed in workplaces, where the passionate engagement of employees fed organization-wide success, happened in towns. In the city with the strongest attachment levels, local GDP — a measure of consumer spending, government spending, industry spending, and exports — grew 6.9 percent over the three-year period of the study; in the city with the lowest, it grew only 0.3 percent. Even during the recession, cities that were beloved by their residents had higher GDP growth per capita than cities that weren't.

Loflin, a native North Carolinian with long, black hair and a sweet-tea accent, began making the rounds to the participating communities to present the results in a series of town hall meetings. Standing in front of her PowerPoint in heels and a blazer, she would explain that when we love our cities, they fare better financially. She would explain that what makes us feel that way aren't sensible things like an effective city council, but little things. A beautiful park. A downtown art fair. Neighbors who say hi.

Residents couldn't believe it. "I always felt dumb for caring about that," they'd say, "and you're sitting there telling me these are the exact things that make me love my place!" It was as if "someone came along and gave meaning and power to those feelings," says Loflin.

Sometimes, Loflin could see a visible wave of emotion wash over the gathered crowd. "I could feel it prickling up the back of my neck, that 'Oh my God' moment: Things just changed, and I witnessed it. Very few of us get to have that moment, where you think, *I've just changed permanently the way people feel, think, and act about something.*"

Because 66 percent of Millennials say they choose the city where they want to live before they find a job there, understanding how they value quality-of-life factors is transforming what mayors and economic development officials do to make their cities attractive to talent. "There was a time not too long ago when economic development was how much land did you have, how cheap could you be, how low is the cost of living, how good for business could you be," says Carol Coletta, the Knight Foundation's vice president for communities and national initiatives. "Price is still important, cost is still important, and being good for business is still important, but what's been added to the mix is: How good can you be for real people? How can you make real people choose your place to live over other places? It's not as if jobs and job opportunities don't matter, but I think we all recognize that that is the paradigm shift."

Twenty-four years ago, Oklahoma City was regularly coming up short in its bid for new businesses, despite a low cost of living, good schools, and hefty tax breaks. In 1991, when United Airlines ignored millions in financial incentives and chose to build its massive new maintenance hub in Indianapolis instead of in Oklahoma City, the company explained why: "At the end of the day, we can't see our employees living [in Oklahoma City]." It was, says Mayor Mick Cornett, "an expensive wake-up call on why place matters."

Since that bleak moment, the city has

presciently rethought its economic development strategy and poured more than a billion dollars into the kind of capital improvement projects that foster place attachment by providing plenty of things to do. They've built a twenty-thousand-seat indoor sports arena, a downtown ballpark, a riverside entertainment district, a seventy-acre central park, a public white-water kayaking facility, and miles and miles of new sidewalks and hike-and-bike trails.

Over time, those additions have changed the identity of the city and turned its weakness into strength. In 2015, Oklahoma City tied with Austin for the lowest unemployment rate in the country among cities its size. For the first time in anyone's memory, "more people from Texas and California are moving to Oklahoma City than vice versa," says Cornett.

Businesses that rely on highly skilled workers need to be located in a place where talented people want to live, which can pose a catch-22 for cities trying to attract both residents and workplaces. Offer tax cuts to lure businesses? Or use tax dollars to improve the city? Jobs follow the talent in the labor pool, and as Coletta explains, "talent moves to the community to get a certain kind of lifestyle. If by cutting your taxes you can no longer provide that lifestyle, if there aren't enough government funds to provide the greenways, parks, schools, and museums, then in some ways you're creating a dilemma."

Oklahoma City has staked millions of dollars on their answer. "The bottom line," says Cornett, "is that we have entered an age when local communities need to invest in themselves."

Not every city can spend so much on new stadiums, boardwalks, or downtown shopping districts — nor do they need to. Here's why: The Soul of the Community study's findings about social offerings weren't empirical in the sense that someone tallied up the number of art galleries and water parks in a five-mile radius. The study measured residents' *perceptions* of where they lived. What mattered wasn't how much there was to do in objective terms. It was how the people who lived there *felt* about it.

In the three years of the study, the very highest emotional attachment score was the 4.07 out of a possible 5 earned by State College, Pennsylvania, in 2010. A university town of 42,000, State College makes regular appearances on lists of the country's safest and smartest places to live. Sometimes people call it Happy Valley. That people loved living there was not a massive shock.

More startling was when below-the-radar towns proved to have a truly attached group of residents, as happened in 2009 when Grand Forks, North Dakota, tied another city for highest level of emotional attachment with a score of 4.01. Grand Forks is, to call a spade a spade, in the middle of nowhere. You can get to Winnipeg in two and a half hours if you drive due north and the roads are clear of snow. They often aren't. With around 56,000 residents, Grand Forks is the third largest city in North Dakota, after Fargo and Bismarck. In Virginia, where I live, that would get eleventh place.

Grand Forks does have a trampoline park, a rock climbing gym, a minigolf course, several theater groups, a youth orchestra, art galleries, splash pads, arcades, an indoor water park, and a town ice rink, making it rather well-endowed in social offerings for its size. On the other hand, it does *not* have the beaches of Miami, the pro sports arenas of Charlotte, or the historical sites of Philadelphia. In the polling, that didn't matter. In 2009, when Soul of the Community asked people who lived there to evaluate the city's social offerings, residents of Grand

Forks rated their town higher than the residents of Boulder, Miami, Philadelphia, Charlotte, San Jose, and Long Beach, California, rated their cities, sometimes by substantial margins.

Big cities may have their fancy art museums, their headliner concerts, and their enormous shopping centers, but in Grand Forks, North Dakota, the prevailing belief was that there are big-city levels of stuff to do. Because residents thought that way, they were more attached to their town. And according to the Soul of the Community findings, having residents who love living there explains why Grand Forks' local economy grew faster than those of the bigger, more amenity-rich cities.

A town is what you think it is, and thinking that your town has plenty to do, even when that might not be objectively true, has a tangible effect on its economic success. It's like our cities can tell that we love them.

SHOW OFF FOR VISITORS

A few months ago, friends stayed with us in Blacksburg for a couple nights on their way from Louisville, Kentucky, to a conference in Philadelphia. We're out of the way enough that we don't get lots of drop-ins, but our thrill at seeing them quickly gave way to a sense of panic. *What are we going to* do *with these people?* we wondered.

Based on past experience, we had only one surefire winner: a grand tour of the Virginia Tech campus. If Quinn expounded at length on the history of the twenty-two-acre Drill-field, the vast lawn that bisected campus, the tour might take twenty minutes. Indulging in a Harry Potter tangent inspired by the way the gray Hokie Stone makes Burruss Hall look like Hogwarts, we could squeeze out another ten.

After that, we came up empty. Did we show them the town library? The park with the old train caboose? Should we give up and collapse in front of old episodes of *Battlestar Galactica*? That these friends were coming from a much larger city only heightened the pressure. What could we possibly show them that they hadn't already experienced bigger and better in their own town?

I grew up nine miles north of Disneyland, and prolonged exposure to the Magic Kingdom had bred in me a constant need for high-quality entertainment and a permanently reduced threshold for boring. Even back then, my easy access to the Magic Kingdom gave me a sense of geographic superiority. It was never lost on me that the place I lived was the place other people came for fun. *On vacation.* My house in Orange County was the geographic nexus of hundreds of high-end, heavily packaged adventures, including multiple theme parks, museums, zoos, the Hollywood Walk of Fame, the Griffith Observatory, Medieval Times, a slightly creepy wax museum, and miles and miles of beaches. When extended family stayed with us in Fullerton, the trick wasn't rustling up enough to do but producing the focus to narrow the list.

In Austin, too, there was no threat of boredom. Our visitors were subjected to a multihour ordeal that might include Zilker Park (with a requisite ride on the Zilker Zephyr train), BookPeople, the Lady Bird Johnson Wildflower Center, the Bullock Texas State History Museum, the quirky shops on South Congress, and the food trucks along South First. Alone, we didn't always want to suffer the crowds, heat, traffic, and expense necessary to do these things, but with out-of-towners in tow, we became show-offy about our good fortune. "You like this? We come here all the time!" we would crow.

Compared to these tourist utopias, Blacksburg felt spare and confining, particularly when the weather turned cold. I felt this keenly on weekends in winter when there

202

was not much to do but order a pizza and binge-watch Netflix, but it struck me most profoundly when guests came to town. How could we keep them occupied? And if we couldn't, what did that say about our town?

It seemed shallow to expect Blacksburg to have a Disneyland or a Statue of Liberty or, like, a Stonehenge replica made out of foam (the way Natural Bridge, Virginia, does). But as the Knight Soul of the Community study proves, believing that your town offers opportunities for enjoyable social interactions beyond your living room is key to how much you feel attached to it. And a good way to pinpoint your own perceptions about the stuff there is to do in your town is by asking yourself, "What would I show off to visitors?"

Imagining how a visitor would view your town is a helpful litmus test because it forces you to don their fresh perspective. Your city's famous statue may have worn out its novelty for you months ago, but would Aunt Margaret enjoy it? In Blacksburg, I wasn't quite sure *what* out-of-towners would enjoy.

It had become such a sore point that a few times that friends had proposed a visit, I'd demurred. "There's not a lot to do here. Maybe we should meet up in your town instead." Last year my Austin friend Amber and her boyfriend stayed in our basement for a few days after hiking a section of the Appalachian Trail. Apart from our standard-issue Virginia Tech campus tour and dinner at a family-style restaurant called the Home-place, the only place we ever took them was Target, so they could buy toothpaste. (On the plus side, they were too exhausted to care.)

Smallish towns like mine often flounder on the "What would I show a tourist?" question. When Kelley Brackett asked this in focus groups in Sierra Vista, a few residents admitted they would drive out-of-towners thirty miles to the old mining town of Bisbee to tour the art galleries, or to Tombstone, where mustachioed actors play out fake gunfights in the street. Bisbee and Tombstone are small towns, too, but they've built a local economy around tourism. Creating social offerings is what they do best.

How could Sierra Vista compete? Could the talked-about laser tag facility or indoor trampoline park turn Sierra Vista into a tourist mecca? When a memorial to the conquistador Francisco Vásquez de Coronado, who traveled through the valley in 1540, hadn't?

Counterintuitively, small towns are often better at making people fall in love with them. In 2011, the psychologist Maria Lewicka asked 1,328 people in Poland how secure and rooted they felt in their town, how proud they were of their community, and whether they missed it when they were away. She found an inverse relationship between community size and place attachment. The bigger the city, the less attached the people who lived there. The smallest villages boasted the strongest neighborhood ties and rootedness. Having lived in both, I suspect that the privacy and anonymity that draw people to big cities may make them feel a bit less like a community.

Even in large cities, sometimes we just don't like what our town is good at. We have a bowling alley; we want a water park. We have a karaoke bar; we want an art gallery. In an attempt to please everybody, large metros like Oklahoma City install such an all-you-can-eat buffet of entertainment offerings that residents and visitors can't help but find something to suit them. Meanwhile, locals sometimes become overwhelmed by the paradox of choice or sense that the amenities are actually meant for tourists. So they stay home, increasingly disconnected and isolated. Bored.

The social offerings in my city weren't something I could readily change. What I *could* change was the story I was telling myself, that *Blacksburg is dull, there's nothing to do here,* which was keeping me from becoming an ambassador for my town, the way the truly place attached are. The idea that emotion follows action seemed key here. For my Love Where You Live experiment, I decided I would find all the fun things in my town and do them. And I'd enjoy it, so help me.

DO WHAT YOUR TOWN IS GOOD AT

I'd already made a start by doing the Walk [Your City] project. Mapping out destinations where people on foot might want to go had forced me to think about which spots in Blacksburg I loved enough to want to send other people to see them. The situation, I'd realized then, wasn't as dire as I'd originally thought.

For this new Love Where You Live experiment, I decided to do something similar with a placemaking technique I'd heard about called "asset mapping." The idea is this: Every community has strengths. You just have to figure out what they are. "It's looking with a new set of eyeglasses," says seventy-five-year-old Mary Nelson, a fellow with the Asset-Based Community Development Institute at Northwestern University.

Some asset maps focus on people as resources, but the kind I was interested in was a literal map of community assets — a street-by-street guide to places in Blacksburg visitors should know about. On my laptop, I popped open a map of the city in Google's My Maps program (you can do this on paper, too), titled it "Blacksburg Stuff to Do," and started dropping markers in spots where I could imagine a visitor passing a pleasant hour or two.

First I added the Walk Blacksburg spots — the Civil War cemetery, the library, the nature center, the duck pond, and the farmers' market — all places I tended to forget or ignore. Then I dropped pins for Imaginations toy store, a few of the town parks, and the aquatic center. Then I was stumped.

One of the challenges for Sierra Vista was that average residents were clueless about interesting goings-on in town, like the annual Cowboy Poetry Festival or Community Night at the observatory. Simply knowing where to go to research local social offerings can help with your perception of your town, and in Blacksburg the flyer-crammed community bulletin boards and newspaper listings had mostly given way to curated online event listings.

I decided to crowdsource my quest for more interesting things to do. On Twitter I asked @Next3Days and @BlacksburgStuff, self-appointed town criers and calendar maintainers, "What's the #1 thing you'd tell a tourist to do in Blacksburg?" For clarity's sake, I added, "Assume it's a boring middle-aged person." Almost immediately, I got responses from both of them:

Tour campus
The Lyric
Donut from Carol Lee
Smithfield Plantation
Lane Stadium/Merryman Ctr FB display
And when the weather is better walk or
   bike the Huckleberry Trail

Ah, the classic campus tour. Done. I'd also already done the Lyric for movies, the Huckleberry Trail for lazy walks, and Carol Lee Donuts (more than was good for me). In my time living in Blacksburg, however, I'd never once been to Smithfield Plantation or Lane Stadium's sports exhibits — never really considered them, actually.

In my mind, Smithfield Plantation, the local historic homestead, carried the undeniable stink of school field trips, of tedium, of second graders longing for their sack lunch and oblivion. Was it worth checking out, even if I wasn't being forced to do so by a teacher? All I knew was that @Blacksburg-Stuff and @Next3Days thought so, and because I'd determined to take other people's recommendations, I took the family one Saturday toward the end of fall, the last weekend before the plantation closed for the winter.

The house was more modest than the word "plantation" might suggest — no Tara-like colonnades, just a row of dormer windows peeking out of a white clapboard colonial. A walkway shunted Quinn, the girls, and me straight to the basement gift shop, where Ruby rapaciously examined plastic-wrapped minié balls and faux-parchment copies of the Declaration of Independence while I arranged for us to join the two p.m. tour of the house. Ella hissed, "Do we have to take a tour? I hate tours." She blanched at the sight of a retiree in a colonial-style dress and a white mob cap waiting patiently on the back porch.

Luckily Felice, our tour guide, turned out to be a gifted storyteller, and soon we were caught up in the idea of the Blacksburg that existed before there was any real town here. These rolling hills, now Virginia Tech's campus, were once sown with flax, hemp, and hops and worked by fifty slaves and a coterie of indentured servants. Beyond the grounds, Highway 460 buzzed past a stockade fence that would have kept out Shawnee warriors in the past. As much as things had changed, it wasn't hard to imagine that two hundred years ago, the plantation was the slimmest margin of civilization in the Blue Ridge wilderness.

The original homesteaders, William and Susanna Preston, built the plantation in 1774 and lived here with their twelve children. Preston used to correspond with fellow Virginian Thomas Jefferson about their mutual love of books. George Washington ate here, though no one can prove he slept here.

Why here? "William Preston had known about this land since the French-Indian War," Felice explained. "He could have built anything anywhere, but he chose to put his home here." Even then, place attachment mattered. All six rooms within its less-than-plumb walls were meant to announce, "We're here and we're going to stay."

Learning my town's history hadn't made it to my Love Where You Live to-do list. Maybe it should have. In California, where I'm from, very little is as old as this house.

To have such a permanent sign of historic settlement a few miles from my very impermanent rental house gave me a thrill of pride. Roots went deep here, even if they weren't my own. Smithfield Plantation went on my asset map.

Lane Stadium, on the other hand, I balked at for a long time. As in most college towns, football is close to a religion around here. The sixty-six-thousand-seat stadium where the Hokies play — big enough to hold the entire town and then some — was listed by the travel website Trip-Advisor as the #1 attraction in Blacksburg. "The team taking the field to 'Enter Sandman' by Metallica is one of those bucket list things to see for hardcore college football fans," writes one reviewer from Canada. A former student in Colorado adds, "The feeling of being home pervades the place." Tweets about games are often hashtagged #ThisIsHome.

Meanwhile, at the one Hokie football game I'd been to, I'm sure I induced rage in the spectators around me by repeatedly asking Quinn, "What just happened? What does that flag mean? Did we just score a goal?" Next suggestion, please.

Rejecting potential sources of enjoyment because they didn't match my existing interests seriously reduced the pool of things to do where I lived. It was also disastrous for place attachment, which thrives on acknowledging your town's gifts as gifts. I could obsess over what I wished Blacksburg was good at (roller coasters, art museums, independent bookstores), or I could learn to love what it was good at right now. And Blacksburg was excellent at rooting for college sports.

Eventually, one drizzly Tuesday, Ruby and I biked to Lane Stadium and spent a half hour walking through the sports exhibits there and in the Merryman Center next door. Trophies, undoubtedly very important ones, were on display alongside 1950s cheerleading uniforms and photo collages about the reign of the women's volleyball team. "Look at this football," I said to Ruby, gesturing to a Plexiglas case, then couldn't figure out why the ball mattered or how to get myself excited about it.

From the outside, the fervor of sports fans makes no sense. Only as you begin to become a fan yourself, embracing the rites, rituals, history, and particular lingo of fandom, do you slowly graduate to insider status. When that happens, suddenly you get it. You love the team. You *are* the team. In extreme cases, you come to define yourself by your team, whooping and cheering and screaming as if you were an actual player. You don't say, "*They* won." You say, "*We* won."

In all these ways — the intense loyalty, the group identity, the sense of ownership — sports fandom is oddly reminiscent of place attachment. Maybe I failed as a die-hard sports fan, but my Love Where You Live experiments helped me see the very real link between rooting for your hometown sports team and rooting for your hometown. Chicagoans don't have to love basketball to cheer the Bulls, and Bostonians don't need to believe in the Red Sox to root for them. They do it because they love their city, and the team's victory is the city's victory. As Movers, they might even find that wearing their sports jersey reminds them of their roots.

Was it ridiculous to think that a T-shirt could make you feel like a member of the club? All I know is that once I bought that "Love VT" T-shirt at the cash mob at Greenhouse, no one could tell I wasn't a Hokie. And once I was passing for a Hokie, the other Hokie-related rituals started to feel like my thing too, regardless of my general football indifference.

When home games were being played a few miles away at Lane Stadium, I could hear the cannon that signified a Virginia Tech touchdown, and I always smiled and checked the score on my laptop. At one point, watching a video of thousands of students in caps and gowns jump up and down to "Enter Sandman" at the 2015 Virginia Tech commencement ceremony made me well up involuntarily. I was crying at "Enter Sandman"! What was happening?

What was happening was that these traditions had come to signify belonging. I had begun to consider myself a Hokie, and by that I mean a member of the community who cares about what happens here. The more strongly connected I felt to Blacksburg, the more its passions mattered to me.

It can take time and effort for your town's things to become *your* things. Realistically, determining beforehand how well a city's social offerings match your interests will increase your chance of loving it there. After all, these are *social* offerings, and social connectedness is at the heart of place attachment. In a new place, you want to find your tribe, that group of like-minded fellow citizens whose interests collide with yours and whose friendship will make you agree with the place attachment scale statement "The people who live here are my kind of people."

These days, you can find your tribe almost anywhere. In Blacksburg, I met a newcomer named Amelie who made her closest friends by playing a GIS-based game called Ingress that's like a sci-fi nerd variant on Foursquare. Players use their phones to physically "capture" places around town by going there. Sometimes Amelie would do that with other locally based teammates, and sometimes she'd meet up with local players for drinks or dinner at night. Ingress is how she met her boyfriend and most of the friends she has in Blacksburg.

A computer programmer, Amelie is exactly the kind of young, bright, tech-savvy Millennial big cities lust after — and she found her tribe in Blacksburg by doing smart, geeky stuff she genuinely finds fun, not faux fun or forced fun. When we're happy, we're happy where we live.

SHOW UP

One day, looking online for things to do in Blacksburg, I learned about an event called New River En Noir. Admission was $60. All that the guests knew in advance was that they were to dress in elegant black, meet in a parking lot in Blacksburg, and be prepared for a festive evening. Everything else was a surprise.

It was as kooky a thing as I'd ever heard of around here, made weirder still by the fact that earlier in the year I'd met a curly-haired South African woman named Suban Nir Cooley who'd done something similar in her adopted hometown of Lansing, Michigan. Like other struggling towns, Lansing had an excess of vacant buildings downtown, and Suban arranged to throw a party in one of them. Guests purchased tickets beforehand, but everything about the event was top secret, down to its location, which was revealed the day of. When people showed up — surprise! — it was a speakeasy party! There was music, dancing, hip flasks, costumes. The event, called Vacant Lansing, was so cool that Suban did it again a few months later, turning an empty warehouse into a 1990s-themed family block party, with break-dancers, hip-hop artists, and an old-school arcade.

In the world of placemaking, there's a sort of cheesy buzzword for this on-the-ground, DIY change: "activation." As in, take a space where not much is happening — a park, an alleyway, a vacant building, an art gallery in the off-hours — and "activate" it by doing something cool to bring it to life.

For instance, an empty three-acre lot in Boston's Seaport District was activated into a temporary park, à la San Francisco's PARK(ing) Day on steroids. Sod was unrolled. Chairs and a stage were installed. Besides a bocce court, Ping-Pong tables, and cornhole games, the main attraction was twenty glowing purple swings sized for adults, who lined up for rides. Anthony Flint, in an article for *CityLab,* commented, "I have no data to support this, but my sense is that [the swings] are the setting of more shots on Facebook, Twitter, and Instagram than anything at least since the silvery bean at Chicago's Millennium Park."

In other towns, activation is simpler and cheaper. Lancaster, Pennsylvania, installed game boards downtown to encourage passersby to stop and play chess. A woman put a Little Free Library on her street in Hutto, Texas. Emily Munroe, of the Canadian urban renewal group 8 80 Cities, calls hula hoops, music, and food "the magic makers" for community activation — and the best part is that they're cheap.

I heard about a group of hipsters in Fargo, North Dakota, who started a project called the Hammock Initiative. It was really nothing more than stringing some hammocks up in a park at a predetermined time and lying in them, but because they'd designed a nice-looking Tumblr site and invited a few reporters, lying in hammocks became more than lying in hammocks. Lying in hammocks became an event. If only the people in Sierra Vista knew how simple it could be to make things happen. As someone in a focus group there said, "Rather than being entertained, you have to be involved, and there are tremendous opportunities to be involved."

With New River En Noir, someone had done all the work; all I had to do was buy a $60 ticket and show up. I chickened out. Later I heard that all the partygoers boarded tour buses to a hip farm-to-table restaurant called the Palisades for dinner and dancing. Looking back, I wished I'd gone. Even if we're not ready to be the ones making the fun stuff happen in our town, we can show up for the people who are. Go to the festival. Buy tickets for the play. Throw a buck in the busker's guitar case. Notice the little things that make your town vibrant and support them. Like the right community brand, it can change your perception of where you live.

In some ways, developing place satisfaction is really a matter of creating a repository of happy memories where you live. Here's where we toured the historic home. Here's where we went on the bike ride.

Here's where we spent the day at the museum/football game/park/nature center. Each shining moment gets pinned to your mental map of your city, and soon it's entirely overlaid with pleasures big and small.

Love Your City Checklist

☐ Develop your out-of-towner list using the Power of 10+ framework developed by Project for Public Spaces. What ten local sites, historic landmarks, tourist attractions, parks, museums, statues, or events can you show off to visitors? Take people to the places that have meaning to you.

☐ Find out what's going on in your town. Most large cities and many small ones have websites, magazines, or newspapers with event calendars or e-mail lists. Online, search the name of your town and a key word like "event." Or download an app like Offline that offers curated lists of cool things to do in selected cities (www.get-offline.com).

☐ Asking people "Where do you take visitors?" is a fabulous ice-breaker, and you may get clued in to some lesser-known spots that will make you feel like an insider.

☐ Do the stuff your town is good at. If the big local attraction is a train museum, go to the train museum. Buy tickets to the football game, at least once, even if it's just the local high school team playing. Learn to like it.

You'll feel happier faster.

☐ Annual festivals are often a focal point of local pride, and they tell you a lot about what your place values and what residents consider themselves good at. Plus, research shows that such community rituals can increase place attachment.

☐ Make your own asset map with Google's My Maps to remind yourself of how much your town has to offer and to plan outings for yourself and visitors. You can drop pins in the map to indicate where to go, then share it with others.

☐ Show up. You don't have to be the one planning the events. Just make a goal to show up to one community social offering a month, even if it's not what you'd normally do for fun.

☐ Create fun for yourself. A shortcut to place attachment is to do the things that make you happy where you live. A local cooking class can increase place attachment for a home chef; a half marathon in town can do so for a runner. Pinpoint the ways you like to spend your time, then search out the right kinds of activities in your town — or make them happen yourself.

CHAPTER SIX:
COMMUNE WITH NATURE

The Internet loves where you live.

At least, I suspect it does, based on the fact that the Internet loves almost every city in America. Congratulations, Seattle, on being WalletHub's best city to find a job! And Pelham, Alabama, for emerging as *Bloomberg Business*'s best town in Alabama to raise a family. And Miami, Cleveland, Pittsburgh, and Fort Collins, all of which have been described on *BuzzFeed* as "the greatest city on the planet."

I'm not arguing with the scientific credibility of these distinctions. At one website, Livability, researchers crunch numbers on health care, school quality, ethnic diversity, crime, climate, and affordability for more than two thousand cities before declaring a top one hundred. *Money* magazine analyzes data from organizations like the EPA, the FBI, Moody's, Trulia, and the League of American Orchestras to winnow down 781 candidate cities into its annual list of the fifty best places to live in America. Even if you don't like the outcome, you can't argue with it. The data has spoken, with results as seemingly inevitable as the answer to an algebra equation.

On the other hand, there's a snarky feature on *BuzzFeed* that invites you to "Generate Your Own Definitive List of America's Best Cities." The winking acknowledgment at the top reads, "These things are all random anyway, right?" It's a reality check that kept me from losing my mind with community pride when I saw that Forbes.com had named Blacksburg one of the twenty-five best places in the country to retire.

Somewhere between the extremes of rigor and randomness is the selection process for *Outside* magazine's annual Best Town Ever, which could most appropriately be described as a popularity contest meets well-informed gut check. The feature runs in the sports and adventure magazine each fall, and to prepare for it, associate editor Jonah Ogles e-mails a group of friends, writers, and fellow editors sometime in the spring and asks, "If you were going to pick up and move to a new place today, what towns would be on your short list?"

"That's how we stumbled onto Greenville,

South Carolina, a few years ago," Ogles tells me. "We have quite a few editors from the Southeast. They were hearing back from their friends that Greenville had this really great restaurant scene and this really awesome park downtown. So I kind of started poking around."

A few weeks of editorial due diligence yields a geographically diverse top ten. In a nod to *Outside* readers' various athletic pursuits, there are beach cities, ski towns, metropolises, rural backwaters, beloved outdoor meccas like Boulder, and underdogs like Fayetteville, Arkansas. The towns are fairly disparate in size, location, climate, urbanity, and cost of living, but they all have one thing in common: easy access to nature. People in a potential *Outside* Best Town Ever want to go outside.

If that seems obvious, consider that twenty years ago, *Outside*'s offices were housed in the Continental Bank building in downtown Chicago. Here was a magazine that worshipped both nature and the daredevils who made a playground of it, that ran articles about Everest climbers and round-the-world sailors, and its editors lived and worked in a sea of concrete. In 1992, when it became clear how ridiculous their setup was (plus the rent was going up), editor Larry Burke began the hunt for a new home for the magazine. The idea was to close the gap between the world they were reading and writing about and the physical world they inhabited.

Most of the well-known outdoorsy towns across the country were considered for the move: Burlington, Vermont. Flagstaff, Arizona. Santa Barbara, California. Burke had almost settled on Jackson, Wyoming, when one day the mayor of Santa Fe, New Mexico, called. Would Burke and his wife want to come for a visit?

No economic development team could have arranged what happened next. "As we crested the hill and got our first glimpse of the Sangre de Cristo Mountains," Burke recalls, "the sun, as if on cue, burst through layered pillows of bleached-white clouds to allow a single beam of light to reveal a cluster of adobes, lit crimson-gold, nestled in the foothills. This was Santa Fe? Our mouths dropped open. We looked at each other as if to confirm that we were both seeing the same thing. I thought, if there truly is a God, He must be commanding our attention to this special place."

Within thirty-six hours, Burke told his wife, "I don't know about you, but this is where I want to be."

Outside's move to New Mexico took three years to engineer, but once the staff left Chicago, all was as it should be. Editors began taking lunchtime runs on the Dale Ball Trails in the foothills of the Sangre de Cristos, or they kayaked on the Rio Grande before work and still made it to the office by nine. "We're able to play the way we want to because we're located here. It actually does happen. It's not really an exaggeration," says Ogles. That's one reason why the Best Town story is such a mainstay at *Outside*. Staffers respect the life-altering power of a new geography because most of them have experienced it themselves.

Readers love the Best Town feature, too — Ogles remembers daydreaming over it in his college library — but apart from the occasional grateful letter from someone who moved on *Outside*'s recommendation, the list is mostly fantasy journalism. That it might serve another, more elemental purpose didn't become clear at *Outside* until 2011, when for the first time the winning city wouldn't be chosen by the editorial staff. Instead, staff would select a top ten, and readers would vote for their preference on Facebook. The place with the most votes per capita would prevail.

Immediately the top ten candidate cities

began drumming up electoral fervor with pep rally stunts, social media campaigns, and beer-fueled voting drives. To clinch a win for Richmond, Virginia, in 2012, a flotilla of kayakers paddled into the James River and spelled V-O-T-E. A year later, Greenville, South Carolina, threw a town parade (and still only came in second place). For a few years after the switch to social media voting, each of *Outside*'s Best Town competitions received between ten thousand and twenty thousand votes on Facebook.

Then in 2014, Ogles had the brilliant brainstorm of slotting sixty-four towns into a March Madness–style bracket. At each level of the competition, people would have five days to vote their town through to the next round. "It was not an original thought at all," he admits, "but we realized we really like brackets ourselves, and we were, like, 'I bet readers will really respond to this head-to-head thing.'"

In less than a month, between May 14 and June 8, 1.5 million votes were cast online at Outside.com. (The print magazine's readership is around seven hundred thousand.) From the beginning, dark horse candidate Duluth, Minnesota, dominated the voting. A city of 86,000 on the western edge of

Lake Superior, Duluth offered excellent trails and trout fishing, as well as single-digit winter temperatures that made it a hard sell. As a midwesterner, Ogles could see its charms, but the city might not have made it into his top ten in the old system. Now, it had just as much a chance at winning as other places, and Duluth wasn't going to let the opportunity pass by without a fight.

To promote their cause, volunteers set up Instagram and Twitter accounts. A graphic designer created a VoteDuluth website. Soon locals began posting their own come-hither images online — a wet-suited surfer carving waves in Lake Superior, a canoe prow cutting through dark water toward a wooded shoreline — each hashtagged #VoteDuluth. Like a community branding effort, the #VoteDuluth campaign forced residents to become vocal ambassadors for what they loved about their town.

The enthusiasm online and off was revelatory. The people who were most excited about the Best Town list weren't the ones who needed statistically driven guidance on where to live next. They were locals who wanted the list to confirm what they already believed — that the place where they lived was indeed the best in America. For residents, having your town make a magazine's top ten list was the publishing-world equivalent of hearing a singer name-check your city in concert. (See: Paul Simon's *Concert in Central Park* album: "It's a perfect night [applause] in New York City [APPLAUSE!!!].") Even better, locals could plaster that name-check all over their Facebook wall.

Facing off in the "Elite 8" round against its own state's largest city, Minneapolis, Duluth didn't falter. Megacities don't do well in this kind of competition, explains Ogles. They're too big. No one cares. "Medium-sized cities that are able to really spread the word almost on a neighbor-to-neighbor basis — those are the towns that do well in our contest. You need those towns where everybody kind of knows everybody and can say to them at the grocery store, 'Oh my gosh, you've got to vote in this *Outside* contest.'"

When Duluth defeated Provo, Utah, for the Best Town Ever title, the city exulted in a blast of unadulterated local pride. Congratulatory tweets poured in from Minnesota's senators, including Al Franken, whose erstwhile Stuart Smalley affirmation could be Duluth's I-think-I-can motto: "I'm good enough, I'm smart enough, and doggone it, people like me." The glossy spread in *Outside*'s print magazine that came along with the win was the kind of publicity that money can't buy.

More important than the businesses or visitors it might attract to Duluth, however, was the morale boost to current residents. In a victory speech posted on Facebook, Mayor Don Ness put it this way: "For decades, a fog of pessimism and defeatism hung low over the city — negative and cynical voices defined our city's conventional wisdom. Too often we simply accepted the fact that Duluth would never fulfill its potential. Today, Duluth is a different place — the optimistic and positive voices are now being heard. . . .

"Is this change real? Ask yourself this question[:] Do you think Duluth could have won this contest 20 years ago?"

Although as far as I know, place attachment researchers have never asked subjects whether they voted for their city in a Best Town Ever contest, the fact that people do offers a clear measure of community loyalty. Who would log on day after day to vote online, post Instagram images of favorite spots, and beg support from friends on social media besides the truly committed?

That made me wonder: Was there something about this particular kind of "best town" that lent itself to place attachment? *Outside*'s contest featured towns that were powerfully connected to the outdoors. Did spending time in nature make you love your town more?

Humans are born with an inborn craving for wildness and green, what Harvard biologist E. O. Wilson calls "biophilia." We are, he says, built for nature. Here's the rub: Towns and cities usually aren't. The earliest settlements were built to beat back the wilderness and its dangers, real and imagined. Today most paved-over urban spaces offer at best minimal contact with an authentically natural world. That problem will only increase as more of the world's population moves to cities, which 85 percent of us are expected to do by 2050. Even now, one out of every eight people lives in a megacity with over 10 million inhabitants, like the metro area of Tokyo, Mumbai, Shanghai, New York, or Buenos Aires.

And yet we still seek green. In New York City, it's a truism among real estate agents that apartments next to even the most minuscule parklet will bear a higher price tag. Desire for green space motivated the tactical urbanists in San Francisco to cover cement with sod for PARK(ing) Day. According to Amanda Burden, the designer who helped turn an elevated New York City railway into the extraordinarily popular High Line walking path, urban green spaces can "change how you live in a city, how you feel about a city, whether you choose one city over another."

Metropolitan areas that satisfy their residents' hardwired desire for nature with pockets of inner-city green space — trees, parks, community gardens, green roofs, and nature preserves — are what University of Virginia professor Timothy Beatley calls "biophilic cities." Places like Portland, Oregon, which has aggressively installed the most acres of park per capita in America, and Anchorage, Alaska, with its mile of trail for every one thousand residents, are "redefining the very essence of cities as places of wild and restorative nature, from rooftops to roadways to riverfronts."

How can you tell if a city is biophilic? One way is to consider its O-score. In 2014, in an attempt to apply a smidgen of rigor to the *Outside* Best Town contest, Jonah Ogles asked a genuine rocket scientist to devise a mathematical formula for rating outdoorsiness. Important factors like the number of outdoors outfitters, breweries, yoga studios, bike shops, miles of trails, and acres of green space in town were taken into account, along with a few stuffier considerations, like unemployment rates and median incomes. In Montpelier, Vermont, the O-score was 74 out of 100. Missoula, Montana, scored an 82. Duluth earned an 88.

Obviously, only a handful of towns have an O-score, and it means something slightly different from city to city. A high O-score could indicate prime wilderness nearby, as in Anchorage, or a lot of urban trails, as in Minneapolis. Maybe you can kayak there, or ski, or surf. The common denominator is simply solid access to nature in some form. The O-score indicates whether a town has effectively married its green and built worlds.

As far as I knew, there wasn't a definitive link between towns with a high O-score and high levels of place attachment. But one of my pet theories about place attachment is that when you're happy and healthy, you're also happy and healthy *where you live* — and a mind-boggling amount of research shows that nature makes people healthier.

Studies have found that spending time in green space improves immune system function, lowers blood glucose levels in diabetics, boosts cognitive functioning and concentration, lengthens attention span, and strengthens impulse control. Residents of counties with a large amount of green space tend to be thinner. On the flip side, a Dutch study found that people who spend less time in nature have higher rates of cardiovascular disease, back pain, migraines, upper respiratory infection, and urinary tract infection and more symptoms of attention-deficit/hyperactivity disorder. Their pulse rates and blood pressure soar along with their stress and anxiety. They're more likely to be clinically depressed.

In one well-known 1984 study published in *Science,* a geographer named Roger Ulrich showed that surgery patients who had a view of a small stand of trees from their hospital beds recovered faster and took fewer painkillers than patients with a view of a brick wall. Merely looking at *photos* of nature scenes made people less stressed and more altruistic. Given $5, they were more likely to want to spend it on others. A scenic view, it seems, makes you a better, healthier person.

Green space also builds social cohesion, the companion to place attachment that we see develop in tight-knit neighborhoods. One study showed that when homes are set among trees and plants, neighbors form stronger social ties and a better sense of community. People who live near parks trust each other more and are quicker to aid their neighbors than people who live farther away.

In a 2001 study, Frances Kuo and William Keller of the University of Illinois at Urbana-Champaign examined the connection between crime rates and greenery around the Ida B. Wells housing complex in Chicago, at the time one of the poorest neighborhoods in America. Of the ninety-eight inner-city apartment buildings Kuo and Keller looked at, some were surrounded by grass and tall trees; others had been paved over to keep maintenance costs down. In an unusual finding, the most lushly planted buildings had 52 percent fewer crimes than buildings with the sparest vegetation.

Our brains and bodies on nature are so much improved that a few scientists have taken to calling green spaces "vitamin G." "Rarely do the scientific findings on any question align so clearly," says Kuo, now director of the Landscape and Human Health Laboratory at the University of Illinois at Urbana-Champaign and a leading researcher on the connection between greenery and human health.

Outcomes like these made me come up with my own hypothesis: that people who lived where they could spend more time in the natural world would feel more enthusiastic about their communities. To find out if I was on the right track, I decided to travel a thousand miles from Blacksburg, to a town whose passion for wilderness is legendary.

SAVE YOUR PART OF THE PLANET

Park City, Utah, won its *Outside* Best Town crown in 2013, before O-scores existed, but everyone told me that if you lived there, it was because you loved the outdoors. You were a rabid skier, biker, angler, jogger, hiker, snowshoer, stand-up paddleboarder, or some combination thereof. Definitely a skier. In a town of 7,500, lifts to Park City's two big ski resorts were no more than five minutes from the downtown's quirky bars and restaurants. One lift was *in* downtown, offering a direct bar-to-powder pipeline.

I visited in midsummer, when the slopes that skiers carom down in winter had shed their thick snow to reveal a complex undergirding of dirt trails. It was up one of these trails, Sweeney's Switchbacks, that Quinn and I were following a hiking guide named Alisha Niswander. We'd met her by the ski lift in downtown Park City. Within a few minutes we'd left behind the boutiques, the art galleries, and the luxuriously renovated former miner's cottages downtown. Almost immediately I was covered in sweat.

I had mentioned on the phone to Alisha, the owner of Mountain Vista Touring Company, that Quinn and I were two clicks from couch potato status. "Go easy on us," I had begged. She undoubtedly was, and that made me even more desperate to maintain the illusion that I could keep up with her. Today's hike would cover almost four miles and gain a thousand feet of elevation. Alisha's well-tanned calves were like rocks. Was it just me, or was the air thinner up here? Why was my breathing so ridiculously noisy? Why was Alisha not breathing hard at all? Would I die, or just humiliate myself?

Loath to ask for a water break (*what would Alisha think?*), it occurred to me to ask for a photo op. We paused. Alisha handed us water bottles from her backpack. When my chest stopped heaving, I finally looked around.

From up here, Park City looked the very picture of a town with a high O-score. Ski lift benches swayed twenty feet away, like an eerie abandoned amusement park ride in an episode of *Scooby-Doo.* Beyond them lay the town, its tilt-shift ski shops and tiny houses set in a bowl, surrounded by mountains. The streets seemed like they might be swallowed by the wilderness at any moment.

Like many *Outside* Best Towns, Park City's unique geography is its blessing and, at least to newcomers, its curse. In February 2015, the median home for sale in Park City was listed at $1.4 million, forever constraining the kinds of people who can afford to live there. From the trail, Alisha pointed out a tiny two-bedroom, one-thousand-square-foot place in the distance. When I asked what it cost, she said, "I'm guessing it's probably worth one-point-five."

"Wait," I said. "One point five million?"

"Yeah," she said. In Park City, the "million" is implied.

Five minutes away, in Summit County, the earth flattens. New housing is being built there along a road that used to close to let dairy cows cross. In Kimball Junction, near the highway and the outlet mall, you can buy a condo for $250,000.

If there's any upside to the ludicrous cost of living it's that the well-off skiers (read: stockbrokers and lawyers) who can afford to live in Park City are also willing to spend their money protecting the area's open space. Cheryl Fox, who moved there from New York in 1983 and now heads the local Summit Land Conservancy, explained to me, "We come because it's beautiful, and people have been really proactive in saving what is beautiful, in saving the most important open spaces and access to them."

One of the most striking findings of place attachment research is that when people are attached to where they live, they're far more likely to protect it. For instance, when visitors to a national wildlife refuge in Minnesota developed an attachment to the place, they volunteered there, organized events, and helped with maintenance — little actions that helped preserve it. In Colorado, teenagers who participated in a short natural-resource-based work program in their town showed higher levels of place attachment and became more likely to behave in eco-friendly ways at home, by sorting recyclables from trash, say, or turning off the tap while washing dishes to conserve water.

In another study, researchers found that the higher residents' levels of attachment were to their small community in Norway, the more strongly they opposed a hydropower development that would cause major environmental impacts there. Maybe that's NIMBYism: "Do it wherever you want, just not in my backyard." Or it may be "solastalgia," a word to describe "the pain experienced when there is recognition that the place where one resides and that one loves is under immediate assault . . . a form of homesickness one gets when one is still at 'home.' "

People who develop a strong affinity for where they live may reel with grief or anxiety at its real or potential environmental degradation, yet from those uncomfortable, solastalgic sensations comes the motivation to fight. Take, for example, the Canadians who protested the Enbridge Northern Gateway tar sands pipeline in British Columbia. Who organized demonstrations? Locals who lived near the proposed route and were desperate to preserve where they lived. The activist Naomi Klein called it "a total celebration of place." So profound is the connection between place attachment and environmentalism that in 2002, the Environmental Protection Agency released a 280-page guide to "understanding a sense of place."

More than dread of change, what drives environmental activism is a sense of responsibility or obligation to places we love, says Jessica Thompson, an assistant professor of communication and performance studies at Michigan State University, who studied participants in a native plant restoration project at the Denver Botanic Gardens. Like solastagia, "that really comes from the bond that we have to places," Thompson told me. "People who recognize the value of places and feel affinity for the natural world, they will sense the potential impacts and losses associated with climate change wherever they are."

It's one thing to understand climate change as an abstract, quite another to notice its effects on your particular place. When you're rooted, you *do* notice. You know that storms are getting fiercer, tides more erratic, or that the lilac that always bloomed the third week of May is now sending up buds in mid-April. You've paid attention, or you've lived there long enough to remember it wasn't always this way. "I don't think you can love a whole planet," says Naomi Klein. "I think what's driving the most powerful resistance movements is love of particular places. That's why Wendell Berry says, 'Each of our jobs is to love our place more than any other place.' And if everybody did that we'd be fine."

In Park City, I could see how living amid the wilderness might enhance that kind of fiercely protective love. Midway up the mountain, the scrubby lower trail entered a ghostly white aspen grove. Pale trunks and knotty black eyes encircled us. Alisha pointed out that "under the ground they're actually one tree, rooted together. The single largest living organism in the world is an aspen grove in Colorado." Every sigh of wind made the leaves rustle and shimmy.

A few minutes later, some mountain bikers rode down the path in our direction. "There's a moose a couple switches back," one said. They meant it as a warning. Moose around here can be aggressive, especially if they're caring for a calf. Alisha reassured us. "I'm sure it'll be fine. I see moose up here a fair amount. But if we do run into it, just go slow. Don't startle it."

A quarter mile up the trail, Quinn whispered, "Mel, a moose, a moose, keep walking, keep walking." When I finally gathered the courage to look back, the moose was bedded in a stand of penstemon beneath the aspens, placidly gazing at us. It was a female with an enormous gray muzzle, motionless and beautiful. If I lived here, I thought, I would want to ensure there were always moose in these mountains. My giddiness at the good luck of seeing her carried me to the end of the trail.

If nature can convert a bystander into an environmental activist, can it also convert a vacationer into a resident? Alisha has seen it happen again and again. She herself grew up on a farm in Ohio, then moved to Park City on a whim thirteen years ago to see the Salt Lake City Winter Olympics; once she was hired as a ski instructor and made some friends, she stayed. She now jokes about missing her true calling as a real estate agent, "because I can sell this town in five minutes. It's insane."

One summer afternoon a couple years ago, on a trail near here, she hiked past a vaguely familiar woman in her late forties. "Wait a second," called Alisha. "Don't I know you?"

"Yes, you were my snowshoe guide last winter. My name's Jenny, and I brought my kids and my husband."

"That's right! What are you doing here?"

"Well, after we talked to you and went hiking that week, we decided to look at property and we moved here."

Their family of four uprooted from the Midwest because while they were on vacation they "just really clicked with the town," Alisha said, "and fell in love with it, which is pretty easy to do."

Traveling lets you feel the first stirrings of place attachment. "I could live here," you think. "I could be happy here." If the outdoors knock you out, you may be right.

ENJOY THE GREEN

I was at a party recently where my friend Christy asked everyone in the room, "What is your absolute favorite kind of nature?" Hers was the beach. Laura and Jolene agreed on the mountains. Lucynthia wanted to return to the coastal beauty of California. I have other friends who, had they been in the room, would have pledged fealty to the red-rock crests of the desert or the flower-spangled Rocky Mountains in summer.

How would you have answered? Now explain why. It's as challenging as verbalizing why you prefer John Steinbeck to Jane Austen, or Bruce Springsteen to Ella Fitzgerald. How we feel about what we see outside our kitchen window is personal and mostly inexplicable. Such preferences just *are*. We're hard-pressed to say why. Why does my friend Christy adore the beach? Because she is who she is.

"Some places move you, touch your soul," is how Jon Montgomery describes it. Fifteen years ago, he felt that soul-stirring on a trip to Hawaii with his wife, Jennifer, for a family wedding. "We were in a van with my parents and my brothers on our way to dinner and I said, 'I could live here.' Everybody, Jen included, said, 'Nah. Wonderful place to visit, but not to live.' "

At the time the Montgomerys were happy living in Pismo Beach, a coastal California town that's no slouch in the looks department itself. But Hawaii! Jon couldn't get out of his head how lovely it was. A year later, as he and Jen prepared to go on the job market with newly minted teaching licenses, Jon suggested applying in Hawaii. Why not? Luck was with them, and they were hired at schools on Lanai, a one-hour ferry ride from Lahaina, Maui.

I'm childhood friends with Jon's wife, Jen, whose Facebook photos of their ritual "Few Rules Friday" — a weekly beach gathering with friends and kids and dogs and beers and pupus and a magnificent sunset — made me wonder how the Montgomerys had ended up living out an HGTV fantasy. (One of the network's endless cavalcade of real estate shows is called *Hawaii Life*.) The answer is that they wanted to, badly. Jobs aligned to allow it, but like the residents of Park City, they've chosen Lanai over bargain real estate and cheap groceries.

Living in Hawaii, where the median home price is $529,800, is pricey and, with grandparents on the mainland, sometimes isolating. In 2008, when their daughter was three, they returned to California to be closer to family, but they missed Lanai too much and moved back the next year. Jon says they're done moving.

Thirteen years after first landing in Lanai, the beauty of the island still broadsides Jon. "We should be jaded," he told me, "but we're still stoked, all the time. I'm not going to try and describe the scenes here in Hawaii. You've seen the pictures. But I can tell you the beauty of a place like Lanai touches you deeply, again and again and again."

There may be a verifiable psychological reason why people like Jon love Hawaii so much: blue mind. That's what marine biologist Wallace Nichols calls the state of increased wellness and peace that stems from proximity to water. "Being by water meditates you," he says. "It puts you in that relaxed state. You don't need to study or practice meditation. You just need to pay attention to the water around you."

When British researchers used a smartphone app called Mappiness to randomly ping sixty thousand adults about what they were doing and how they felt, then connected their responses to GIS data about their location, they found that people experienced a significant happiness bump near water. "It was the largest effect of any natural environment we looked at," says

George MacKerron of the University of Sussex.

The Montgomerys weren't consciously thinking about the calming benefits of blue mind when they decided to move to Hawaii, nor the seemingly related fact that, according to Centers for Disease Control and Prevention data, people living in Hawaii have the lowest levels of mental distress in the nation — 6.6 percent, compared to 14.4 in Kentucky. They just thought it was beautiful.

To become truly rooted, we know from the Knight Soul of the Community study, people need to feel that where they live is aesthetically pleasing. Beauty is mostly perception, and I'd already learned that how we *think* about our town matters. So it's simple. Just find the place whose beauty bowls you over, and move there. Maybe Hawaii.

Except there lay my problem. I didn't live in Hawaii, or Vermont, or Rapid City, South Dakota, or any of the other places whose natural beauty had stunned me in the past. I lived in Blacksburg, Virginia. And though I knew that other people thought my town was lovely, I didn't, not quite, and I could barely put into words why.

Let me tell you about the day we first

drove into Blacksburg. It was July, and muggy, and after driving for hours we finally crossed the Virginia state line in the late afternoon. Highway 460 wound toward Blacksburg past a string of tired-looking towns — Pearisburg with its cigarette filter factory, Narrows with its lone Burger King. The hills that rose sharply on either side of the road were thickly furred with trees. The trees themselves were practically hidden beneath mounds of kudzu vines.

The New River Valley, the broader area that encompasses Blacksburg, was so green, everywhere green, it was like the mother-lode of vitamin G. According to all the research, I should have felt amazing — all blissed out and anxious to help a neighbor. Instead something in me bridled against these mountains. Everything was so creepily *lush,* like the wicked forest in a Grimms' fairy tale. I couldn't quite put my finger on why, but for months afterward driving through the mountains northwest of Blacksburg made me faintly uneasy.

My Love Where You Live experiments were designed to change how I felt about my town. But this? My reaction to how my town looked? How its nature made me feel? That felt as much an honest manifestation of who I was as my proclivities for British detective shows and Kate Atkinson novels. Was it possible to cultivate a taste for *Game of Thrones* and World War II biographies instead? Are our preferences for natural landscapes as immutable as they feel, and as core to our personalities? Where do they come from, anyway?

Andrew Lothian, owner of Scenic Solutions, a consulting firm based in Adelaide, Australia, says that our feelings about landscapes are primal. Evolution has given humans an attraction to topography that makes successful human habitats. We want places that are safe and that allow us to see without being seen.

The most desirable of these, to our ancient brains, resembles the savannas of Africa, with parklike grasslands that offer both a few large trees for refuge and occasional vantage points for eyeing predators. We've unconsciously mimicked the savanna form for centuries in all kinds of artificial landscapes, from the gardens of Pompeii to the great estates of Europe to modern parks, backyards, and even shopping malls.

Water is also universally beloved, not just because of its soothing blue-mind properties, but because it whispers of survival. "If you want to improve the landscape, just add water," Lothian told me. "And trees are the same. If you can add vegetation and trees, they will tend to always enhance landscape quality. A barren landscape is universally disliked."

For one project, Lothian, who has a PhD in landscape quality assessment, had 430 UK-born respondents rank photos of England's Lake District. Mountains, fittingly, emerged at the top of the heap, with a score of 7.05 out of 10. Empty plains were at the bottom, with a 4.15. In dozens of studies comparing the landscape preferences of people from all over the world, similar results emerged time and again.

Gray-haired, with the mild, bespectacled look of a civil servant, Lothian explained that most of us are more mainstream in our perceptions of landscapes than we'd expect. "You know, there's the saying that beauty lies in the eyes of the beholder, which tends to suggest that every person sees beauty differently. They don't." In fact, when you ask people to rate the appearance of different types of landscapes, the responses usually look like a U-curve: a few outliers at the extremes, but the vast majority meeting somewhere in the middle in agreement about the desirability of water and trees, prospect and refuge.

It was odd to see how Lothian's color-coding system for landscape ratings made an aerial map of the Lake District look like an infrared schematic of military targets. Just that quickly, Lothian reduced centuries of Wordsworthian lonely-cloud wanderings to statistics. Yet it was also comforting to learn that some of my preferences were biological. Without knowing it, I'd internalized prospect-refuge theory, the evolutionary desire for both a view and a hiding place. Of course Blacksburg's thick forests made me nervous. Too much refuge, not enough prospect. The geography kept me from getting a bead on whatever imaginary predators my brain still watched for.

A few individualistic factors also play into our preferences for natural landscapes. In 2012, a pair of Swedish environmental psychologists asked 1,325 people about the type of landscape they grew up in and where they chose to live as adults. The relationship between the two was undeniable. Of people who grew up on the coast, 73 percent later settled in a coastal area; 63 percent who grew up among forests settled in a similar landscape later on.

The natural elements of our childhood environment imprint themselves on us, forming our earliest memories of what a place should look like. One woman I talked to, Susan Auten, moved home to the three-hundred-acre farm where she grew up, in Buckingham, Virginia, because "I love this farm like it's a member of my family. I love having my own space. I love the safety I feel here. I love the scenery and just the comfort of knowing this is my past and my future. There's something so comforting knowing you are where you're supposed to be."

Landscape preferences may also be plainly practical. Maybe we get seasonal affective disorder in gloomy climates or humidity makes our hair frizz. In 2012, "change of climate" was the least common reason for moving given on the census, and yet it tells you something that six times as many Movers headed to Sun Belt cities where the January high temperature was over sixty degrees than moved to cities where the high was below thirty-five degrees.

In the spirit of a Love Where You Live experiment, I tried an exercise similar to the ones Lothian used to gauge a landscape's attractiveness. On Pinterest, I did an image search using terms like "natural landscape," "scenery," and "places." Up popped photos of mountains, waterfalls, pine forests, lavender fields, and beaches where tidal pools reflected the clouds. I saved the ones I liked best, and at the end of a half hour I reviewed the collection. What did they have in common? Would I see patterns that indicated to which version of nature I gravitated?

My pictures — places like Gimmelwald, Switzerland, and Kenai Peninsula, Alaska, and Mount Hood, Oregon — weren't exactly the same, but I noticed broad similarities. There was usually a body of water, like a lake or a river, and often the kind of tree-speckled grassland that evolutionary biologists say I'm primed to like. A mountain generally loomed in the background. Given the calculus of landscape preference that Andrew Lothian explained, apparently I'd be happiest in either the parkland my DNA craved, near water, or in a mountain valley straight out of *Heidi.*

I'd been reading *Heidi* aloud to Ruby, and I was struck by how much the happiness of the little girl depended on her return to her beloved Swiss mountains: "She had no need now to wander about, for the great burning longing of her heart was satisfied; she had seen the high mountains and rocks alight in the evening glow, she had heard the wind in the fir trees, she was at home again on the mountain."

Our feelings about natural beauty are quantifiable and fairly predictable — and yet we talk and write about nature in such soulful ways! Novels and nonfiction glorify a Prince Edward Island spring or a pond in Massachusetts. In ballads, singers croon the praises of "Carolina in My Mind" and "Southland in the Springtime" ("With the farmland like a tapestry passed down through generations / And the peach trees stitched across the land").

The magazine *Orion* runs a column called "The Place Where You Live," in which writers extol the graces of their towns in melting prose. In one piece, Jenna Sammartino, a Cape Cod National Seashore ranger who grew up in Colorado, describes her experience of her town: "Surrounded thus by seawater, I've felt my molecules slowly rearranging over the years, the ocean seeping its way into me. . . . I realized long ago that this was something I couldn't be without — the smell of the sea."

Would my molecules slowly rearrange over the years, too? It wasn't impossible. Nonhuman organisms acclimate to their environments all the time, sometimes making physical alterations to meld body and place more seamlessly. Perhaps I, too, would evolve in time. Lothian agreed. "I've found in all of my studies that familiarity can increase ratings by up to 5 percent, maybe even more in some places," he said.

Having lived through a few rounds of seasons in Blacksburg, I'd already learned to appreciate localized spots of beauty. I knew where the daffodils would burst out of the ground and when to expect to smell the lilacs. Maybe eventually things would be all right. Of course, eventually wasn't the time frame I was after. I wanted to speed things up. It was time for a Love Where You Live experiment.

TAKE A HIKE

A good starting point: the website Scenic Seven.com. A few years ago, the New River Valley Economic Development Alliance created the site as a PR come-on to potential new residents and investors. "You don't have to travel far to experience breathtaking natural beauty," it declared. "The Scenic Seven are seven locations in the New River Valley of Virginia that showcase the natural wonders of our region. Take a tour of the Scenic Seven this year."

The argument was a twist on "Blacksburg isn't boring" — this time, "Blacksburg isn't ugly." The Economic Development Alliance believed it could prove it to you, if only you would take the Scenic Seven Challenge and explore the following local outdoor attractions:

- The Bear Cliffs Trail at Mountain Lake Conservancy, a nearby nature preserve
- The Black Ridge Trail on the federally funded Blue Ridge Parkway
- The Joe Pye Trail at Pandapas Pond
- A waterfront stroll along the New River in Bisset Park in nearby Radford
- The ten-mile stretch of the New River Trail between Pulaski, Virginia, and Claytor Lake
- The Huckleberry Trail in Blacksburg
- The Cascades Trail in Pembroke, Virginia

The challenge was to hike or bike all seven trails. Do it and you'd get a free Scenic Seven T-shirt. Boom. Gauntlet thrown.

Around here, everyone hikes the Cascades. We'd gravitated there for a family walk or two already, and the two-mile trail's dim, Pleistocene dampness enthralled us. Texas had been in severe drought when we moved away. We'd been unnerved to see the water levels in Lady Bird Lake dropping, dropping, dropping. Here the burblings of Little Stony Creek provided the kind of white noise nature soundtrack I listened to as I worked. In its presence I could feel calm settling over me.

Inevitably by the second mile of the hike Ruby would decide that death-by-exhaustion was imminent, and Quinn and I would have to carry her, cajole her, and/or lie to her about how much longer and — oh my gosh, is that Hogwarts around the corner? All my calm would evaporate.

When at last we'd reach the sixty-nine-foot Cascades waterfall, the trip would seem worth it anyway. Even Ruby would be stunned into cheerful nonwhining. The girls would peel off their shoes and wade into the shallows, while Quinn and I sat and watched the water boil down the rocks. Perhaps, I would think, where we lived would be okay.

The Cascades were a half hour from our house, and they were excellent public relations, which made me think that as place attachment strategies go, the Scenic Seven Challenge was a smart one. Wisely it fostered something called "place dependence," a subset of place attachment that emphasizes feelings of reliance on a landscape. Farmers and ranchers develop place dependence as they work the land for their livelihood. In their own way, recreationists rely on places, too. Think of a skier moving to Park City for the easy access to the slopes, or a surfer who settles in La Jolla, drawn by the waves.

The kayakers, mountain bikers, anglers, and ultrarunners who vote in *Outside* magazine's Best Town Ever contest have pastimes that require a particular geography. The most avid choose where they live because of it. They depend on their places to do what makes them happy and so develop an ongoing, rewarding relationship with the local outdoors. That makes them attached.

Like North Star Destination Strategies' community branding efforts in Sierra Vista, Arizona, the Scenic Seven Challenge targeted current residents as much as future residents. Would participating in the challenge as a Love Where You Live experiment increase my attachment to Blacksburg? According to Gerard Kyle, a professor in the Department of Recreation, Park and Tourism Sciences at Texas A&M, yes — and even more if I did it with other people. "It's the activity, the experience, and who you share that experience with. So if you enjoy the activity and you enjoy it with significant others, then the meanings you attach to those relationships often become embedded in the place."

To fall in love with your town, do what your town is good at — preferably with other people. Here in southwest Virginia, most of the people I'd become friends with hiked for entertainment. Soon the Scenic Seven Challenge was generating excited discussion on Facebook. The consensus seemed to be: "Let's go get our free T-shirt."

My friend Michelle organized the first official Scenic Seven outing. Winter was wearing off, and nine or ten women, eager for spring, showed up to hike the Joe Pye Trail at Pandapas Pond, a nature area a few miles up Highway 460 past Blacksburg.

Between us we'd brought thirty or so kids, from babies to teenagers. Most of the children, at least one of whom was wearing sparkly Sunday shoes, ran ahead, so ecstatic to be outside in each other's company that they forgot to complain. The women walked behind, bunching into knots of two or three, stopping to help our little people cross swollen streams, then clustering again to carry on paused conversations.

Every last woman on that hike was a Mover. We all came from other places — California, Utah, New York, Washington, Montana, Texas. Some had lived here for years, some just a few months. We talked about kids and schools and church and books, so drunk on sunshine that, like our kids, we were hardly aware of the miles passing.

A few months later, my friend Laura and I took our kids on the three-mile Black Ridge Trail on the Blue Ridge Parkway — another of the Scenic Seven challenges. From the first, the hike seemed doomed. We'd walked about one hundred feet when Laura's youngest had a potty emergency. Another mile after that it was Ruby's turn. ("Drink less water," I chided.) Somehow we managed to lose the trail, only noticing when we emerged onto the Blue Ridge Parkway. The maps we'd found online were no help. Where did we go next? Were we really meant to walk through a cow pasture?

We were. The cows parted for us like the Red Sea. And just as we were congratulating ourselves on our sense of adventure, the skies blackened and it began to rain. "Great, I'm wearing a white T-shirt," Laura lamented. Our children screamed and galloped away like startled deer. The rain thickened. The trail dissolved into rivulets of mud beneath our feet.

Luckily, hiking disasters were our favorite stories. Every so often one or the other of us would say, *Remember that time we walked through that cow pasture? Remember when we got lost?* I'd think about the rainbow that appeared right as we ended our hike, the wisps of steam that exhaled from the pavement as the sun came out. Gerard Kyle, the Texas A&M professor, had been right. When I hiked with people who were meaningful to me, the places we went absorbed meaning by osmosis.

As a Love Where You Live experiment, the Scenic Seven Challenge wasn't an unmitigated success. For months I chipped away steadily at each of the seven hikes. Then I stalled out on the ten-mile bike ride of the New River Trail. I couldn't find the time or a way to get my bike to the trailhead. I still haven't earned my Scenic Seven T-shirt.

Did the Scenic Seven Challenge work anyway? Did I learn to "experience breathtaking natural beauty" in the New River Valley? At first, what all those walks in the woods taught me was to admire my area's physicality the way a runner admires her body after a marathon. I appreciated what my area allowed me to *do,* and so I could ignore its appearance.

Paradoxically, being bodily present in the woods, doing happy things with people I liked, gradually bled the woods of their eerie

Grimmsian connotations. My brain subconsciously formed new mental associations, and soon a kudzu-beribboned forest no longer prompted a PTSD flashback from childhood viewings of *The Watcher in the Woods.* It summoned up the pleasant associations of good, hard exercise, birdsong, the sounds of water and laughter.

Andrew Lothian had told me that most people found familiar landscapes more desirable than unfamiliar ones. Spending time hiking in the forests around Blacksburg hastened the process of familiarization. Pretty soon, I knew half of the New River Valley by my experiences: "Here I played in the stream with Ella and Ruby." "There we saw the waterfall." "That's where the kids played hide-and-seek in a cave." As I'd learned with my last Love Where You Live experiment, a town is what you think it is. In the same way, a town looks like what you think it looks like. I understood now why people thought it was beautiful here.

That day that I looked through online photos of different landscapes, I stumbled on a picture of the Blue Ridge Parkway, which intersects a town about forty minutes from mine. A flare of evergreens spiked in the foreground. Beyond, layers of dark mountains receded into the horizon, each crest growing fainter, as if drawn in ever-lighter pencil. It looked very much like the views I see around Blacksburg. And my heart jolted, and I thought: Home.

LOVE YOUR CITY CHECKLIST

☐ Make a list of your town's natural assets. If you live in a city, are there parks nearby? Secret gardens? What makes you feel close to nature where you live? What do you like looking at?

☐ Learn the names of the flora and fauna in your area. Check out a book on the subject, or connect with the Master Naturalists or Master Gardeners in your town.

☐ Find ways to do the outdoorsy things you love where you live. Even in cities, you can walk through parks, bike greenbelts, or dangle your feet in ponds. Spending time in nature is soothing (remember vitamin G) in a way that makes people feel better about their surroundings.

☐ Invite friends for a hike, since doing something in nature with people you love creates a happy place anchor.

☐ Go geocaching or letterboxing, as an easy way to get into natural spaces in your town. The more your hobbies rely on where you live, the more place dependent you'll become, which makes you love your town.

☐ So you're not outdoorsy. That's fine.

Figure out one beautiful place in your town — a creek, a park, a river — and spend some time there. Go for a drive and enjoy the view.

☐ Protect where you live through small acts of daily responsibility — picking up litter, buying low-energy compact fluorescent lightbulbs, recycling, turning off the water when you brush your teeth, remembering by some small miracle to take your reusable shopping bags to the supermarket. If you want to be place attached, act like someone who loves where they live.

CHAPTER SEVEN: VOLUNTEER

When you're an event planner, people expect you to throw yourself a rock-star birthday party every year. In 2010, Robyn Bomar wasn't sure she wanted to. "There's nothing special about turning thirty-eight, but it felt like a lot of people were, like, 'What are you going to do?' " Finally she said, "Let's do something for someone else."

No party. No guests. Robyn decided she would spend the day doing thirty-eight random acts of kindness, one for each year she'd been alive.

She and her family began right after breakfast on her birthday. They loaded bags of groceries into shoppers' cars at the supermarket. They fed parking meters around Destin, Florida, where they lived. They hid gift cards between the books at Barnes & Noble, passed out Tootsie Pops on a playground, and paid for the cars behind them at a toll bridge. They delivered balloons to hospital patients and dragged a neighbor's garbage can up the driveway for her.

Strangers were sometimes hesitant. "Why are you doing this?" they'd ask. "What organization are you with?" Robyn's three daughters were under strict instructions not to tell anyone it was their mother's birthday, so they'd simply say it was a little something to brighten their day.

July 17, the day we moved to Blacksburg, also happened to be the day I turned thirty-six. Festive birthday highlights included a seven-hour drive through Kentucky and West Virginia, topped by a celebratory signing of contracts at the electric company. I made Quinn vow that, to make up for it, he'd turn my next birthday into a bacchanal of indulgence, or at the very least bake a homemade cake and do the dishes afterward.

I would have held him to it, too, if he hadn't registered for an out-of-state conference that week. Good-bye, homemade cake. Hello, dishes. I braced myself to spend birthday #37 wallowing in self-pity.

To cheer myself up, I contemplated taking Robyn Bomar's approach, which she had turned into a national movement called the Birthday Project, and which I had written about for a women's magazine. Building some good place-karma here in Blacksburg might be more rewarding, I thought, than passing my special day in a Facebook coma. Inspired, I settled on completing seventeen acts of kindness, a number that seemed propitious for a July seventeenth birthday.

Robyn Bomar, ever the event planner, had plotted and prepped her thirty-eight good deeds beforehand. I, too, brainstormed a list of possibilities, starting with a few basic questions: Who in Blacksburg would be cheered by a surprise hit of affection? What good deeds might make my birthday feel like a party? Once I'd decided what to do, I spent a few days gathering supplies (gift cards, quarters) and mapping the most efficient routes around town.

The July humidity sets in early in southwest Virginia, so not long after eight a.m. on my birthday, Ella and Ruby and I were heaving a cooler full of water bottles toward the Huckleberry Trail, the paved path where I'd posted the Walk Blacksburg sign. Our first act of kindness was modeled on one of Robyn's. Destin, she'd said, was full of walkers and joggers, so she and her family handed out water bottles. I figured we could mount a low-effort version on the Huckleberry. We left the cooler next to the trail with a construction paper sign that said, "Good for you for getting outside! Enjoy some cold water on us." Then we ran back to the car. The ding-dong-ditch aspect electrified us. By the time we were buckled in we were practically hysterical.

After that, each little random act of kindness tumbled efficiently into the next, like we were working our way through the best list of errands ever. Deliver Carol Lee donuts to the library and the fire department. Stuff vases with flowers and get the nurses at Lewis-Gale Medical Center to deliver them to patients. Tape $1.50 in quarters to a hospital soda machine. Leave a buck on the claw machine in the supermarket, with a note advising the finder to play a game. Check, check, check, and check.

Robyn had said that as her birthday wore on, she paid more attention to who was around them and what they really needed. That, she said, "was the biggest learning experience of all — to not be so random about kindness and be more intentional." Like her, I tried to keep my eyes open to genuine distress. We saw a homeless man with a "Need Food" sign on a bench downtown. When I handed him a bag of donuts and a paper carton of milk, he nodded wordlessly, as if he'd been expecting us.

The librarian, on the other hand, squealed like a teenager: "Donuts? For us?" More than I'd expected, people in Blacksburg were willing to roll with the oddness of the moment when a stranger assaults them with goodwill. That morning, I'd spotted a Volunteer Rescue Squad truck parked on the side of the road, and I'd run up and thrust a box of donuts through the window (donuts being the ultimate happiness maker). "This is a random act of kindness!" I exclaimed. "Thanks for your service! Share them with the rest of the rescue squad!"

The driver, a middle-aged man with a mustache, blinked at me, then laughed. "Are you serious? Wow."

I'd like to think that at dinner tables around Blacksburg that night, people told crazy stories. *Can you believe that lady with the donuts?* they'd say. Or, *Hey, I finally got to play the claw machine!* I imagined them saying how it made their day.

It more than made *my* day. About half of our random acts of kindness were designed for anonymity. These were the sneaky ones that Ella and Ruby loved best, like hiding dollar bills among the play equipment at Nellie's Cave Park or tucking an Olive

270

Garden gift card into the door of a young couple we knew from church. We always left before we could see their reaction. Sometimes the reaction found us anyway. In the afternoon, when we circled back to the Huckleberry Trail to pick up the cooler, I found a couple bucks and a thank-you note inside.

Even in anonymity, the seventeen random acts of kindness we did made me feel more seen in Blacksburg. We had made something good happen. We had thrown a pebble into the pond and watched the ripples fan out.

FIND A REASON TO GIVE

I probably don't have to convince you that doing nice things for others makes us feel better in all sorts of ways.

Physically, community service is as satisfying as gorging on burgers and as calming as a session of yoga, but without the nasty side effects of Zoloft. In one 2013 survey, more than a third of American volunteers said that volunteering lowered their stress levels and made them feel better. Volunteers have higher self-esteem, more optimism, and better social skills. They're less anxious and depressed. They wow doctors with their lower blood pressure and healthier hearts. In studies, they're less likely to die at any given moment than nonvolunteers.

"When we do good deeds," explains bio-ethicist Stephen G. Post, coauthor of *Why Good Things Happen to Good People,* "we're rewarded by a dopamine pulse. Giving a donation or volunteering in a food bank tweaks the same source of pleasure that lights up when we eat or have sex. It's clear that helping others, even at low thresholds of several hours of volunteerism a week, creates mood elevation."

Volunteering in your hometown, you reap a double-whammy benefit: Helping out makes you feel better while simultaneously making your city a better place to live. Think about it. Every time you pick up litter, you make your city more aesthetically pleasing — one of the three most important factors in place attachment, as the Soul of the Community study taught us. Every time you volunteer to pass out T-shirts at a town festival, you help your city increase its social offerings — more place attachment. When you hammer nails into a Habitat for Humanity house in your town, your city becomes welcoming for all kinds of people. Still more place attachment. What's good for your community is also good for you.

In 2005, researchers from the National Conference on Citizenship started measuring the number of nonprofits in 942 metro areas and 3,100 counties across the country. A few years later, the recession hit. That allowed them to uncover this startling piece of information: People who lived in towns with a higher number of nonprofit organizations — a symbol of how service minded the town was — were less likely to become unemployed during the recession than residents of towns with fewer nonprofits. Just one extra nonprofit per one thousand people added up to a half percentage point fewer out-of-work residents. A similar effect was seen among cities that had a greater number of citizen volunteers.

Why did community service help cities do better economically? One reason suggested by researchers is that volunteering increases place attachment, and place attachment to one's town can "increase the odds that one will invest, spend, and hire there."

As taxpayer dollars peter out, the list of what unpaid volunteers do for cities has grown long and kind of appalling. Volunteers don uniforms and patrol neighborhoods with the city police force in Pasadena, California. They man the front desk of the Naperville, Illinois, city hall. They direct lost passengers around the airport in Philadelphia and write parking tickets in Deer

Park, Texas. In an ideal world, municipalities would never have to recruit volunteers to handle the filing, maintenance, gardening, cleaning, and caring that should probably be the domain of full-time city employees. On the other hand, volunteers free up cash-strapped governments to maintain basic or extra services. If American volunteers were paid for all the service they gave in 2013, it would cost an estimated $173 billion.

So substantial is the good that cities can eke out of local volunteers that in 2009, then mayor of New York Michael Bloomberg and the Rockefeller Foundation funded an organization called Cities of Service, to teach cities how to galvanize volunteers and use them more effectively. More than two hundred mayors across the United States and the United Kingdom joined the Cities of Service coalition, pledging to, in the words of Mayor Bloomberg, "harness the power of the civically minded to help solve our most pressing local challenges." Two dozen cities, including Baltimore, Houston, and Richmond, were given grants to hire a chief service officer, a senior official who would develop a citywide volunteer plan and champion it through the highest levels of city hall.

Two days before Laurel Creech was set to start work as Nashville's first chief service officer, in May 2010, the city was hit with a thousand-year flood that killed eleven people and caused $6 billion in damage — a baptism by fire if ever there was one. Before the flood, Creech says, Nashville "already had a pretty good culture of service in our community. Postflood, that has increased dramatically."

As chief service officer, Creech launched the Mayor's Workplace Challenge to encourage businesses to prioritize employee volunteerism, and she helped create an accreditation program for nonprofits that train and treat volunteers well. In a city that's expected to triple in size over the next twenty-five years, volunteers now do more of the heavy lifting with city-run initiatives like the Home Energy Savings Program, which retrofits low-income houses to make them more energy efficient. By signing up for Cities of Service opportunities, residents are essentially saying, "If the city thinks it's important, so do I." That, says Creech, "enhances the pride and value of being in Nashville."

One of the by-products of volunteering in and for your city can be a sense of "place identity." The idea is that, in the same way you might self-identify as a parent or a lawyer or a dog lover, volunteering helps you see yourself as a valuable part of your town. You join the collective "we" of your place, a sentiment that's summed up tidily in this statement from the place attachment scale: "Where I live tells you a lot about who I am as a person."

One woman, a self-described "chronic volunteer" who spends six hours a day running the free community toolshed in Flint, Michigan (a Cities of Service program), explained why she didn't just hand the job over to city government: "*We* are the city of Flint. This is our responsibility. We have to take care of our home." For the place attached, volunteering for your town feels as natural and obligatory as Saturday chores around your house. The more you give, the more firmly you feel that way.

The cycle goes something like this: You volunteer, so your town becomes better, which makes it easier to love, which makes you more attached to your town. As Abraham Lincoln purportedly said, "I like to see a man proud of the place in which he lives. I like to see a man live in it so that his place will be proud of him."

That your city wants you to volunteer in some capacity is a no-brainer. Of *course* it does. Nashville, which rates a middle-of-the-road twenty-second place for volunteering among the fifty-one largest cities in the country, is desperate for it. So why don't Americans do it more often? In 2014, only about a quarter of Americans volunteered. Those who did gave a median fifty hours of service — impressive, but that still leaves three out of four Americans who never volunteered during the year. Not even once.

How geographically mobile we are may explain some of our reluctance. In one survey of why metro-area Atlantans gave to charity, 83 percent said they did so "out of a sense of community." Implied is that if you don't have a sense of community, you may not be motivated to give. Other studies show that Movers are less philanthropic than Stayers, and that towns with more Stayers tend to have more volunteers.

When we move, our volunteer habits from wherever we lived last often carry over to our new town, says Becky Nesbit, an assistant professor of nonprofit management at the University of Georgia, who studies volunteerism. So if you volunteered for the animal shelter in your old city, chances are good you'll sign up with another animal shelter after you move.

Some Movers, however, wait for an invitation to volunteer, which means they have to develop a social network first. Others have a tough time finding the right fit. They track down the soup kitchen, "but it might be kind of cliquey and they feel left out, so they stop because it's not the same positive experience it was before," says Nesbit. Or they want to volunteer for the local arts organization but find it poorly managed. Sometimes they inquire about volunteer opportunities and never hear back. "There are a lot of barriers to people successfully reconnecting to volunteering [after a move]."

Nesbit herself, who's lived in Indiana, North Carolina, Kansas, and Georgia in the last ten years, says that the painful process of getting your feet under you in a new place can be enough to kill the time or desire to volunteer. "My last few moves, I haven't been there very many years. I haven't made as much of an investment in place. I thought for a long time I'd like to be a CASA volunteer, but I just haven't done that. I don't know all the reasons why." She hasn't found her forever place, and "there's this reluctance to make a deep [volunteer] commitment unless I know I'm going to be there for a while."

By those lights, Minneapolis–St. Paul,

Minnesota, is something of an outlier. It's one of the fastest-growing metros in the United States, with more new move-ins than move-outs. Yet the Twin Cities also have one of the highest volunteer rates in the country. Nationally, about a quarter of Americans volunteer. In the Twin Cities in 2013, 35.8 percent did.

How does a city filled with Movers get people to volunteer? My hypothesis was that it might have something to do with how much people liked living there. In 2014 the Twin Cities scored fourth place in Gallup-Healthways' well-being poll. Wages are high, 23 percent above the national average, and it's relatively inexpensive to live there. Other studies back up just how happy and healthy locals seem to be — more physically active than most of the nation, more well-read, more likely to feel safe.

Did people in the Twin Cities volunteer because they were so bowled over by their hometown's splendor that they just had to give back? Or were Minneapolis and St. Paul amazing because they were packed with the kinds of people who volunteer no matter what?

In the 360 acres that constitute the Minnesota State Fair (tellingly referred to as the "Great Minnesota Get-Together"), you can admire abnormally large zucchinis and eat vast amounts of cheese curds. You can watch white-clad 4H-ers lead their heifers around the cattle barn while judges make lurid-sounding pronouncements about the second-place cow's "awful good udder." And still I feel confident saying that one of the more unusual displays of state pride is found in a barn across from the Red Hot Chicago Dog booth. "Hey there, welcome!" a man cried into a microphone as I wandered inside. "We're doing a little volunteering today! Come join us!"

I had found the KARE barn, where each Saturday and Sunday of the Great Minnesota Get-Together, fairgoers can complete a small volunteer project for a Twin Cities nonprofit. One day they were making blankets for people in hospice care, the next assembling journal kits for the children's hospital. Today's goal: decorating holiday boxes, which in December would be filled with food and delivered to clients of the Aliveness Project, a charity that serves Twin Cities residents who have HIV/AIDS. "In just ten minutes," said the guy with the mic, an Aliveness Project staffer named Tim Marburger, "you can help us make someone's holiday a little brighter this year. Last year, we helped seven hundred families."

Outside, there were alligators to be admired and corn dogs to be devoured. A community service break seemed like a lot to ask. Yet a couple dozen people were splayed across benches, drawing out-of-season snowmen and sleighs on white boxes. Volunteers ferried around plastic cups of crayons and markers. Everyone seemed happy to be there.

Why did Minnesotans at the fair take the time to volunteer? When I asked Patricia Garcia, a staffer with local volunteer network Hands-On Twin Cities, cosponsor of the speed volunteering event, she said, "It's the whole concept of 'Minnesota nice.' It's important to us to have a close-knit community."

"There's a culture of giving back," added Meghan Morse, the center's special projects director.

I had of course heard about "Minnesota nice," the famed midwestern brand of bland, nonconfrontational pleasantness so well-known that it merits its own Wikipedia entry. Was the reason Minnesota ranked second in the nation for number of volunteer hours per resident because Minnesotans were just plain nicer than everyone else?

When I ran this theory by Kristin Schurrer, executive director of Hands-On Twin Cities, she was incredulous. "No!" she blurted. "Have you driven on our roads?" Minnesota nice — really an excruciatingly reserved social politeness — wasn't the same thing at all as being fundamentally kinder than the rest of America.

Schurrer's theory was that the prevailing ethos of community service was ingrained in local culture by the area's Scandinavian immigrants. They valued mutual aid, trust, and social connectedness — antecedents for volunteerism that were cemented by Minnesota's harsh weather. Pioneers literally had to help each other survive.

The same prosocial characteristics can be seen in other bitter-cold states. North Dakota, South Dakota, Minnesota, and Vermont excel on measures of social capital where Sun Belt states like Nevada, Tennessee, Georgia, and Alabama do poorly, prompting social scientist Robert Putnam to point out that "the best single predictor of the level of social capital in American states is distance to the Canadian border."

If anyone embodies the genuinely good side of Minnesota nice, it's a woman named

Jenny Friedman — which is odd, since Jenny's originally from St. Louis. She moved to Minnesota for college as an eighteen-year-old and immediately fell in love with the state. "It was a feeling I got when I got here, that it just seemed to fit me," she says. After a stint in graduate school in Chicago, she and her husband settled in a homey neighborhood of Minneapolis three blocks from Minnehaha Creek.

Not long afterward, Jenny volunteered to deliver for Meals on Wheels. She and a friend piled into Jenny's tiny car, a stack of hot tin-foiled dinners between them and their kids buckled into the back. At each stop, one of the women would escort a child to the front door to present a meal to a grandmotherly senior. The experience became a mission; Jenny went on to found the family volunteering nonprofit Doing Good Together. But she remembers that first foray into volunteering as a direct response to her joy at living in Minneapolis. "I felt like I was incredibly blessed, like life had handed me this great place," she recalls. "Here I was in Minneapolis! I loved it. I was just happy. So I wanted to do something."

Though the Twin Cities have a lot going for them, they are not Shangri-La. Like any major metro area, they deal with their fair share of crime, drugs, gangs, violence, poverty, racial inequality, and all-purpose hard times. For residents, volunteering is a concrete, positive way to deal with their city's problems so they don't overwhelm them.

Through Doing Good Together, Jenny organizes an annual Family Service Fair, with booths where grade schoolers can assemble sandwiches for a homeless shelter or design a card for a hospitalized child. So many people cram into the Midtown Global Market for this little carnival of idealism that "it's like all these people shining lights into the darkness," she tells me. "It makes you feel good about people in general, and about your city and the place you live."

One man I met in Minneapolis moved to the city's north side precisely because it was one of the most economically disadvantaged and troubled parts of town. Brian Mogren is a lanky, forty-eight-year-old white guy who looks not unlike the dad from *Family Ties.* In 2008, he quit his job as an art director for Target to turn his Craftsman-style home in the Near North neighborhood into a "house of hospitality." The idea was to provide a safe, light-filled gathering place in a part of town where crime is not uncommon.

In practice, that means a literal open-door policy at his home, called St. Jane House. The book- and candle-bedecked living room hosts a local meditation group, monthly ukulele sing-alongs, and a support group for women who have lost children to violence or prison. People pray there. They hold hands and hug. The day I was there, a couple of schoolkids, Devon and Lazell, did homework in Brian's kitchen after school, raiding the fridge at will and complaining about the snacks. (Lazell: "Aw, man, these Oreos are stale!" Brian: "No, they're not. I just bought them." Lazell: "They're stale, Brian.") Brian, who has no kids of his own, relishes the part of godfather, buying the brothers school shoes and cajoling them about their grades.

To manage St. Jane House full-time has required sacrifice. No more 401(k), health benefits, financial security, or Target employee discount. The differences between Mogren and his neighbors are sharp enough to cut yourself on. He's conscious of the fact that some people probably see him as another white do-gooder. But he firmly believes that "this is what it's all about — connecting across differences and discovering our common humanity. It's hard to build community from the outside."

I can hardly think of a more demanding way to invest in where you live. Yet Brian radiates joy. He insists he's never been happier. He was frenetic about introducing me to his friends and mentors, including the Visitation Sisters of Minneapolis, a group of white-haired "nuns in the hood" with their own open-door policy a few blocks away. "My life is so great because I'm surrounded by great people," Brian told me about ten times.

One of the friends Brian wanted me to meet was Don Samuels, a former Minneapolis city council member who was recently elected to the city's school board. Sitting at Brian's kitchen table, Don told me that after immigrating from Jamaica as a twenty-year-old, "I made the commitment that I would always live in the inner city." His first house, in Providence, Rhode Island, was in a neighborhood so bad that no one else would live there. Even as Don's career as a toy designer took off, he settled his family in poor, mostly African American neighborhoods every time he moved, in Boston, Southern California, New York, and elsewhere.

Living in rough neighborhoods meant his four kids had few playmates. On the sidewalks there were guys with guns instead of children on bikes. In Minneapolis, the real estate agent refused to show them houses in the high-crime, low-income Jordan neighborhood that Don and his wife, Sondra, targeted. "You don't want to live there," he said. They bought a place in Jordan anyway.

Don and Brian had turned their entire lives into placemaking tools, and their commitment astounded me. When I pointed out that they might be the only people in America who took this half-crazy approach to house hunting, Don laughed. "I'm not trying to find the toughest neighborhood to beat up on myself," he said. He believes that the number one reason inner-city neighborhoods are struggling is that the middle class, and specifically the black middle class, won't live there. To survive, the bad parts of town need to become more stable and economically diverse. How could Don make that happen? Live there himself and hope others followed. That's what it has taken to put his ideals into the kind of lived, daily action that helps him sleep well at night.

For Don, changing underserved communities by choosing to live there is the ultimate expression of loving where you live. "Lots of people would like to see neighborhoods change," he says, "but they don't want to have to change their own life to modify them."

Occasionally some of Don and Sondra's well-off friends are beguiled by their philosophy. "You know, the kids are leaving," one woman said. "We might do this!" She pointed at a rehabbed house on a tough street and said, "I like that house. Can I see it?"

"I'll give them the property and Realtor information and they seem genuinely inspired to make the move," says Don mildly, "but nothing comes of it. It often comes so close, but it's a hard decision to make. The barrier between us and the future we want to see is as thin as a membrane."

JUST GIVE CASH (THE RIGHT WAY)

Stories about selfless Good Samaritans like Don, Brian, and Jenny are inspiring and depressing in equal measure. The idealistic jolt they give me quickly dissolves into lassitude. *I can never be like that,* I think. *I can barely be nice to my own kids some days.* The thought of trying to solve someone else's problems while I'm being pulverized by my own seems a laughable act of hubris. Despite seeing how good volunteering is for us and our communities, sometimes I can't resist the guilty satisfaction of locking myself in my house and muttering, "Maybe next time."

Volunteering is, by definition, the thing we don't *have* to do, unlike working, eating, parenting, sleeping (maybe), and trying to maintain some semblance of a life. As our day-to-day schedule becomes chaotic, volunteering is naturally the first commitment we jettison — or else it becomes the commitment we agonize over and learn to resent. In Blacksburg, I volunteered to organize a readathon fund-raiser that made $10,000 for Ruby's elementary school. Still, whenever Quinn saw me staying up late to work on it, he would say, "You've got to quit the readathon. It's too much. Tell them you can't do it. Someone else can take it on."

Except there *was* no one else. Even in the Twin Cities, only slightly more than a third of residents volunteer — and that's a staggering amount for the United States. If you are among the two-thirds of nonvolunteers, no judgment. I get it, I really do. When you're overworked or stressed or don't know how to help, sometimes it's easier to not do anything.

Here's a thought. Just give money.

Each of my Love Where You Live experiments had taught me that the more I gave to my city, the more I got back from it.

When I invested time, curiosity, and enthusiasm, I *felt* more invested. The act of giving increased my commitment and my place identity — the sense that there's a holistic relationship between who I am and where I live. That we're in it together.

Why not write a check, then? The local nonprofit isn't asking for blood. They want cash. Just as investing in American Airlines stock makes us pay a lot more attention to how American Airlines is operating, and probably makes us more likely to fly American ourselves, I figured that investing my hard-earned money in Blacksburg could increase my ratings on place attachment measures like "If something exciting were happening in this community, I'd want to be involved"; "I'm really interested in knowing what's going on here"; and "I care about the future success of this town."

I thought I'd test my theory out. In 2013 the Lyric, the restored Art Deco movie theater in downtown Blacksburg, needed to upgrade to a digital projection system. The change would cost $120,000 — wildly expensive for an operation that relies on volunteers to sell the peanut M&M's. Still, they'd managed to raise all but the last $50,000, and for that the board of directors launched a civic crowdfunding campaign on Kickstarter.

The Lyric is one of Blacksburg's hubs, where standing in line for cheap buckets of popcorn is akin to community social hour. Back when Quinn and I didn't know anyone in town ourselves, we felt wistful about all the people calling out greetings around us. Now that we'd made more of an effort to make friends, we sometimes ran into people we knew there, and every time it happened I got a place attachment buzz. *Yes. We know them. We belong here.*

The Lyric was one of the places that made Blacksburg Blacksburg, and so it felt important to give to the Kickstarter campaign. Ours wasn't a particularly liberal donation, just $25 or so. As studies predict, donating gave me a brief sense of satisfaction. That was it. No big deal.

It wasn't until a few months after the fund-raiser ended, when the Lyric began scrolling a "thank you" trailer of the names of the donors who'd coughed up a total $58,561 in pledges, that I felt differently. The list had 844 people on it. It took *forever,* so many people loved this movie theater. Sitting with my hand in my popcorn, I searched for our names, and there they were, *Quinn and Melody Warnick,* a big-screen sign that we were part of the community. Our $25 investment made the theater — and thus a bit of Blacksburg — feel like it belonged to us.

Kickstarter and Indiegogo are by now familiar venues for crowdsourcing. Sites that raise money specifically for community projects are proliferating as well. The websites ioby (the letters stand for "in our backyard"), Citizinvestor, and the UK-based Spacehive have helped towns and nonprofits crowdfund bike lanes, dog parks, fireworks festivals, playground renovations, and community arts centers, the kinds of placemaking projects that make towns more lovable.

Rodrigo Davies remembers his shock at hearing in 2012 that Spacehive had crowdsourced £792,000 for a multipurpose community center in remote Glyncoch, Wales, thirty minutes from the working-class mining town where Davies grew up. That civic crowdfunding would catch on in San Francisco was predictable. But Glyncoch, a town in terminal economic decline? "These are areas that have been depressed and had chronic unemployment for decades," Davies explains. "If it can work in a depressed mining town in Wales, something transformative is going on."

In research he later conducted at MIT,

Davies found that civic crowdfunding succeeds better in small towns than large cities, for the same reason that smaller cities do better in *Outside*'s Best Town Ever contest. Human connections matter. "I think often people assume, well, you introduce a technology platform and it's the great anonymous masses who are going to make it happen," he told me. "Money is just going to come from people on the Internet." Not true. Money for community projects comes from people in the community. When residents know who's running the fund-raiser, or they know how their place will benefit from it, they're more likely to donate.

The powerful effect that civic crowdfunding had on places intrigued Davies so much that he took a job with a company called Neighborly, which once functioned as a typical civic crowdfunding site but now takes the fresh approach of allowing small-scale, individual investment in municipal bonds. Munis aren't charity. Cities use municipal bonds to raise money for large-scale public projects. They're a government-backed investment vehicle with a 99 percent on-time repayment rate.

And yet, like civic crowdfunding sites, Neighborly is making munis a way for locals to change where they live for the better. This is the big stuff: $100 million to improve a health care center in Livonia, Michigan (population 95,000); $31 million for water system upgrades in Tigard, Oregon (population 50,000). Investing in a local muni, or donating to a crowdfunded local project, is like paying self-imposed property taxes that happen to show you exactly how your money improves your quality of life. That's empowering.

Because sites like ioby and Spacehive show you how much has been donated, and sometimes who's doing the donating, you're not just blindly slipping money into a closed pot. You see that there are like-minded individuals out there, as I did with the Lyric Kickstarter, and that helps you feel part of the community. As Davies explains, "Effectively this says, 'Look, we're all doing this together.' That's the kind of connection that I think people really crave, especially if they're new to a place. They're trying to get a foothold. They want to feel like they belong. This is a way to get there."

Finding a local cause to support requires determining what you value in your town, a kind of charitable asset mapping. Should you support the cancer care center? The public gardens? Back when I started to shop at Imaginations toy store, I learned that if you don't want it to go away, you should spend your money on it. Donating to organizations whose services you benefit from, like a public radio station or a community orchestra, is sometimes called "philanthropic consumerism." That has a materialistic ring to it, but for Movers it's a helpful way to get started.

Another way to donate locally is through a giving circle, like the one retired teacher Fran Bussey started in Liberty, Missouri. In a giving circle, members each donate a set amount of money per year, then collectively decide which local charity will receive the funds. As a member of several nonprofit boards, Fran knew "there is always a big need for a really good dose of cash to help a nonprofit be really successful." So she asked three of her neighbors to join the circle with a $302 donation apiece, then those four invited more women.

Eventually the Liberty Giving Circle grew to more than two hundred members. Since 2006 they've pumped more than $250,000 into eight local charities, including a transitional home for homeless families and a program for autistic children. Circle members vote on grant applications, and the Greater Kansas City Community Foundation manages the money.

A University of Nebraska study found that giving circle members were highly engaged in their communities, regardless of how long they had lived in town or whether they were homeowners. By requiring friends and neighbors to cooperatively make charitable decisions, the Liberty Giving Circle increases social cohesion and collective efficacy, those forerunners of place attachment. Fran says it gives members a way to "be philanthropic in their hometown."

I would never say that someone should confine all their charitable giving to their hometown. The world is full of places that need Americans' money far more than Americans need it. Give to them, and then, to increase your rootedness, support a local cause, too. Donate to the new community theater. Help remodel the hospital. Pitch in for the Kickstarter to build a mountain bike skills park. (I did, in Blacksburg.) Money changes your town. Giving money changes you. When you invest, you feel invested.

FIND YOUR VOLUNTEERING COMMUNITY

Right after moving to Blacksburg I started showing up for elementary school PTO meetings. That's a form of volunteering that Becky Nesbit says is especially easy for

Movers because it transfers so seamlessly from place to place. Your kids attended school in your last town, and they attend school here.

It's also like a gateway drug for community social cohesion. Most volunteerism involves human contact, the very thing that newcomers (and everyone else) require to feel rooted in their community. By introducing me to that most vital milieu, the parents of my kids' friends, my hours of shelving books and chaperoning field trips paved the way for relationships at a time when I desperately needed them. After a few years and a couple readathons, I was firmly attached to the school.

Then Quinn had to point out that helping with the PTO was a rather cloistered way to give back. "That's not really the same thing as volunteering in your town, is it?"

Since my goal was to attach to Blacksburg, he gently suggested that for a Love Where You Live experiment, I find a way to volunteer for the town as a whole, or at least a slightly larger swath of it. Of course, whatever new volunteer gig I picked up would be in addition to what I was already doing. I needed a low-commitment kind of commitment, something less random than the acts of kindness I'd done on my thirty-seventh birthday, but just as rewarding.

The Town of Blacksburg didn't use volunteers that I could see, so I looked on the VolunteerNRV website for opportunities to help nonprofits. Some of the jobs I was vastly unqualified for (Habitat for Humanity plumber). Some didn't appeal (data entry for a hospice). The one that did strike my fancy was packing bags of food for Micah's Backpack, a nonprofit that sends disadvantaged Blacksburg schoolchildren home with something to eat over the weekend, when they don't get a free school lunch. The group helped all the kids in town, not just the ones in my neighborhood. The packing sessions were once a week. There was no formal commitment. I could just show up.

Everything about this plan seemed brilliant to me, until the evening Quinn and I drove the girls to St. Michael's Lutheran Church to help load the bags, and everyone in town showed up, too. A long line of volunteers snaked through the hall and into the chapel. We waited five minutes for the chance to drop a few granola bars in a grocery bag. Not only did I feel redundant, I felt like, by adding to the crowd, I was actively making other volunteers' experience worse.

I tried elsewhere, taking a once-every-three-months shift at the Interfaith Food Pantry. Many of the clients were working poor who couldn't make ends meet despite having full-time jobs. Some were ill or unemployed. Helping them fill grocery bags with Cheerios and ground beef felt like I was doing something valuable, but like Micah's Backpack, the food pantry had such a surfeit of volunteers it didn't need me very often. (Educated people volunteer more often. Hashtag college town problems.) I was encountering exactly the challenges that Becky Nesbit said kept Movers from volunteering where they lived.

In my utopian fantasies, I'd wanted my volunteering to help Blacksburg residents who needed it most. I knew there were poor people here, kids without enough to eat, people living in desperate circumstances. Couldn't I find a way to make life easier for them, and simultaneously make my town more welcoming? Ninety-five percent of us feel like our volunteering makes a difference in the world, a sensation that is both the impetus and the payback for our acts of charity. We *have* to feel like that or we wouldn't bother. So maybe it's ridiculous that, in the end, the place where I ended up volunteering the most happily was the Lyric.

I know what you're thinking: The movie theater? Really? Of all the noble causes in Blacksburg that really, truly need your help and money — all those hungry people, abandoned animals, struggling kids — you're helping at a movie theater?

Here's why. The Lyric was something I loved and valued. In the same way I didn't want Imaginations toy store to go away, I didn't want the Lyric to go away. I tried to go to movies and concerts there when I could, and I never snuck in candy. (There's a circle of hell reserved for people who sneak candy into a nonprofit movie theater.) Volunteering was just the next step in my existing commitment.

Also, volunteers at the Lyric always looked like they were having an incredibly good time. The people who handed over our popcorn and Sprite were a good-humored group of college students, grandparents, middle-aged folks, and men with crazy handlebar mustaches. Behind the counter, they laughed and chatted. They got free popcorn and soda. Forgive my shallow motivation, but I wanted to join the party.

I started on a winter Saturday morning at a free family matinee of *Hook*. While Ruby and Ella claimed seats in the empty theater, Betty, the cheerfully competent projectionist, showed me how to pour the proper amount of kernels into the popper, press the green button to squirt in a stream of oil, and add a dollop of salty popcorn flavoring. "Make sure the agitator is on," Betty said, "and when the pops are seven seconds apart, dump it and start again."

Despite some initial panic (*When do I press the button?*), I soon developed an easy rhythm with the two other women working concessions — me filling popcorn tubs, someone else handling soda, the third taking orders, all of us in constant motion, like ballerinas. Later, in the dark theater, I felt a bizarre pride listening to the crunch of popcorn around me. *That's my popcorn, people,* I thought. *I made that.*

Most shifts were already taken by regular volunteers, so I made a habit of signing up to volunteer at special events, like a midweek showing of a documentary about pilgrims along the Camino de Santiago in Spain. Since volunteers were always invited to see the show for free, a few minutes after the screening began I fumbled my way to a seat in the dark balcony to watch a film I never would have bothered to see otherwise. In one scene, a hiker speaks exuberantly about the transformative powers of the camino journey. "I came on the camino hoping my

301

brother would change," she said. "But instead, I changed."

Her words made me wonder: Am I changing? How were all my Love Where You Live experiments adding up? Did I really feel differently about my town?

Changes were happening in subtle ways. I had more friends, or at least more people that I recognized, including women like Betty. Volunteering, getting to know my neighbors, hiking, and most of my other experiments had increased my social capital. My numbers on the place attachment scale were steadily going up. I not only knew my way around, but I was genuinely interested in what was going on, and I knew that if something exciting was happening in this community, I'd want to be involved. I identified more with Blacksburg; I felt a part of things. In small ways it felt like I was having an impact on my town, and that felt good.

A few weeks after I started at the Lyric, I received an e-mail inviting me to march with other Lyric volunteers in the Blacksburg Holiday Parade. Quinn, Ella, and Ruby categorically refused to go with me. I contemplated saying no, then I reminded myself of a principle I'd learned from my earlier Love Where You Live experiments: to feel attached, you have to act like an attached person. Was there any question that a person who loved Blacksburg would march in the holiday parade?

That night, Betty the projectionist was the first to see me searching for the Lyric group among a coiled line of floats and marching bands. "Hi, Melody!" she called. "We're so glad you made it!" As I waved at the gathered volunteers with a mittened hand, someone instructed me to put on my cat ears.

The Lyric is a nonprofit. It wasn't going to miss a chance at free advertising, holiday theme be damned. We were all marching in the parade dressed as cats to promote the Lyric's upcoming Internet Cat Video Festival. Someone donned a Nyan Cat costume, a piece of cardboard painted to look like a pink Pop-Tart, with rainbow streamers drooping out the back. The rest of us strung signs around our necks that said things like, "Nom nom nom" and "I can haz cheezburger." Our entire motley crew of concessions volunteers was a walking Internet meme.

I can verify that not everyone in Blacksburg is familiar with the corpus of cat-themed Internet memes. For every spectator who yelled, "I don't know, *can* you haz cheezburger?" there were five that squinted in bafflement. "What *are* you, anyway?" they called as we hustled past, flinging our candy canes willy-nilly.

By the end of the parade, I had a new theory: The crazier you act in loyalty to your place, the more attachment you build. Once I'd worn cat ears in front of ten thousand Blacksburgians, I had a stake not only in the Internet Cat Video Festival (to which I took Ella and Ruby the following day — wouldn't miss it), but in the Lyric movie theater and the whole of Blacksburg.

In Minneapolis, I had met a twenty-five-year-old woman named Jennifer Prod. Over donuts and macaroons at the Wuollet Bakery, she told me the story of how she had moved to the Twin Cities a year earlier with her husband and basically become a professional volunteer. In addition to working with official charities like the Junior League, she developed a sideline doing what she called Random Acts of Happiness — like my birthday acts of kindness, but wackier and more creative.

Jennifer had balloons printed with encouraging messages she had written herself — "A day without you is like a morning without coffee," or "Your smile made me forget my parking ticket" — and she tied them in random spots around town. She passed out homemade cookies on a street corner in honor of Thoreau's birthday. One afternoon, she walked around downtown Minneapolis taping jokes to signs and planters, doozies like "What does a nosy pepper do? Gets jalapeño business." Strangers started following her around to read the next one.

I asked her if doing her Random Acts of Happiness had made her love her city more. She thought about it a second, then said she didn't think so. It wasn't like she was doing those things because she wanted to like the city more. She was just doing them to be (Minnesota) nice. And yet she did love her adopted city, passionately so, and I couldn't help thinking those Random Acts of Happiness were part of the reason why.

There are a million good reasons to volunteer, one of them being that "you don't have to move out of your neighborhood to live in a better one," as urban activist Majora Carter has said. Falling in love with where you live is simply a side benefit.

LOVE YOUR CITY CHECKLIST

☐ Consider the things about your area that break your heart, like the homeless guy on the bench or the packs of teenagers you see shuffling around at loose ends. "Once you know where your grief lives," says Kathy LeMay, author of *The Generosity Plan,* "you can lean into it," using those feelings to guide your contributions. Or you can work to enhance the things that bring you joy, by volunteering for a gardening club, for instance, or starting an after-school ballroom dance program at the local YMCA.

☐ Find a place to volunteer. Big cities offer endless variety, so it's easy to find a match for your skills. Smaller towns often have their own volunteer centers. Or check a national website like VolunteerMatch.org or the local branch of the United Way to track down interesting opportunities.

☐ Check your city's website to see if your city government needs volunteers. The work (ahem, filing) might not be glamorous — or then again, it might (forensic work with the police). Bonus: You'll develop a greater appreciation for where your tax money goes.

☐ Perform random acts of kindness, either on a special day like your birthday or a day you're bored. RandomActsof Kindness.org lists dozens of ideas, which you can filter by cost or time investment. Other resources include Robyn Bomar's TheBDayProject.com and Jen Prod's website, StudioKindred.com, which includes details on more than fifty clever and very nice acts of happiness.

☐ Donate. If it's tough for you to give regularly, save change in a jar and let your family decide which local organization to donate to once it's full. Touring the organization's building or volunteering there will enhance the place attachment premium.

☐ Give to a civic crowdfunding project. Find one at Kickstarter, ioby, or Citizinvestor.

☐ Join or start a giving circle. Giving Circles.org spells out how to do it.

CHAPTER EIGHT:
EAT LOCAL FOOD

The Bite into Maine food truck has a blessedly slim menu. A kid's grilled cheese. A few sides like potato salad. Whoopie pie for dessert. The real star is the lobster roll, a toasted New England–style bun piled with lobster that was crawling in Casco Bay this morning. Bite into Maine offers a lavish six varieties, including Connecticut style, dripping with hot butter; Wasabi, slathered with a spicy, Japanese-inflected mayonnaise; Chipotle; Curry; and the Picnic lobster roll, dolloped with melted butter, creamy coleslaw, and celery salt.

For purity's sake, I went for the Maine-style roll, a version with heaps of delicate pink claw meat bound together with a healthy serving of mayonnaise. It seemed the right thing to do in light of the truck's location.

All summer long, Bite into Maine parks a few hundred yards from the Atlantic Ocean in Cape Elizabeth, Maine, up the hill from one of New England's most photographed lighthouses. The day I was there, the Portland Head Light towered in glorious Instagrammability. Waves hit the shoreline with a washing-machine rumble. Inside the gleaming aluminum trailer, Bite into Maine co-owner Sarah Sutton assembled my Maine roll with a generous heap of lobster and a pinch of fresh chive, then handed it to me with a pack of Cape Cod potato chips and a bottle of Maine Root root beer. I sat at a nearby picnic table and took a bite.

I'm not from Maine. For that matter, neither are the couple who own the Bite into Maine food truck. Sarah Sutton and her husband, Karl, are midwesterners who met while working at a high-end camera store in Minneapolis. In local parlance, they're from Away.

To be clear, being "from Maine" is not as simple as it sounds. Anyone from Away is obviously off the list, but among hard-liners, not even being in possession of a Maine birth certificate is enough. They don't consider you truly part of the fold unless your family goes back a few generations. Either way, the Suttons aren't even close. They're from *away* Away.

And yet somehow their little food truck

managed to capture the essential flavor of their adopted state. This lobster roll represented how Maine was meant to taste — fresh and sweet and briny. A little bit unctuous, a little bit ocean kissed. If I had only two hours to spend in the entire state, I thought, this is what I'd do. I'd go to Cape Elizabeth, grab a stack of napkins, and eat a lobster roll with mayo and chives.

Maybe I'm perpetuating a mythological version of the Maine coast, but Sarah Sutton understands that urge. She was born and raised in Wisconsin but had long nurtured an "East Coast fantasy about lobstermen and cable-knit sweaters." In 2001 she and Karl scheduled a trip to Acadia National Park. "We came to Maine on vacation and fell in love with it," Sarah told me. "We had that 'If we ever move anywhere, we would really like to move here' thought." They visited again in 2002. "Then it was one of those things where we pined over it. We just had this sense that life was better here."

When Sarah's job relocated to New York, they were faced with a decision: move to New York, find a different job in Minneapolis, or take the severance package and run. They chose option C, and in 2004, when Sarah was twenty-nine and Karl was thirty-one, they moved to Portland, Maine.

When I asked Sarah what pushed them toward Portland, she mentioned its manageable size (a metro-area population of 200,000) and winter weather that wasn't as freakishly cold as Minnesota's. Also: food. Karl and Sarah considered themselves, if not foodies, then people who really loved to eat delicious things. They had a fundamental appreciation of Portland's swelling restaurant ranks, from glam upscale oyster bars to old-school diners that served blueberry pancakes to lobstermen at four a.m. "Generally speaking," Sarah said, "if the food scene in a city or a town or wherever you live has something that you identify with or it's vibrant, that's a really good indicator of other elements of that town."

"Come for the food, stay for everything else" is a pretty good theory when it comes to place attachment, and it was more or less why I'd gone to Portland, a city whose national identity now revolves around eating and drinking. As a mecca for back-to-the-landers, Maine got a head start on the local food trend. By the 2000s, Portland was attracting chefs from New York and Boston with its less-frenetic pace and cheaper kitchens, eventually accumulating more restaurants per capita than San Francisco. *Bon Appétit* called it America's "foodi-est small town."

Restaurants are a bellwether of a healthy local economy. According to the National Restaurant Association, about one in ten jobs in the United States is in a restaurant, and when restaurants do well, their employees and owners spend more money in the community. The truly great restaurants — and Portland has them — attract tourists, who sometimes turn into residents.

As the reputation of Portland's restaurants rose, the city began appearing on such a glut of best cities lists — *Forbes*'s most livable, *Parents'* third best place to raise kids, *Travel and Leisure*'s fifth best city for hipsters — that two local newspapers ran stories exploring the phenomenon. ("Talk about a model city!" crowed the *Portland Press Herald.* "Portland corners the market as magazines and websites rank locations for livability.") More restaurants meant more places to go, stuff to see, good meals to be had — the kinds of social offerings that create place attachment.

Though the Suttons had never owned a food business, they saw how passionate locals were about eating and sensed that the food truck movement could catch on here. Their first day sitting inside their $25,000 custom Mission trailer, in 2011, "we ate more than we sold," Sarah said, laughing. Eventually social media, word of mouth, and mentions by Gourmet.com and *Food and Wine* rallied customers. In 2015, Bite into Maine was the only eatery in the state to earn a spot among Yelp's top one hundred in America. On warm days between May and October, the line at the food truck, fed by busloads of tourists coming to gaze at the Portland Head Light, can stretch hundreds of feet.

Good food makes cities wealthier and more compelling, but there's another reason why what we eat makes us love where we live. Food has an inimitable sensory power to connect us to place. What's New Orleans without gumbo and po'boys? Kansas City without barbecue? Baltimore without crab cakes? By dint of longtime association, some foods have their own natural habitat, as if they're meant to be devoured in one spot on earth and nowhere else. You can get a lobster roll almost anywhere in the country, but it won't taste nearly as good as one eaten on the shores of Casco Bay.

When I spoke with Bonny Wolf, a food journalist based in Washington, D.C., and cofounder of the American Food Roots website, about why we invariably connect

313

cities with particular dishes, she waxed lyrical about the wild rice and Nut Goodies that defined her Minnesota childhood, and the brisket and chili of College Station, Texas, where her family lived later. Wherever she happened to land, food offered an entry point to her community, and often a history lesson or a narrative of her place, too. (The omnipresence of chicken paprikash in New Brunswick, New Jersey, for instance, denoted a large community of Hungarian immigrants.) "When you go to a place and you find out these things, it not only makes you feel like a part of the community, it makes the community feel like you're trying to fit in," Wolf said.

A few years ago, she wrote a story about Baltimore coddies, the fried cod-and-potato-cake sandwiches that were once the 5¢ after-school snack of choice for Baltimore schoolchildren. Spread with mustard and sandwiched between saltine crackers, coddies sound pretty horrific, and they're virtually extinct today. But two years after publishing the coddies piece, Wolf was still getting e-mails almost daily from former Baltimoreans who remembered buying them at neighborhood drugstores. "It just touches a nerve," she said.

Anthropologists have noted that community members gravitate toward foods that reinforce place identity. In a 2013 study of more than eight hundred residents of Aragón, Spain, researchers found that 80 percent enjoyed heritage foods that provided a sense of belonging, like *ternasco* lamb and *migas,* a breakfast dish made with leftover bread and ham. More than a third said that local foods were their favorites.

In some towns or regions, a well-loved food becomes a symbol for place attachment. "Drive down any road in the province of Alberta, Canada, and you are likely to spot an automobile with an 'I Love Alberta Beef' bumper sticker," notes Gwendolyn Blue, a geographer at the University of Calgary, who points out that beef there has become a metaphor for the other aspects of place that locals value, like "a folk tradition of wholesome cowboys" and "wide open spaces."

Food is impossible to divorce from the welter of emotions it evokes. More than fuel, food is culture, history, memory. Even across years, it can conjure the places we've lived. For me, the thought of fried avocado tacos makes me long to visit Austin, by far the foodiest town I've ever lived in. Flaky Dutch letters filled with almond paste evoke Ames, Iowa. Fresh apricots from a backyard tree are Fullerton, California, where I grew up.

Taste provides my most insistent sense memories of places where I've lived and traveled. When I move, it's often the thing I miss most. (Whither the good queso and brisket we left in Texas?)

Food was so central to how I felt about every other city where I'd lived that I knew it presented a perfect vehicle for strengthening my allegiance to Blacksburg. Here was the focus of my next experiment: to channel my natural proficiency at eating into place attachment. Could food make me feel like a Virginian? Or would the inevitable dress size increase be for nothing?

SHOP AT YOUR FARMERS' MARKET

French winemakers figured out long ago that where food grows informs its flavor — a concept described by the fancy French word *terroir,* which loosely translates to "the taste of place." As Rowan Jacobsen writes in his book *American Terroir,* terroir is reflected in foods that "celebrate the best of what the land has to offer." That's "land" broadly defined. For years, most Americans cared about the birthplace of their food only if a particular locale had a reputation for producing a tastier version — peaches from

Georgia, say, or strawberries from California.

In the first decade of the twenty-first century, the same cultural shift that made "locavore" the *New Oxford American Dictionary*'s 2007 word of the year created a new idea of terroir: We want "the taste of place" where we live. Here. Foods that grow well in our town, right now.

Most conventional foods travel a gas-guzzling 1,500 miles to land on our plate. One study showed that a carton of mass-produced strawberry yogurt represented a collective 2,211 miles of travel for only its three primary ingredients, milk, sugar, and strawberries. (Presumably high-fructose corn syrup added a few more.) Local foods, on the other hand, average just 44.6 miles, meaning that a meal made from locally grown ingredients uses much less energy and far fewer greenhouse gas emissions.

Less-traveled food also tastes better. Foodies can't stomach the rock-hard Central American plums and anemic tomatoes that huddle, cold and unappealing, in industrial supermarkets. Yet in most places it's easier to buy an international jetport of exotic edibles than to find products from your own town or state. In a quick tour of my pantry I discovered Nutella from Canada and

317

applesauce emigrated from France, along with oatmeal from Illinois, crackers from New Jersey, and refried beans from Nebraska. It made me think of the commercial where a group of rough-looking cowboys discovers that the cook has served them salsa made in New York City. "Get a rope," growls one.

If you want to eat local food — and energy, the environment, factory farming, frightening product recalls, and (horror of horrors) withering flavor all present reasonable motives — you must work at it. Even a $6.1 billion local food market doesn't make it a cakewalk. The author Barbara Kingsolver famously committed to a year of eating only local, mostly homegrown food not far from here in Virginia. In order to even begin the experiment, her family had to uproot from Tucson, Arizona, which "might as well be a space station where human sustenance is concerned."

To keep to a self-imposed ten-mile food perimeter around her home in Whidbey Island, Washington, the writer Vicki Robin arranged to purchase all her grains, beans, greens, meats, eggs, honey, and milk from local farmers. Anything that didn't grow locally she tried to at least buy locally, sourcing flour from an island bakery, for instance.

Nuking a frozen burrito from Walmart wasn't an option.

For a while I imagined that I, too, could draw a circle around a map and declare that none of my food would come from farther than Galax, Virginia. Au revoir, French applesauce. Hello, enormous place attachment payout. When local crop conditions determine what you ladle onto your dinner plate — when, like Kingsolver, you're subsisting on last winter's potatoes until you forage enough rhubarb for a pie — you pay attention to where you are. Vicki Robin had said that her ten-mile diet, which she called "relational eating," created an intense version of place dependence. She described "a profound sense of belonging that arose as I ate the food of my place on earth. I'd never felt so at home."

Yes, please. I very much wanted those feelings of being at home. Except I was painfully aware that I lacked the required willpower to sacrifice out-of-state granola bars or forage for locally milled flour. Wasn't circumscribing my food world so severely a bit . . . extreme? What I needed, and what I thought other novices might need, was a realistic starting point for using food as a way to embed myself in my place. I needed a low barrier to entry.

I was going to shop at my farmers' market.

You probably have. At this point, most of us do shop there, at least on occasion. In 1994, there were 1,755 farmers' markets in the United States; by 2014, that number had exploded to 8,268 — an almost 500 percent increase. If you haven't already gotten on the bandwagon, there are a few reasons to consider it now.

First, the kinds of small, slow transactions that farmers' markets represent are the unmechanized anomalies of the sales world, and they're more pleasant for it. You're not manhandling a Costco shopping cart filled with a stockpile for your bunker; you're filling your arms with the food you'll eat for dinner tonight. It's a French village way to shop, simpler and sweeter than most Americans are used to.

Second, like other forms of buying local, buying your groceries at the farmers' market returns more money to the town you live in. Farmers usually pocket only 16¢ of every dollar that their produce sells for at a supermarket, the rest to be consumed by wholesale distributors and the store itself. When they sell directly to consumers, they keep most of what they make, minus farmers' market fees. As one Cumberland County, New Jersey, farmer explained, "I got $6 wholesale for a crate of lettuce that cost me $7.20 to grow. I got $24 for that same crate from people who buy from me at the Community Farmers Market." Like other local retailers, they're more likely to spend their earnings in town.

One of my overarching principles of loving where you live had become *If you love your town, you should do what's good for it.* Here in southern Virginia, if we all agreed to spend 15 percent of our weekly food budget on locally grown food products, it would generate $90 million in new income for area farms. Not industrial farms halfway across the country. Farmers who live right here.

Third, the farmers' market is decidedly social. In supermarkets, three-fourths of shoppers arrive alone. At farmers' markets, three-fourths come with someone else, suggesting that we treat the supermarket as a chore, the farmers' market as an event. Another study showed that at community farmers' markets, people had ten times as many conversations, with vendors and other patrons, as they did in supermarkets.

Richard McCarthy, executive director of Slow Food USA, a nonprofit that champions local food cultures, told me that "when you go to a supermarket, it's extremely ef-

321

ficient. They have it down to a science. There's one checkout line, and you don't have to talk to anyone, you just go through. At the farmers' market, there are as many checkout lines as there are vendors, which means you are forced to have social interactions. And not just with farmers but with the people in line. That democratizes things. The guy in front of you is dressed well and is holding a bunch of kohlrabi and you ask, 'What in God's name is that? I've never seen that,' and he starts to tell you about it. That builds a sense of community and a sense of shared learning."

The intimate, unplanned exchanges that proliferate at the farmers' market — the jabbering with strangers about tomato blossom end rot, the sharing of recipes for arugula — are really a community's social lubrication. They bind us together as townspeople. As I'd noted with each Love Where You Live experiment, my relationships with other people were what made me feel most at home in a place. The genius of the farmers' market was that you strengthened relationships while doing something as practical and necessary as buying groceries.

Like the restaurant scene that Karl and Sarah Sutton scrutinized in Portland, Maine, farmers' markets epitomize a town's vibe. That can be especially helpful for Movers. McCarthy, who founded the Crescent City Farmers Market in New Orleans, said that "especially on Saturday mornings, we would field so many questions from newcomers to town asking, 'Is there a co-op in this city? Do you know of any pick-your-own places? Is there a bicycle club?' It was amazing the number of questions we'd get from people trying to navigate 'Where do I fit in in this town?' "

In a study of 1,300 residents of the Mid-Hudson region of New York, sociologists Brian Obach and Kathleen Tobin measured whether people who participated in "civic agriculture" — by joining a community-supported agriculture program (CSA), shopping at the farmers' market, or buying produce from a locally owned store — were also more likely to be engaged in their communities than people who bought their food from more conventional supermarkets. In most cases they were, by large margins. Seventy-one percent of civic agriculture participants volunteered in the community, compared to 48 percent of the general population. When asked, "Overall, how much impact do you think people like you can have in making your community a better place to live?" 76 percent of the civic agriculture shoppers said, "A big impact." Only 32 percent of regular shoppers agreed.

Importantly, the civic agriculture participants also liked where they lived better. Seventy-seven percent rated their community as either "excellent" or "very good," compared with only 64 percent of the general population.

This might be, as Obach and Tobin write, a question of "Which came first, the (free-range) chicken or the (organic) egg?" It's hard to prove causality. Maybe the people who had the energy and disposable income to join a CSA were already town boosters. But it's reasonable to assume that "civic agriculture is fostering, or at least reinforcing, heightened community engagement." Food is the perfect venue for it, simply because everyone's gotta eat.

At Blacksburg's Wednesday and Saturday farmers' markets, the rules are firm: Vendors are primarily producers — the people growing, raising, and/or making what they sell — and production has to happen within a fifty-mile radius of town. In winter, that meant a handful of chapped-cheeked vendors stood hopefully behind tables laden with the few food items that were impervious to cold: local honey and jam, some fall apples and squash, coolers of eggs and beef and chicken.

In summer, however, it was a different story. The pavilion in Market Square Park overflowed with vendors. Everywhere were piles of fresh fruits and vegetables, paper cartons of blueberries, ziggurat stacks of corn. No hermetically sealed plastic containers here! In the warm air, the raspberries and basil were irresistibly redolent. Beyond the electric chill of the supermarket, shopping for food became the multisensory experience it was meant to be. Everything was bright and beautiful, fragrant and delicious, sold by vendors with evocative names like Merry Peas, Gnomestead Hollow Farm and Forage, and Under the Green Umbrella.

While I probably wasn't as religious about shopping at the farmers' market as I should have been, for the same reasons I sometimes struggled to shop locally in general — too expensive, too hard to get there, etc. — when I did go it felt so *right* that I considered it one of the very best things about Blacksburg. The farmers' market made the otherwise uneventful experience of buying food into a lovely, sensual, social experience, with the added perk that you got to taste what you bought.

Last June I chaperoned Ruby's class of

wriggly first graders on a field trip to the farmers' market. Her teacher had been conducting a unit on economics, and the market offered a real-world chance to put their skills to work. Clutching Ziploc baggies of dollar bills, the kids shuffled past the stands looking for something homegrown to buy. Naturally, Ruby passed up the squash and beans to spend her $3 on a little cup of homemade mint chip from Big Lick Ice Cream Company. I helped her polish it off, then pulled another $3 out of my wallet for a cardboard pint of fresh strawberries from Indian Valley Farms. Food miles traveled: 34.3.

The berries were jewel red and the size of postage stamps. They were still warm from sitting on a table in the sun. Ruby and I couldn't stop eating them. As we walked back to the elementary school, her friends crowded around us, eager to taste.

GROW YOUR OWN

When I lived in Ames, Iowa, my friends Rachel, Brittany, and I chipped in $7 apiece to subdivide a ten-by-forty-foot plot in a town-owned community garden. We each got a little patch of dirt tilled by the city, and after advice from serious gardener friends, we installed a makeshift chicken-wire fence to keep the rabbits out. The Iowa soil was so fertile that by summer I was managing the miracle of a thriving little colony of basil, green beans, and cucumbers. *I made stuff grow!* I thought in disbelief.

Studies have shown that people who garden or farm have higher levels of neighborhood attachment; the act of literally putting down plant roots extends metaphorical ones as well. In Blacksburg, though, a garden wasn't going to happen. No time. No space. I hadn't even managed a plot of basil on the patio (although that's good for place attachment, too, the way it leads you to watch the weather and figure out the microclimate of your town). An every-other-week visit to the farmers' market would have to suffice. Then Sean Hagan started telling me about his CSA.

The route thirty-three-year-old Sean Hagan took to Left Field Farm in Bowdoinham, Maine, was so circuitous that he helpfully includes a little map on his website to clarify things. First: California, where he was raised. Second: college in Connecticut. Third: a year working on a farm in Hawaii. Fourth: five years managing an urban farm in Sacramento. Fifth: a year at Foxglove Farm on Salt Spring Island, in British Columbia, Canada.

That last one, Sean said, was "one of the most beautiful places I've ever been, just gorgeous. I met some great people and they're still really good friends, but I had no connection to it. It was a weird situation, feeling just not drawn to stay there." As he thought about where to go next, he remembered childhood summers he'd spent at his grandparents' home in Kennebunkport, Maine.

The state was, for Sean, what its license plates boast it is: Vacationland, with loads of extended family and everyone in a good mood. "It's funny, when I was living in California, every September I would get homesick for Maine — which makes no sense in that I'd never lived here. Maybe that's the other reason we end up where we end up. We're trying to remind ourselves of happy times." Full of nostalgia, Sean moved east in May 2012, got a job on a farm in Bowdoinham (pronounced *Bode*-en-ham), and eventually leased the land to start Left Field Farm on his own.

The afternoon I visited him there, Sean looked like the kindergarten flash card version of a farmer: a plaid shirt worn thin and soft; muddy jeans and boots; a thatch of brown hair stuffed under a baseball cap. We walked past the autumn rows of leeks and carrots, then he showed me his two white hoop houses, filled with racks of onions and gray-green kabocha squash, the antidote to Maine's notoriously short growing season. "Whereas in California," he said, "you just threw it in the ground."

Besides selling his produce at a couple different farmers' markets nearby, Sean had seventy people who paid either $340 for a small share or $550 for a large share of Left Field Farm veggies as part of its community-supported agriculture program. CSA initiatives allow consumers to contract at the beginning of a growing season for shares of a farmer's forthcoming produce, and, like farmers' markets, they've surged in popularity in recent years. In 1990, only 60 farms nationwide operated CSA programs. In 2012, more than 12,600 farms did.

For twenty weeks between June and October, Sean packed bags with whatever surprise mix of produce was ripe at the time: beets, tomatoes, garlic, basil, collards, chard, zucchini, lettuce, squash. An e-mail let everyone know what was coming; if a CSA member shared a recipe, Sean passed it along. For an extra fee, members could also get fresh cheese from Winter Hill Farm in Freeport or bouquets from East of Eden

Flower Farm. A few times a year he included a piece of original artwork, like a postcard-size map of Left Field Farm that he made himself on his own printing press.

The concept of the CSA, where you commit up front to support a local maker and in turn receive the fruits of the harvest, isn't limited to leafy greens. There are CSAs for eggs, fish, apples, ice cream, beef, pork, blueberries, bread, pie, flowers, and chocolate. In Seattle, you can join the Urban Bee Honey CSA and get a one-pound jar of honey (delivered, ahem, by Beecycle) once a month. In Chapel Hill, North Carolina, the Short Winter Soups CSA will give you a quart of soup a week, in flavors like sweet potato and beet minestrone, for $115. Here in Blacksburg, a former Tech student named Jess began baking bagels and selling them at the farmers' market. For $15, you could join the Blacksburg Bagels CSA and pick up a dozen each week without the risk of running into a "Sold Out" sign.

Supporters of local eating are sometimes accused of being elitist or exclusionary, or of tethering themselves to a leash like a dog who won't leave the yard. Yet most people don't join farm CSAs because they're obsessively counting food miles. One study found that members were most motivated by the idea of eating nutritious, in-season produce that tasted the way food was meant to taste — not a mealy supermarket Red Delicious but a Cumberland so crisp it practically bit back. They wanted to know where their food came from, *who* it came from. They wanted to shore up the local economy and say to local farmers, in effect, *I want you to succeed here.*

"A lot of belonging to a place is that that place has meaning to you in some way," says Steven Schnell, a professor of geography at Kutztown State University in Pennsylvania. "Part of the way you gain that meaning is having a sense of the story and uniqueness behind that place. People fundamentally get meaning out of storytelling and narratives — and ones they can place themselves in, especially. It's a means of a place becoming more than just a location where you happen to have a house that you live in."

Schnell first noticed the power of story to connect food and place in 2003, when he studied microbreweries. Why were they so popular? Well, better-tasting beer, for one, but most were also distinctly place based, selling craft brews whose names and packaging referenced local figures, sites, or events. Sometimes only insiders could make heads or tails of a name like Cream City Pale Ale or Obsidian Stout, giving them a sense of being in the know that fostered feelings of place attachment.

CSAs and farmers' markets offer a similarly meaningful local narrative, Schnell told me. "It's knowing the story of where your stuff is coming from. These aren't just tomatoes, they're heirloom tomatoes that were raised by John and Amy down at this farm, and I know them, and I know their kids. It's trying to make economic relations more than just an economic exchange. It's bringing community back into it."

Bowdoinham resident Kate Cutko was part of the town microfinance group that helped Sean Hagan purchase his greenhouses. Buying a farm share from Left Field Farm was, for her, another way to encourage Sean to put down roots and stay in town. Kate lived close enough to Left Field Farm that Sean delivered her CSA bag to her doorstep. The greens, root vegetables, peppers, and occasional berry were "gorgeous stuff, and nothing too bizarre," she said.

Eating what her neighbors had grown, understanding the seasons, knowing not to ask for sweet corn in May or expect buttercup squash until late August all made Kate feel more rooted in her place. "We pass their tractors on the dirt road where we live, we walk our dogs past their fields. They are our neighbors and their farmland is our landscape. With the exception of growing them myself, I can't get much closer to the source than buying CSA shares from Sean."

Kate is from Away, but she knows the story of her food, a feat CSAs make possible even when you can't see the farmland from your front porch. You meet the growers. You see the shifting of the seasons in what shows up in your CSA bag. You eat produce bursting with your town's terroir. You become *part* of the story. Kate Cutko's words about feeling close to the land and supporting local growers rang in my ears. Wasn't that the essence of loving where you live?

I'd always been a bit frightened to join a CSA. Ella despised salad. Ruby's pickiness had veered into extremism. (Cheerios: gross. Cheese sticks: gross. Jam: gross.) For months after my trip to Portland, I hesitated over the online sign-up for the CSA of Glade Road Growing, a four-acre farm in Blacksburg.

Booking a trip to Disney World a few years ago taught me the valuable life lesson that paying a large lump sum up front is less agonizing than doling out dribs and drabs of cash. By keeping me from weekly sticker shock at the farmers' market, CSA membership would force me to do the thing I believed was right but sometimes struggled to do. With the hope that eating locally more often would also help me feel that much more attached to Blacksburg, I finally pulled the trigger, submitting $350 through PayPal for a six-month farm share. This would be a very experimental Love Where You Live experiment.

The following Saturday, a brisk day in April, my family and I wandered over to Glade Road Growing's booth at the farmers' market. When I announced to the curly-haired guy working there, "We just joined your CSA!" he seemed pleased. Jason Pall ran Glade Road Growing with his wife, Sally Walker, on a patch of land on the north side of town, where the landscape was just flat enough for a large garden, and chickens, cattle, pigs, and goats roamed the rolling hills around it. "We don't really get going till later in the summer," he said. "Spring is pretty slim pickings. But take one of these tetsukabuto squash. They're the tail end of the winter squash. And take a bag of salad greens, too." Jason waved off our payment.

That night, Quinn roasted the squash,

splashed with a little olive oil and brown sugar. We tossed the greens in our salad spinner. Alongside grilled steak and kid-friendly plain white rice, the produce from the CSA was delicious. The weird-sounding squash that I never would have bought on my own was my favorite part.

BECOME A REGULAR

In her 2014 book *Delancey,* the writer Molly Wizenberg describes running a pizza restaurant in Seattle with her husband, Brandon. Amid the elation and anxiety, the streaky wineglasses that kept her up with night terrors, one unmitigated bright spot was the presence of regulars, "strangers who'd quickly become our friends. . . . There's the couple of regulars who come in once a week and bring us homemade jams in the summer, another couple whose dog is our dog's best friend, the neighbor who called once to tell us that he'd caught a salmon and wanted to give us half."

This was a revelation. In my many years of restaurant patronage, I had not for one single second considered bringing a restaurant owner a gift besides my credit card to pay the bill. I'd never known the name of a waitress who wasn't also my college roommate.

Perplexed, I asked Sarah Sutton about it. She said regulars were integral to Bite into Maine's success. "We've had people that, within that first season, we've known their names, what they're going to order, what's going on in their life," she said. Her husband, Karl, made it a priority to remember their regulars' names; the loyalty card the Suttons introduced — buy eleven lobster rolls, get the twelfth free — acted as a useful memory jog. "It's something sacred to business owners because those are the people that are your soldiers," Sarah said.

It's a symbiotic relationship. Restaurant staff make customers feel like they've wandered into the proverbial Cheersian establishment where everybody (or at least somebody) knows their name. Customers, in turn, treat their favorite cafés, bars, and lobster roll carts as hangout spots that are neither home nor work but something in between — what Ray Oldenburg, a professor of sociology at the University of West Florida, terms a "third place." "At the risk of sounding mystical," says Oldenburg, "I will contend that nothing contributes as much to one's sense of belonging to a community as much as 'membership' in a third place." It's tough to have a bad day when you're meeting a friend at the coffee shop.

In 2002, a professor of marketing at Northern Illinois University named Mark Rosenbaum began researching third places after his newly widowed mother became a regular at Kappy's, a former Big Boy in Morton Grove, Illinois, with a high-end diner menu of burgers and omelets alongside spanakopita and gluten-free chicken chipotle salad. Almost 60 percent of Kappy's patrons ate at the restaurant at least five meals a week. Most knew the waitresses by name, bet on the Chicago sports teams with the guy at the next table, and swore they'd come even if the food wasn't delicious (thank goodness it was). The owner, George, excelled at matchmaking friendships among patrons — widows with widows, veterans with veterans. The ultrafaithful were rewarded with nameplates on "their" table.

So connected were the patrons and staff that one recently widowed woman called a Kappy's manager when her car door lock froze and she didn't know what to do. Another confessed, "Kappy's was closed Christmas and New Year's Day, and I felt lost. George said I should come to his house for dinner. So I did."

"In marketing we always talked about loyalty," Rosenbaum told me, "but my mom used to have to call the restaurant if she was going to miss a night so that they didn't come look for her. When she decided to sell her house after my father died, she actually didn't want to move too far from her restaurant."

Has anyone ever experienced this at a multinational chain restaurant? And if not, why, when we're in an unfamiliar town, do so many of us gravitate toward the glowing red Outback sign or the enormous plastic crustacean hovering over a Red Lobster? In a hypermobile society, uniformity passes for familiarity. There's insta-comfort in knowing just what the Cheddar Bay biscuits are going to taste like. *Here's a place we've been before!* we think. *We're not totally lost!*

By definition, third places have customers who return again and again, so naturally chains like Starbucks are eager to create a third place vibe. *Come in! Stay awhile! Our barista will remember that you want a venti skim latte!* Even Burger King and Mc-Donald's, once known for using lurid colors that would drive people to eat faster, are testing new design concepts, like comfier upholstered chairs and mellow Starbucks-style lighting, not to mention robust free Wi-Fi, that will get customers to stay awhile. The third place strategy seems to be working; sales at the average made-over Burger King have increased by 10 to 15 percent.

Here's a tip: If you want to experience an authentic bit of local life, don't wander into the nearest Burger King. Yelp a restaurant or bar you've never heard of but that locals love — *their* third place. A great local diner, drive-in, or dive can act like a proxy for a town at large. It offers a way of seeing what a community is about. When you have a great experience there, you like the town more. Plus, places thrive economically because of what makes them distinct. Generic eating and drinking establishments might feel comfortable, but they do nothing to build affection toward a place.

Falling in love with a restaurant isn't exactly the same thing as falling in love with your town. But it's close, both because it presses us into the social web we need to be happy in our towns and because it gives us a concrete surrogate for the town itself. When you fit at the coffee shop or the diner, by extension you fit where you live. If you can't imagine life without Kappy's, then you won't want to move away anytime soon. Good burgers and a friendly waitress may not be a lot to build a life around, but they're something.

One night, cleaning up the dinner dishes after homemade chicken tortilla soup, I announced to Quinn, "I've got a new Love Where You Live experiment. I think we should become regulars at a restaurant."

"What do you mean?"

"I think we should pick a restaurant in town and just keep going back there until they know our names. It'll be like Cheers."

Quinn loaded a pot into the dishwasher and said, "I'll eat out as much as you'll let me." So that was settled.

How, exactly, does one become a regular at a restaurant? For once, there wasn't any helpful advice online. Did you just show up over and over again? Was there some minimum threshold for regularity? "Appropriation increases with familiarity," writes Oldenburg. "The more people visit a place, use it, and become, themselves, a part of it, the more it is theirs." How much was enough? My gut told me that, ideally, we'd show our faces at our chosen restaurant four or five times a week, like the old ladies at Kappy's. But ours was a world constrained by English professor/writer finances. Once-a-week dinners out would be all that the budget allowed.

"How long do you think it will take before they recognize us?" Quinn asked. I was uncertain. I'd spoken with a North Carolina woman named Helms Jarrell, who for Lent one year devised something called Within One Mile. She challenged herself to limit all her purchases and outings to stores and restaurants within a mile of her home. "For the past five years I've been the copastor of a church on the physically and demographically opposite side of town from where we live," Helms explained. "It's fifteen minutes to drive to church, and everyone at the church is middle- to upper-class older white folks, while almost everyone in my neighborhood is younger, lower income, and African American. So I think over time my own personal identity as a resident of this neighborhood had sort of lost its strength." It was time to reinvest in her neighborhood.

Immediately, Helms saw the social benefits of her shopping perimeter. "Almost anytime I went into any store I saw someone I knew. Because it was within a mile, I could just walk [to stores], so I was also walking past other neighbors that I know." On only her second visit to the diner down the street, the waitress remembered her drink order. Her Within One Mile challenge unwittingly made her a regular, and fast.

A mitigating factor: Helms has pink hair. What about us less memorably coiffed locals? Was there a math equation for figuring out how soon waitstaff would remember me?

"I have no idea how long it will take," I finally told Quinn. "At least six weeks, I'm guessing."

First Quinn and I had to decide *where* to become regulars. Under normal circumstances, becoming regulars happens organically over time. You eat at a restaurant, you love it, you eat there again. In my accelerated timeline, I had to choose. Gillie's? Green's? Our Daily Bread? Obviously the food had to taste good, and the menu had to vary enough that we wouldn't go crazy eating there week after week. Close to home was a bonus. Most essential was that the restaurant existed only in Blacksburg. We might experience the social benefits of a third place at a Golden Corral, but we'd feel zero local pride eating there.

After some back and forth, we settled on Lefty's Main Street Grille, a slightly upscale restaurant in a former Long John Silver's on Main Street. The menu was a zany multicultural mix of burgers, shrimp and grits, steak au poivre, and Caribbean salmon. I was already in love with their cashew chicken sandwich slathered with pesto and golden raisins. We could walk there in ten minutes. Lefty's existed at the just-right confluence of convenience and craving, and only in Blacksburg, unlike, say, the gas station Subway.

For our first official visit under the auspices of the Love Where You Live experiment, we grabbed a table under the framed pictures of famous left-handers (Bill Clinton, Beethoven, Ned Flanders) and ordered everything from a chips-and-guac appetizer to an apple-cinnamon bread pudding. Elliott Smith and Counting Crows played on the stereo, a promising sign. Every time our waitress, a college girl in short shorts, swerved through the overcrowded dining room toward us, we beamed up at her, giddy for approval and recognition.

By the second visit, I could tell we'd made a miscalculation. Mark Rosenbaum, the marketing professor, had told me that the employees who were most likely to engage their customers and become part of their social network averaged sixteen years working at the restaurant. "So if you've got a transient employee staff, you're not going to have a third place."

No one working at Lefty's, from the waiters to the chefs wielding sauté pans in the kitchen, looked to be over the age of twenty-five. An ever-rotating cast of college students took our orders. They were perfectly nice, but never the same person twice.

Because Lefty's was a seat-yourself establishment, we couldn't even request to sit in a particular server's area. One drizzly Friday night, we grabbed a table, only to realize that we were being served by a new guy in plaid bermudas, while last week's waitress hovered at the table next to ours. "All this regular business is for nothing!" Quinn cried in mock despair. "You don't know how hard we've worked. We were here six days ago! *Six days!*"

Whenever I mentioned the poor progress of this particular Love Where You Live experiment, people threw out ideas for making ourselves memorable. Leave a big tip, recommended my friend Megan. At the bagel shop where she once worked, a customer regularly tipped $20, and "we used to fight over who got to serve him." Proportionally, a $20 tip on a bagel would translate to around $165 on a dinner at Lefty's. That was practically M.C. Hammer–level money — weird, not to mention unaffordable. Quinn and I stuck with a trying-to-be-generous 25 percent, with no noticeable reaction.

Chat up the waitress, advised our friend Neal, who himself possessed a preternatural ability to befriend service workers. The next time we went to Lefty's, I managed this much repartee with the waitress: "How's it going? You seem really busy tonight." Then the forced conviviality fell apart. Squeezing out conversational bon mots every time the waitress refilled our water glasses left me feeling tense and drained. It also irked the guy at my table. "I'm on a date with you," Quinn said. "I don't want to talk to the waitress!"

As the idea that we would ever have anything like a third place experience at Lefty's dissolved, going there for dinner — *again* — began to feel like a whole lot of bother for nothing. Were we really regulars if the only people who knew about it were us? Couldn't we skip it and go to Marco and Luca's this once?

And yet eating at the same restaurant week after week, I found myself studying the minutiae that make a restaurant what it is. The regular additions and subtractions to the chalk wall menu. The dark wood tables left over from the building's Fried Fish Platter days. The stack of mismatched coffee cups by the bathroom. One night we sat at the bar — another recommendation for becoming regulars — and got an insider's view of the chef and sous chef in the minuscule kitchen, frying and ladling, swerving and avoiding collisions.

In a Florida State University study of third places, 38 percent of coffee shop regulars hardly ever spoke to anyone. They sat alone, content to see "familiar strangers." A modicum of social interaction — sometimes just "Can I take your order?" — was all that was required for "their existence as a member of the community [to be] confirmed."

Perhaps, I thought, being recognized didn't matter as much as doing the recognizing. So what if I ordered the same chicken cashew sandwich five times in a row and an employee didn't congratulate me on my steadfastness? I could still enjoy feeling like it was *my* sandwich, the same way I could still feel like this was *my* restaurant, even if no one who worked there cared.

All over this country are would-be third places — not just coffee shops and diners but potlucks, bean suppers, church dinners, and chili cookoffs — that can make us feel like we belong where we live. During the summer, the Blacksburg Ruritan Club hosts a monthly fish fry at a church off Mount Tabor Road, $8 for all-you-can-eat white-fish, fries, lemonade, and slices of home-made cake. You load up a foam plate, then sit at crowded picnic tables while the community band plays.

Once at the fish fry, Ruby spotted a girl that she'd met at a concert in the park a few days earlier. "Can I go play with her?" she cried. When we nodded, she dashed off.

I wish it were that easy for adults; I'd tap one of the old ladies in a windbreaker and say, "Wanna be my friend?" Instead, I contented myself with being among familiar strangers, eating good food.

LOVE YOUR CITY CHECKLIST

☐ Try strEATing, the practice of turning an average street or public place into a quick, cheap social eatery. Get a group of friends together and a city permit or two and you can make an event of it, the way the artist Hunter Franks has with his 500 Plates project. Or just put a picnic table somewhere unexpected. Everything tastes better eaten al fresco.

☐ Make dinner into a mini block party by eating on your front lawn. Maybe neighbors will stop and join you, and you'll build social capital, or else you'll simply create an experience for yourself in a way that builds happy memories and thus place attachment. (Put a pin in your mental map. . . .)

☐ Find a place in your town to become a regular. Clues: Google the name of your town with "hidden gem," "local," "secret," "neighborhood," or "undiscovered."

☐ Shop regularly at your farmers' market or join a CSA. LocalHarvest.org keeps a database of them, or just search online for your town and the words "farm share" or "CSA."

☐ Try a one-week "25-Mile Challenge,"

eating only foods grown within twenty-five miles of your house. Seeing how well you eat (or how close you come to starving to death) will make you feel more invested in supporting local agriculture as well as give you a stronger sense of place dependence, a variety of place attachment.

☐ Plant a garden, a fine way to get in touch with your area's growing season and planting cycles. Your local chapter of the Master Gardener program can provide resources to get you started.

☐ Follow restaurants on social media. One woman I met told me that she makes a point of Instagramming or tweeting about a good meal at a local restaurant or leaving a positive review on Yelp. When I saw that a couple new restaurants were opening in Blacksburg, I started following them on social media, an approach that earned me an invite to Wicked Taco's soft launch.

CHAPTER NINE:
GET MORE POLITICAL

Fifteen minutes before class started, I collected my name tag lanyard and scanned the room. We'd been told to come early to the Blacksburg Motor Company, a former car dealership turned LEED-certified meeting space, so we'd have time for dinner. A few punctual souls were now scattered among long tables, eating pizza from paper plates. Five o'clock traffic crawled past the windows. A pull-down screen glowed with a PowerPoint slide:

2015 Citizens Institute
Welcome

My own plate of pizza in hand, I took a seat next to a young woman who looked like she'd rushed straight from the office. "So," I said, "what made you sign up for this?"

The woman blew out an apologetic breath. "Well, first I should tell you that I never,

ever, *ever* thought I'd be living in Blacksburg." By her own confession, Cassie was a transplant from Richmond who, in marrying a Virginia Tech professor, had reluctantly committed herself to Blacksburg for the foreseeable future. "I miss all the restaurants and stuff to do that Richmond has. Blacksburg is a lot smaller than I'm used to. But my husband really likes his job, and I decided I needed to have a better attitude about being here."

"Oh, honey," I wanted to say, "I sat next to the right person." A better attitude about Blacksburg was pretty much the reason I did anything these days. Signing up for the Blacksburg Citizens Institute was merely my latest effort.

I'd seen the flyer for the Citizens Institute, a civic education program offered by the town government, on the bulletin board at the public library a few months earlier. In some of the hundred or so U.S. cities that host such courses, they might go by names like "citizens academy," "neighborhood college," or "Town 101." All operate with the same basic objective: to let average residents take a look inside the gear works of their town government.

Here, participants spend nine spring Mondays cycling through Town of Blacksburg departments for a weekly lesson in what government employees do all day. On Housing and Neighborhood Services night, we'd tour low-income housing complexes. Police Department night would feature a canine officer demo. If some small part of me might once have been reluctant about the wonkiness of a nine-week civics class, it had been overshadowed by the recognition that Citizens Institute was exactly what you would do if you really cared about your city. *If you want to love your town,* I reminded myself, *act like someone who loves your town would act.*

Anyway, I needed the education. My admittedly naive view of local government was derived largely from viewings of the NBC sitcom *Parks and Recreation,* about a city parks and rec department in fictional Pawnee, Indiana (slogan: "First in Friendship, Fourth in Obesity"). Overeager deputy director Leslie Knope, played by Amy Poehler, serves her city with almost pathological good cheer. At one tense public meeting, Leslie shrugs off the invective hurled by citizens, saying, "These people are members of the community that care about where they live. So what I hear when I'm being yelled at is people caring loudly at me."

Meanwhile, Leslie's antigovernment boss,

Ron Swanson, works on bleeding the beast from the inside. "I have so many ideas," he says at one point. "Some are simple, like take down traffic lights and eliminate the post office. The bigger ones will be tougher, like 'Bring this crumbling to the ground.'"

I wanted to be Leslie Knope when I grew up, at least the part where she was wildly committed to her town. And yet for all the time I'd spent thinking about Blacksburg, I'd failed to think much about the capital-*T* Town itself. How it worked. Who made it run. What the quiet background thrum of government meant for my happiness where I lived.

In my defense, most of us don't ponder the parks department or the police force unless it fails us (*Why haven't they plowed the snow yet?*). The better bureaucracy works, the less attention it draws. If we do think about government workers and elected officials, we tend to view even the local ones as faceless bureaucrats. They're people we know *about* but don't really know, which makes them easy to hate. Kind of like the Kardashians.

Citizens Institute's simple remedy: Get to know government employees. "It's really easy to have a negative perception of government when you don't know the people behind the scenes and don't know how things operate," says Heather Browning, Blacksburg's community relations manager. "But it's hard to fuss too much about the horrible recycling program when you meet the five people who operate our recycling program and see how hard they work."

That first Monday night in the Blacksburg Motor Company, Citizens Institute successfully made me not hate the town manager, Marc Verniel. That was not, I learned, a universal feeling. Verniel's was one of the very public faces of the town, so every time Blacksburg attempted to make a major change, he was the guy people "cared loudly at." *You want to widen Main Street? You want to turn College Avenue into a pedestrian plaza? What??* Even the plans for the now-beloved Market Square, where the farmers' market meets each week, spurred livid complaints about the removal of precious parking spaces downtown.

Listening to Verniel talk, I came to two realizations. First, good towns don't just happen. They're planned into existence, against all odds and opposition.

Second, making decisions that keep all kinds of residents satisfied is incredibly difficult. To underscore that point, we played a planning-themed board game called Built.

Seven of us circled a game board, a seven-by-eight grid, and arranged cardboard tiles labeled to represent elements of a town — Hotel, Small Business, Gas Station, Strip Mall, Bakery, Train Station, Empty Lot, and so on. The goal was to create a simulacrum of a place we wouldn't mind living in.

Right away it got tricky. Where did we want the poultry processing plant? The prison? All the players had to set down paper tiles with our own names on them as well; essentially, we had to live in the world we were creating. I ended up insulated by a live theater, a coffee shop, and a pharmacy (Walker's Paradise!), while next to me Skip's property value was being dragged down by an unfortunate adult bookstore.

No matter how thoughtful we were about placing the train station next to the county transit hub so it was convenient for commuters, and lumping the power plant, car dealership, and light manufacturing into an industrial zone, life interfered. "Here are six more squares to find spots for!" a city employee would cry, or "Change any five squares in the next three minutes!" Moving one tile created ripple effects elsewhere. Someone always wound up in the bad part of town. Though Skip, a real estate agent, was sanguine about his seedy game-board neighborhood, if real property values were at stake, I'm guessing he might be the one writing angry e-mails to Marc Verniel.

Studies show that Americans feel a lot better about local politicians than national ones; in one poll, 72 percent of Americans said they trusted their city government to do the right thing, while only 19 percent said the same of the federal government. The trouble is, we trust our leaders just enough to stay completely uninvolved until we're angry about something. Our first introduction to someone like Verniel is often when we're ready to shove his awful road-expansion project down his throat.

Citizens Institute defuses that tension by inviting residents like me to a massive brag session, where city employees get to yammer about their successes to a willing audience. One evening we rode a bus around town while Matt Hanratty, the Housing and Neighborhood Services manager, told us how his team developed beautiful, sustainable homes for low-income residents. He was so earnest, so morally upright about it. *I love this man,* I thought.

A few weeks later we met with the volunteers who run the fire department and the rescue squad, and I thought, *No other humans in the world are as fundamentally good as these.*

Hang out with people who share only good news and you're bound to feel enthusiastic. Maybe I was too Leslie Knope–naive, too eager to drink the government-authorized Kool-Aid. Yet every single Monday for nine weeks, I'd trundle off to class and have the same unvarying reaction: *The people who run Blacksburg are pretty awesome.*

The bus drivers. The parks and rec director. The lady who handles building permits. The SWAT team member who abandoned his twins' birthday party to answer an urgent call. The mayor, who sat next to me in a mock town council meeting. I adored them all. Week after week, I became more besotted with the people running my town. Naturally, that made me feel pretty good about the town itself. (Also, at one Citizens Institute session I got to ride on a fire truck, and there are few circumstances in which a grown woman gets to realize that ambition.)

So many of my Love Where You Live experiments had worked because they managed to make me like people in Blacksburg. Citizens Institute accomplished that more successfully than anything else I'd done.

"I think town employees are the unsung heroes," says Rick Morse, an associate

357

professor of public administration and government at the University of North Carolina at Chapel Hill, who studies citizens academies. "They're always in the background working, and people don't realize that all in their life is convenient and good because of what these other people do. For citizens, it's kind of this aha moment: 'Oh wow, these are good people, and they're doing good things.' "

Their ability to do good things matters more than you might expect. After Somerville, Massachusetts, famously surveyed its citizens about their happiness in 2011, researchers found a correlation between life satisfaction and certain well-run city services, including traffic and parking enforcement, code enforcement, and the appearance and maintenance of parks. "It's possible that happier people have a rosier view of the city," a report noted, "but in this case, it is not a stretch to imagine that living in a clean, beautiful, efficiently run city is making people happier."

For cities, making residents happier is a few levels up the Maslowian hierarchy, the kind of goal to consider once the proverbial trains are all running on time. But it makes sense that cities want to shoot for it, since residents who are happier with their city are more likely to be attached, and attached residents are more likely to get involved.

In 2004, a sociologist at Sam Houston State University named Gene Theodori quizzed the residents of two small Texas towns. Had they ever attended a public meeting on town or school affairs in their community? Had they worked with others in their community to try to solve community problems? Had they participated in any type of community improvement activity?

Then he asked them questions likes the ones from the place attachment scale: How much did they feel like they belonged? How meaningful were their friendships in the community? Did they want to stay, or were they eager to move away? The more attached people were to where they lived, Theodori found, the more civically involved they were. The two went hand in hand. When you love where you live, you care what happens there. You want to get involved, and cities thrive on that involvement.

At the first Blacksburg Citizens Institute meeting, Verniel, the town manager, told us up front that getting us to serve the city was part of the master plan. "We have more than thirty boards and commissions in the town, and our Citizens Institute graduates are a really good pool of people to pull from, because you have shown interest in the town and you know about it. So don't be surprised if you get a call from us sometime."

The majority of Americans are crap at civic engagement, the process by which we citizens participate in the running of our town in an effort to make things better — happier — where we live. Very few of us get involved in local politics. Movers are far less likely than Stayers to do so, perhaps put off by the notion of city government as an impenetrable good ol' boy network. Maybe they're simply not attached enough to care.

Would you run for office where you live? The truth is, you have to be incredibly dedicated to your town to want to, but once you're elected, there's an enormous place attachment effect. That's especially true for Movers. Sam Colville, a town council member in coastal St. Marys, Georgia, where he moved in 2009, said, "I had forty years within which to get to know and to feel a part of Kansas City. I don't have forty years left to spend on doing that in St. Marys, so it's a fast track to getting to know the city and to really enjoying its assets." Dick Goodman, who ran for city council in Suwanee, Georgia, two and a half years after retiring there, joked that "according to my wife, I'm a walking chamber of commerce for Suwanee." (Indeed. His e-mail signature includes Suwanee's rankings on the *Money, Family Circle,* and *Kiplinger* best places lists.)

Stayers experienced an attachment bump as well. My friend Emily became a member of the school board in Huntington, New York, because it felt like a debt she owed the hometown where she grew up and has spent most of her life. "I feel much more pride about where I live now than I necessarily did when I was living here as a kid growing up," she says. "I am Huntington's biggest cheerleader, particularly for our school district but in general our town."

I spent five years as a member of the town library board in Ames, Iowa, a position for which I applied and was appointed as a relative newcomer. Sometimes when I was elbow-deep in policy documents at an all-day community charette, I wished I'd had the strength of character to ignore the board recruitment notice like everyone else. Yet nothing I did in Ames made me feel more connected to my town. Along with a seat at the table and a highlighted copy of the budget, the library board gave me the feeling of being on the inside of things. As a board member I was a necessary, voting part of the organization and, by extension, the city. I mattered, and feeling like you matter makes you feel like you belong. No wonder Ames was the town I left most regretfully.

Jeff Coates, a program director with the National Conference on Citizenship, compares the effect of public service with going to college. "People become very attached to the place where they did their undergrad. I went to the University of Oklahoma. I'm a Sooners fan. I love watching Sooner football. Why? Because I invested a lot in that university, and when you invest a lot, you *become* that place. The same thing can happen when you invest a lot into a community."

Exhibit A: Matt Tomasulo. A year after the creator of Walk [Your City] first showed me around Raleigh, I started getting e-mails from the Committee to Elect Matt Tomasulo. He was running for Raleigh City Council, with a platform of prioritizing close-knit, walkable neighborhoods. (Other ideas: more tiny houses and a "City Hall to Go" mobile services bus.) I totally would have voted for him.

PUT PARTY POLITICS ASIDE

Americans take flack for being politically apathetic, so it's ironic that politics is also blamed for stratifying the country into warring red zone/blue zone camps. With the persistent bleating of the twenty-four-hour news cycle, "Republican" and "Democrat" have become convenient shorthand for explaining what we care about, in politics and everything else.

To create its top ten lists of conservative and liberal cities, the website Livability looked not only at voting patterns but at consumer preferences. Apparently, California Pizza Kitchen and Romano's Macaroni Grill are favored by liberals, O'Charley's and Cracker Barrel by conservatives. Car-buying patterns are revealing, too. Liberals want to drive Honda Civic Hybrids. Conservatives want to drive Ford Mustang convertibles.

Like our buying habits, our place preferences are closely aligned with our politics. In a 2014 survey of over ten thousand Americans, the Pew Research Center found that liberals want smaller houses, urban settings, and walkability. Conservatives prefer larger houses in smaller towns or rural areas and don't mind driving from place to place. The more liberal or conservative people skew, the more pronounced their predilections along those lines become. It's both clichéd and confounding. Pew's report concludes, "If people living in 'deep red' or 'deep blue' America feel like they inhabit distinctly different worlds, it is in part because they seek out different types of communities, both geographic and social."

Theoretically, we like our cities better when they embrace a diversity of residents. Remember, openness to all kinds of people was one of the three main factors that generated place attachment in the Soul of the Community study. In reality, living among people who share your political views — and more than a quarter of Americans admit it matters to them — creates a comforting Us vs. Them echo chamber. As a Democrat living in Hoboken, New Jersey (one of the most liberal towns in the country), or a Republican living in Benton, Arkansas (among the most conservative), you get away with thinking, *Everyone here agrees with me! What's wrong with the rest of you?* Life can be a lot easier when we live among people who are like us.

If we cluster geographically by politics, we also cluster by personality. One miserable winter afternoon, I took a free online personality test at a website called Outof

Service.com. For each of forty-six statements like "I see myself as someone who is talkative" and "I see myself as someone who tends to find fault with others," I had to rank myself between a 1 (strongly disagree) and a 5 (strongly agree). Once I finished, the program would tell me who I was based on psychology's Big Five personality traits (with the helpful acronym OCEAN):

- **Openness**, or curiosity and creativity
- **Conscientiousness**, or responsibility and diligence
- **Extraversion**, or friendliness and talkativeness
- **Agreeableness**, or helpfulness and caring
- **Neuroticism**, or moodiness and anxiety

Simply taking the test revealed something important about me: I have no idea what kind of person I am. Waffling over whether "I see myself as someone who worries a lot" deserved a 1 or a 5, I realized that my grip on my own identity was disturbingly loose. Did I worry a lot? Sure, sometimes. Then again, not always. How about "maybe"? Was "maybe" good enough?

The only piece of requested data that was

easy to provide was my zip code. Happily, University of Cambridge social psychologist Jason Rentfrow could tell a lot about a person from his or her zip code.

Rentfrow is one of the major researchers of place-personality theory, the idea "that people in certain parts of the United States may have slightly different personality traits, and that may contribute to differences in industries and economy." As a child growing up in the American South, Rentfrow moved a lot, and he'd always wondered why different towns seemed to have their own idiosyncratic personalities, reflected in the character of the people who lived there.

Then, in graduate school at the University of Texas, Rentfrow read a book by Richard Florida called *The Rise of the Creative Class,* which pointed out the curious fact that creative and high-tech industries were concentrated geographically in certain regions of the United States. Why? Creative types probably moved to Silicon Valley because jobs were easier to find there. But was it bigger than that? Did place-personality theory explain the variations among towns that Rentfrow had observed moving around as a kid? Did cities have personalities the way people do?

Rentfrow happened to have a ready-made

data set to test the idea, in the form of 1.6 million personality tests like the one I had completed at OutofService.com. That website was created by Rentfrow's adviser, University of Texas social psychologist Sam Gosling. Because users provided their zip codes, Rentfrow and Gosling could geocode the results.

In their fascinating findings, Rentfrow and his fellow researchers discovered that personality types indeed clustered geographically. Residents of Wisconsin were the most extroverted, residents of Vermont the most introverted. On conscientiousness, South Carolina rates highest, Maine the lowest. Utah is both the most agreeable and the least neurotic; on the other side of the country glower neurotic West Virginia and disagreeable New York. Washington, D.C., is most open, followed by California and New York, as you might expect. Least open? North Dakota, by a long shot. It was as if places had their own temperaments.

How do places develop such strong constellations of Big Five personality traits? Blame history, climate, economy, aesthetics, topography. There's a whole stew of possibilities. One explanation for why Rust Belt states like Ohio and Michigan scored high on conscientiousness but low on openness, for instance, is that their economy for years centered around assembly-line jobs where focus mattered more than creativity.

Or maybe it's social contagion, a theory developed by Nicholas A. Christakis, a physician and sociologist at Harvard Medical School, and James H. Fowler, a social scientist at the University of California, San Diego. Using data from the Framingham Heart Study, Christakis and Fowler found that happiness and unhappiness occur in geographic clusters. When friends or neighbors within a mile of you become happier, your chance of becoming happier increases by 25 percent. "We catch the emotions of the people we have relationships with and the people they have relationships with," Rentfrow explains. "Anecdotally, it's pretty obvious to those of us who have been in close relationships or have worked with difficult people, if you spend some time with someone who's an asshole, that will affect you." It's not much of a leap to suggest that other emotions, behaviors, and attitudes — personality traits, essentially — are passed like a virus among people who live in the same town.

Also at play is the concept of person-environment fit, a term for how well your personal characteristics — your values, goals, abilities, needs, interests, preferences, and traits — correspond to those of where you live. We search for cities where we can see something of ourselves in the locals, and we're more likely to find that when more residents do our kind of work for a living. Hence, creative types flock to the coasts, and then more creative types follow suit because they like to live around other creative types (and because they have more creative-type job opportunities there). The prophecy becomes self-fulfilling.

"At the end of the day," Rentfrow told me, "your personality is going to be a strong determinant of how happy you are where you live. If you're able to find an environment that satisfies your psychological interests and needs, that can have a positive impact on your daily experiences."

When we pick a place to live, we usually don't know how our town ranks on Big Five personality traits. Have we fallen in with the Relaxed and Creative types — low on neuroticism, high on openness — that Rentfrow says cluster in the West and the Carolinas? Will we be living among the Temperamental and Uninhibited Americans — more neurotic, less agreeable — found primarily in the Northeast? Sometimes personality is something we can sense. It's a large part of what draws us to certain places. Feeling, even instinctively, that the people who live in your town are like you makes you feel like you belong.

The trouble is, we're not always sure who we are. That was my fundamental problem with the Big Five personality test I took. After bungling through the survey, I balked at the results. Twenty-second percentile for agreeableness? Twelfth percentile for extraversion? That meant 88 percent of test takers were more outgoing than I was. "That's not me!" I thought indignantly. "Could that be me?" Maybe it wasn't, because when I retook the test at OutofService.com in sunnier weather, my agreeableness score rose to 50 and my extraversion score to 22. Still low, but not fetal-position low. I apparently changed my personality as easily as I changed clothes.

Even when we know who we are, we don't always know what we want. Humans are notoriously poor predictors of what makes us happy. In place terms, that suggests we're clumsy at identifying a good person-environment fit. We hope that a small town will mellow us when we're too neurotic for the slow lane. We move to a wild city but we're too introverted to adore it. Eagerly we take "What City Should You Actually Live

In?" quizzes, hoping the results will point out something about our personality we haven't noticed yet. (According to BuzzFeed .com, London was my destiny. Southern Living.com advised — wait for it — Austin, Texas.)

Most of those quizzes are click-bait fabricated by twenty-year-old website interns. The "What Town Matches My Politics?" quiz on the website of Clarity Campaign Labs, a political research and consulting firm based in Washington, D.C., seemed more legit. I selected my home state and answered seven simple questions about my politics and my feelings about climate change, gun control, abortion rights, taxes, and urban living. With eerie precision, the site's algorithm used my answers to pair me with a town in my state that leaned left in a socially conservative way: Horntown, Virginia, population 574.

Our political philosophy reveals something about who we are. It's at least as indicative of our personality as our agreement with a Big Five test statement like "I see myself as someone who remains calm in tense situations." If we want to land in a town that's a good person-environment fit for us, it's not ridiculous to take the area's voting patterns under consideration.

I find it hopeful, though, that in Blacksburg and many other locations, town council candidates run without party affiliations. The Democrat/Republican divide cedes importance to simply making stuff happen. "Mayors are pragmatists, they're problem-solvers," says Benjamin Barber, a political analyst and author of *If Mayors Ruled the World.* "Their job is to get things done, and if they don't, they're out of a job." There's no time for filibustering and gridlocking. Schools need to function. Potholes need to get filled. Trash needs to get picked up.

No one likes to feel that they don't fit in with the prevailing politics or personality of their city. I've talked to people who have confessed that, despite the time and concerted effort they've put in, their city has never felt like home. In those serious cases I usually blame a poor person-environment fit.

When you live in a town where people are not like you, politically or otherwise, you can feel isolated and alienated. The antidote, and the way to experience more place attachment where you live, is twofold. First, learn to appreciate other residents for who they are and what they do for you, as I did at the Blacksburg Citizens Institute.

Second, work with others to make good

things happen in your town despite your differences. That's collective efficacy, and it's the aim of entering the civic life of your town. Your personality and beliefs matter, but maybe not as much as the fact that you owe your city something. That you are, in the words of the American Democracy Project, a "steward of place."

USE CIVIC TECHNOLOGY

How exactly does one steward? The National Conference on Citizenship offers a few questions that make for a good civic engagement gut check:

- Have you ever contacted a local government official about an issue that's important to you?
- Have you ever boycotted or protested in your town?
- Have you ever attended a local public meeting?
- Do you talk with friends and family about politics?
- Have you attended a political rally or speech where you live?
- Have you signed a petition, online or off?
- Do you keep up on the news?

- Have you worked or volunteered for a political party or candidate?

Such behaviors are the equivalent of putting a dog in the fight. They make you care more about the outcome, which makes you feel rooted where you live. Yet very few of us perform these basic acts of local civic engagement.

In hotly contested presidential elections, only around 60 percent of eligible voters cast a ballot. We're even less likely to vote in local elections. In mayoral races from 2008 to 2011, no major city mobilized more than 45 percent of its voters. In a few places, including San Antonio and El Paso, turnout was in the single digits.

To be fair, city politics can be hard for Movers to grasp. It usually takes me a few years after I move to a new state just to remember the name of my governor. (Just Googled Virginia's. It's Terry McAuliffe.) If we're paying attention at all, it's to bark about national issues while roundly ignoring the municipal traffic projects, business permits, housing developments, and recycling programs that influence our lives on a daily basis.

It's not that way everywhere. In Japan and France, more citizens vote in local elections than national ones. But in America, unless there's a sex scandal or a proposal to legalize marijuana, local politics operate in an "equilibrium state." That's code for "We don't care that much." Perhaps it's too confusing or frustrating, or we don't know where to begin. Much easier to stay home, cuddling our laptops.

Good. Stay there. Digital placemakers are effectively bringing the mountain to Muhammad in the form of civic technology. That's an umbrella term for the way coders, hackers, entrepreneurs, policy makers, and politicians are huddling around computers, trying to reinvent the way cities interact with their citizens.

Most governments are late to the technology party. Check out your city's website. Does it look like it's been updated in the past five years? Can people apply for food stamps or business permits online or pay the electric bill with an app? No? Civic technologists want to change all that by applying a start-up mind-set — quick action, little red tape — to making government services more accessible and public life less arduous.

The best success story in the field comes from the San Francisco–based nonprofit Code for America. Nicknamed "Peace

Corps for Geeks," the group annually sends a cohort of fellows into cities across the country to create custom technology that's responsive to local government needs. In 2012 in New Orleans, Code for America fellows built the website BlightStatus (now Civic Insight) to track more than thirty-five thousand vacant lots in the city in real time. The following year, fellows in Louisville designed a criminal justice dashboard to monitor local jail occupancy and offer incarceration alternatives. Other apps and websites developed under Code for America's auspices help users map public art, locate social services, and figure out where to get a flu shot in their town.

Some civic technology apps are just fun, in a community-minded way. The website Blockee lets users "pimp" their neighborhood by adding GIF planters, bike lanes, and other "civic bling" to Google Maps images of their street. Click-That-Hood is an online quiz that tests how fast you can name your city's neighborhoods. When I played the version some coder had created for Blacksburg, names of neighborhoods like Miller Southside, McBryde, and Ellett Valley flashed across the screen, and I scrambled to match them to the right locations on the map. I got all twenty in under two minutes, surprised at how well I knew where things were now. (Thank you, mental map.)

Annually, Code for America holds a National Day of Civic Hacking, a marathon session where programmers use publicly available data to design websites and blitz-code local apps. More than ninety in-real-life events were held in 2015, from Silicon Valley's heartland to the nation's capital. The group also runs a business accelerator, and one of its first picks in 2012 was a company called MindMixer (now MySidewalk).

A couple of Omaha-based urban planners, disgruntled by low turnout at public meetings, started MySidewalk as a kind of twenty-four/seven digital town hall to make it easier for residents to voice opinions without leaving the house. That was a problem in desperate need of a solution. Nationwide, less than a quarter of Americans go to public meetings, a figure only slightly less appalling than the 19 percent of us who have contacted a local elected official to express an opinion.

With my personality (sixty-ninth percentile for conscientiousness!), I can't help wanting everyone to be a good citizen in the classic ways the National Conference on Citizenship measures. Write those letters! Sign those petitions! Storm that city council meeting and wait a few hours for a turn at the microphone. It's your civic duty.

On the other hand, this is not 1988, and "Come see us in person" shouldn't be a city's only communication strategy. For each of its 1,300 clients, MySidewalk creates online forums where local users can opine on questions like "How can we make Southfield [Michigan] a 21st century city?" or "Is there a program or activity that another library does that you would like to see at Kearney [Nebraska] Public Library?" Sometimes residents earn reward points for submitting ideas, redeemable for prizes like city pool passes or an outgoing voice-mail greeting from the mayor. Decision makers, whose photos appear on the site, respond in real time.

According to MIT researcher Ben Armstrong, who compared MySidewalk comments with the ones heard through the microphones at a Pittsburgh town hall meeting, "the people who show up in person are older, and they are probably more willing to spend an evening at a local community center." He added, "We know from a variety of research that those who participate online are typically younger and wealthier."

The hope is that, slowly, demographic shifts and technology begin to reach citizens who might otherwise be on the civic margins — people who don't have transportation, can't find child care, or can't get away from work. If, for instance, a time-strapped young mom posts online about a local park, then the play equipment she recommended gets built, "this changes her feeling of civic engagement in her community because she was directly involved," says Emily Olinger, vice president of client experience for My-Sidewalk. "As the park changes, she gets to say, 'I shared my idea of how my child uses the playground and where I think things should be, and it's happening.' " Once someone sees that their voice is being heard, civic engagement clicks.

Civic technology doesn't have to be bound by geography. Programmers too far away to join a Code for America hackathon can log on to its Civic Tech Issue Finder and solve tech challenges for projects in other countries. It works best, though, when local people solve their own problems, as over fifteen thousand coders and hackers do as part of Code for America brigades.

In late 2014, a programmer named Ben Schoenfeld happened to start a brigade in my town, called Code for NRV. (NRV stands for New River Valley, Blacksburg's broader metro area.) At weekly civic hack nights in a coworking space above PK's Bar & Grill, members sit around with their laptops and work on the group's ongoing projects. Money from the national Code for America organization buys pizza, soda, and beer.

In Blacksburg, Ben says, there isn't the low-hanging technological fruit you see in some cities. The town's website is fine. There's already an app for the Blacksburg Transit bus system. So the group has focused on developing apps that make life better, like a safe streets crime mapper and a multicounty park finder.

For someone with a very particular set of skills, Code for America projects are precisely the kind that foster place attachment. You're working with people who are like you. You're solving a problem together (collective efficacy!). You're making your city more open, responsive, or beautiful. As Ben, who looks like a slightly nerdy George Harrison, told me, "I haven't found [another] project in Blacksburg that makes me feel more connected to the region."

Most of us, however, do not have that very particular set of skills. We're the end users of the world, not the coders and designers.

For us, civic engagement comes from using technology to connect with our town government, as with MySidewalk, or to connect with fellow citizens, with a company like Nextdoor. Since Nextdoor's launch in 2011, about 40 percent of U.S. neighborhoods — more than six hundred thousand in all — have signed up to create online Nextdoor "neighborhoods," digital communities that function a bit like private, hyperlocal Facebook pages.

Typically a resident starts a Nextdoor neighborhood by personally recruiting a critical mass of neighbors and starting online conversations. Anne Clauss, who spoke to me about the Nextdoor neighborhoods she started in Hamilton, New York, and Swarthmore, Pennsylvania, said she and a friend invited everyone they knew in the neighborhood, then preloaded the site with questions: *What time is the school play tomorrow night? Does anyone know a carpenter?* "I never needed a carpenter," Anne said. "You ask dumb questions and you look dumb. People start to respond because they want to help. 'Oh, Anne, I know a good carpenter.' 'Oh, Anne, the play is at seven; you can get tickets from my daughter.' " By seeming vulnerable and accepting assistance, Anne says, "all of a sudden you have an instant bond." (Not bad advice for neighbors in general.)

Nextdoor fosters the kinds of useful interactions — borrowing a hedger, selling a bike, discussing a park cleanup — that create the collective efficacy towns need. As of 2015, more than 870 agencies in 630 cities used Nextdoor to broadcast government, police, and fire department updates to Nextdoor members in town. In Sacramento, California, as Nextdoor membership soared and the police department used the site to connect with citizens, crime dropped by 15 percent.

In civic engagement, social cohesion matters. That's why the state and city Civic Health Indexes created by the National Conference on Citizenship measure not only how often people write letters and vote, but how often they talk to friends and family, exchange favors with neighbors, and work with neighbors to solve a community problem. It's all interconnected. Be social, and you're likely to want to do the harder civic engagement actions. Sarah Leary, one of Nextdoor's cofounders, said she'd lived for three or four years on her block in the Cow Hollow neighborhood of San Francisco and knew exactly one person. Since starting a Nextdoor neighborhood there, she's gotten to know dozens of people. Not coincidentally, she's also volunteered for the neighborhood emergency response team.

Toward the end of my weeks in the Blacksburg Citizens Institute, I saw that the city had set up an online survey to elicit feedback about its website. Riding the high of my government-employee lovefest, I tried to remember that there was a human behind this survey who was trying to do his or her job well.

I had also read a few things recently about Code for America's Digital Front Door Initiative, which proposes redesigning municipal websites to make them more transparent and welcoming. Thus emboldened, I spent ten minutes poking around Blacksburg.gov and brainstorming ways to make the site more like the Code for America ideal. It took me another ten minutes to answer eleven survey questions about how I use the city's website and what I thought should change. (Hot tip: Pick fonts that don't look like they were stripped from my high school term paper.)

I'm not going to lie. As Love Where You Live experiments go, completing an online survey was . . . kind of anticlimactic. No warm fuzzies. No burst of satisfaction. That's okay, because I'm guessing it mattered to someone in my town. Sometimes placemaking is just doing the boring stuff our towns need from us.

LOVE YOUR CITY CHECKLIST

☐ Follow your mayor and city councilors on social media. (First you'll have to find out who they are. For that, visit your city's website.)

☐ Figure out when your next election is and vote, even if it means you have to spend thirty minutes cramming on the issues.

☐ Join your local citizens academy, if your town or county has one. They go by many different names (citizens college, neighborhood university, and so on), so e-mail your town clerk and ask about local availability.

☐ To keep up-to-date on what's happening in local government (plus new restaurants, volunteer opportunities, and a place attachment bonanza of additional information), read a local news source, online or in print.

☐ If you have coding skills, join a Code for America brigade where you live, or sign up for a one-off civic hackathon. Code for America hosts a National Day of Civic Hacking once a year. Find an event near your town at HackForChange .org.

☐ Run for an elected town office, or just

volunteer for a city board or commission. Cities are mostly grateful for the help.

☐ Download and use civic apps for your town. To find them, Google the name of your town plus "app."

☐ If there's something in your place that's driving you nuts — a pothole, a broken light — go on your city's website and figure out who can help you get it fixed. Corollary: If there's something in town you love, write about that, too. City employees aren't overwhelmed with positive feedback. This will make someone's day, and you'll feel amazing.

☐ Attend a city council meeting. Just one. Try it.

CHAPTER TEN: CREATE SOMETHING

One day in the spring, my daughter Ella looked up from her Instagram feed. "You know what we should have in Blacksburg?" she said. "A sidewalk chalk festival."

"Like they had in Texas?"

"Yeah. That was awesome."

A couple years earlier, our family had gone to a street painting event in Round Rock, a city north of Austin. On parking space–sized sections of the main downtown avenue, artists were drawing gorgeous pictures with chalk, in colors that blazed like lightning strikes against the black asphalt, illuminating dreamy landscapes or Van Gogh's *Starry Night*. We watched for a while, then paid a few bucks so our girls could get a box of chalk and a small square of street to try out their own drawings. Ruby, a preschooler then, mostly scribbled stick figures, but Ella, who's been the best artist in our family pretty much since birth, worked with the concentration of Michelangelo. In the past she'd tried oils, acrylics, and pencils. "Sidewalk chalk," she said, "is my true medium."

A box of it went with us when we moved to Blacksburg. For as long as the warm weather and the sunlight lasted, our driveway was tattooed with schools of koi, flowers, trees, and Totoro. The chalk sticks crumbled in her hands. A rainstorm cleaned the slate. She drew more. I loved that it looked like someone was filming a Beatles movie out there.

Still. When one's twelve-year-old expresses a passing interest in having a chalk festival in town, one does not bother to look up from one's novel before offering an appropriately vague and noncommittal response along the lines of "That would be fun." Describing that day in Round Rock, Ella sounded languorously nostalgic. Nothing indicated that the chalk festival was more than a random memory flitting across the screen of her mind. Under normal circumstances, I would have nodded and moved on. Except these were not normal circumstances.

On a reconnaissance trip in 2014 to gather place attachment research, I'd grabbed a seat in a conference room in Detroit's GM

Renaissance Center for a presentation by Lyz Crane, the young, dark-haired deputy director of ArtPlace America, about a national movement of creative placemaking. ArtPlace, Crane explained, was a ten-year collaboration among eight federal agencies, six major banks, and thirteen of the wealthiest foundations in the country — an august group put together by the National Endowment for the Arts. "So far," she announced to the standing-room-only crowd, "ArtPlace America has made $42.1 million in grants for creative placemaking — for all kinds of things where you use art to change a place. That's 134 grants, given to 124 different organizations in 79 communities across the United States." Within a few months, another round of grant making would bring the total to $56.8 million.

Back in 2010, when the concept of creative placemaking was first gathering steam, the NEA's chairman was a dapper former Broadway producer named Rocco Landesman. He'd spent most of his career backing Tony winners like *Angels in America* and *The Producers.* Cobbling together resources was what he did best. And so he saw opportunity in a 2009 White House memo encouraging federal agencies to create place-based initiatives to "target the prosperity, equity, sustainability, and livability of places — how well or how poorly they function as places and how they change over time."

Creative placemaking, Landesman figured, offered exactly what the Obama administration wanted — a tool to restore and reimagine American communities. He'd seen it in his work, the way theaters changed their towns. Even without a theater, every town in the country had artists. Why not tap their creativity to fix real problems in real places? Kickstart economic development by, say, funding maker spaces for creative entrepreneurs? Make a community more liveable by building an outdoor stage as a gathering place? To truly change, Landesman thought, towns had to put the arts on the agenda.

Culture and creativity also happen to be excellent at fostering long-term attachment to places. Aesthetics, social offerings, and openness — the three elements that made people want to put down roots where they lived — were pretty much its inevitable natural by-products. To Jason Schupbach, director of design programs for the National Endowment for the Arts, the Soul of the Community findings "said something huge — that if you are trying to build a community, you need the arts at the community development table." You still needed strategies for jobs and safety and education and transportation, but creative placemaking could help with those, too.

By 2015, fifteen federal agencies, including the Departments of Agriculture, Transportation, and Housing and Urban Development, had deployed twenty-nine place-based programs in cities all over the country. On a map produced by the White House, a rainbow of colors indicates where in the nation's geography your tax dollars are at work. Counties with Promise Neighborhoods show up in lime green. Towns with a Local Food, Local Places grant from the Department of Agriculture are tomato red.

Purple denotes the NEA's contribution, a creative placemaking grant program called Our Town, started in 2011. With an average of $75,000 to grant recipients, Our Town has funded projects like an arts festival on an abandoned college campus in Sitka, Alaska, and a program to coach fourth graders through a place-based writing curriculum in Missoula, Montana. The $26 million investment is flecked in purple all over the map, through communities in all fifty states and Puerto Rico.

The same year that the NEA launched

Our Town, Landesman used his considerable producing prowess to convince some of the wealthiest foundations in America, including the Bloomberg Philanthropies, the Ford Foundation, and the Kresge Foundation, to help fund the new creative placemaking collaborative called ArtPlace America. "Suddenly the budget expanded incredibly versus what the NEA could do alone," explains Anne Gadwa Nicodemus, principal of Metris Arts Consulting and one of the coauthors of the original "Creative Placemaking" white paper that inspired the program. In its first round of grants, ArtPlace funded thirty-three creative placemaking projects, including programs to provide affordable apartments for artists, help makers train as entrepreneurs, and stage operas based on local oral histories. These projects weren't just art for art's sake. They were art for the sake of large-scale community needs like housing, economic development, and social cohesion.

At the National Main Streets Conference, where deputy director Lyz Crane was speaking, this was incredibly good news. Most of the attendees worked for one of the two thousand Main Street organizations around the country — an official designation bestowed by the National Trust for Historic

Preservation on communities that commit to revitalizing their historic downtowns. Main Streeters' local pride is as fierce as their money is short, hence the lineup of conference sessions like "Tapping Federal Financial Incentives to Support Rehabilitations" and "Why Aren't You Asking for Year-End Gifts?" Now, hearing that ArtPlace had the private-sector freedom and capital reserves to lavish millions on projects that tightfisted local governments scoff at, members of the audience gaped. Lyz Crane was the fairy godmother who was going to make all their dreams come true.

She told us about a few of her favorite projects. In Newark, New Jersey, $240,000 in ArtPlace money was helping convert an eight-story building facade — the last stand of a fire-gutted church — into an outdoor performance space and urban farm that would increase community cohesion and local food security. In Lexington, Kentucky, forty shotgun-style houses were being remodeled into a neighborhood of live-work spaces for creative types, a visionary approach to economic development and housing affordability.

The projects were thrilling — wildly inventive and substantial enough that I could imagine them changing an entire town's identity, or at least catalyzing the transformation. The Main Streeters could imagine it, too. When Crane ended her presentation, attendees scrambled to extend their business cards.

BECOME A CREATIVE INITIATOR

Of the laundry list of places that Crane rattled off in her presentation at the National Main Streets Conference, the one I couldn't stop thinking about was Prattsville, New York, a zero-stoplight town of 450 in the Catskill Mountains. Most people had never heard of it until 2011, when flooding from Hurricane Irene destroyed 40 percent of its homes. A year later, ArtPlace America awarded a Prattsville resident named Nancy Barton $200,000 to convert a rickety hardware store there into a community art center.

Crane had said the Prattsville Art Center was one of her favorite projects, and on the phone a few weeks after the conference I asked her, "What about it stood out?"

"I did that site visit," she told me, "and on this little tiny main street, there's this little diner, and half the town came out. I had half the town telling me about how important this project was going to be for them, going around the room one by one sitting in the diner. Even the pastor was like, 'A lot of folks come and spend time in the church, but I'd love for there to be another space where folks can come and hang out and talk and have that central gathering space.' It was one of those experiences where I was like, 'Take all my money.' "

In the photos I found online, ArtPlace's $200,000 didn't appear to have gone far. The Prattsville Art Center was a ramshackle two-story building with peeling green siding and a tie-dyed, hand-lettered banner. It looked pleasantly bohemian, but also jerry-rigged. Two years into the ArtPlace grant, the building had only just gotten water and electricity.

On paper a homegrown art center in a storm-torn town hit all the right buttons for my neolocal idealism. But the pictures gave me misgivings, hinting at the less-romantic reality of too much physical labor and not enough money. What was ArtPlace America's poster child like in real life? Was Prattsville as kumbaya as Lyz Crane thought it was? Or was the art center merely the pained last gasp of a dying area?

And what about Nancy Barton, who wrote the proposal that won the grant? I had a mental image of a placemaker as a selfless, self-actualized superhero who was so rooted in her town she was compelled to better it. Who exactly was Nancy Barton? I wondered. And why in the world was she doing this to herself?

Even before Hurricane Irene, everyone in Prattsville recognized Nancy. "[My husband and I] are not normal-looking people," she told me in a voice tinged with Valley Girl, like Phoebe Buffay's from *Friends*. "When we first got here [in 2001], I'd walk into the market and everything would stop."

Right away I could see what she meant. I'd booked a plane ticket to upstate New York to find out for myself what creative placemaking looked like, and Nancy had met me at the art center wearing a voluminous lime green jacket and high-tops that looked like they'd been stolen from a Harajuku-obsessed nineteen-year-old. As she delivered her origin story, she blinked at me through cat-eye glasses that sparkled with fake diamonds. A fifty-six-year-old professor of art at New York University, Nancy is sometimes described in posts on RateMyTeachers.com as "eccentric." Considering New York's traditionally high bar for eccentricity, that tells you something.

She's not the kind of person you'd think would be attracted to life in Prattsville. While neighboring villages like Hunter and

Windham draw city dwellers with their upscale cheese stores and antiques shops, resolutely blue-collar Prattsville refuses to pretend at urbanite sophistication. It has no movie theater, no bowling alley, nothing remotely hip. Just two bars, a couple of churches, the Zadock Pratt Museum, and a Great American grocery store on Route 23.

Still, when Nancy and her husband, another artist, stumbled across Prattsville on a weekend outing from Manhattan, the attraction "was almost an unconscious thing, like when you fall in love with somebody." The place's "take me as I am" authenticity — its fundamental weirdness, like something out of a John Waters movie — fascinated her. A few months later they bought a small house across Scoharie Creek from Route 23.

Since then, the couple had split their week between their two homes — usually Tuesday through Thursday in their cramped NYU faculty apartment 140 miles away in Manhattan, the other days in Prattsville. Even without the wacky glasses, Nancy was an outsider and a part-timer among families who had lived on the same land for generations. She mostly kept herself to herself.

Then in August 2011, Scoharie Creek rose fast with runoff from Hurricane Irene. A bridge near town clogged with debris and began shunting water onto Main Street. Soon the creek was rocketing past the diner, the grocery store, and the gas station at a speed, several people told me, to rival Niagara Falls. Houses were washed clean off their foundations. Many of the homes that still stood were rendered uninhabitable by broken windows and waterlogged basements.

Nancy's home was fine, but the damage to the town shocked her — all those collapsed buildings, the trailer park scattered through the streets. She urgently wanted to help, so she showed up at a few community meetings where residents were talking about how to build a new-and-improved Prattsville. "After the flood, the place was so devastated," she recalled. "Really, just so many things were lost. And going to the meetings and kind of hearing what people needed and what they didn't need — so many people complained about the youth not having anyplace to go or anything to do. And I thought, 'Well, that is something I know about.' "

How about an art center? she suggested. With a gallery! Workshops for adults and kids! Artist residencies! Few people at the meetings knew Nancy personally, but her neighbors were enthusiastic, and the concept evolved as others latched on to it. Let's make it into a teen hangout space, they decided. Maybe add a coffee bar. A local man offered a flood-damaged, 3,500-square-foot former hardware store rent free. Nancy wrote the ArtPlace America grant application. When the $200,000 came through, she bought the building outright and started repairing it with the help of some of her NYU students.

By the time I visited in late 2014, the art center looked less scruffy than it had in its online photos. The siding had been repainted a fresh khaki green, with variegated stripes around the door and window frames. Two red silk Chinese lanterns hung in the front windows. Paper signs taped to the window said, "Welcome to the Art Center" and "Free art classes Saturday and Sunday." They looked like they'd been drawn in Magic Marker by a teenager, and probably had been.

Two years earlier, before the hardware store had running water and bathroom trips required a dash to the fire station across the street, Nancy recruited artists from around the country to stay in the center's dusty upstairs bedrooms or in loaner cottages. They alternately created their own art, taught workshops to locals, and helped repair the building. Many formed lasting friendships. Nancy proudly mentions one of her students, a gay black man, who takes in Rockettes shows with a Prattsville woman who lives in a trailer park around the corner.

Not everyone could handle the chaos. One woman, a former NYU student from Los Angeles, was horrified by Prattsville's poverty. "Oh my God, people here need other things besides art!" she wailed.

"Yes," Nancy replied, "but they don't want to just have charity." At the art center, classes were free, giving everyone the dignity of doing something productive and imaginative. The process was the point, not the product. In the art center's beautiful white gallery space, paintings by professionals hung side by side with paintings by Prattsvillians. One wall held a series of pencil drawings by a local woman in her sixties. To me, the angels, horses, and UFOs looked like the doodlings from a middle schooler's notebook, but Nancy displayed them without irony or explanation.

Hours at the center were still loose, schedules not being Nancy's thing. Everything ran with what she called "the Little Rascals school of management: Hang up a sheet and put on a show!" (Literally. Someone offered a sound system and a projector and suddenly summer music and movie nights were on the docket.) Anyone who wanted to come and make something happen was welcome. "We basically have a no-assholes policy," Nancy said. "If you are a wonderful person and you come in here, whatever you're interested in can be a part of what we do."

One afternoon, Nancy buttonholed a gray-haired woman named Christl who had come to see the art center. "Are you into sewing?" Nancy asked.

"I sew a lot," Christl conceded.

Grinning, Nancy revealed that upstairs was an armada of donated industrial sewing machines, awaiting someone to teach people how to use them. "If you would like to be involved with that, I would love it. What days would be good for you?" I watched Christl hem and haw for a few minutes. It was clear to me that she was unwilling to commit, but Nancy didn't seem to notice her lack of enthusiasm.

The next afternoon, a senior citizen with an oxygen tank got a similar treatment. When Nancy found out that he'd spent his career as a metalworker, she immediately asked, "Is that something you'd be interested in teaching here at the art center?"

Every creative placemaking project has a creative initiator, a leader who comes up with a bold idea and has a strong enough vision to see it through to completion. Most artists are used to the relatively instant gratification of finishing a painting or a sculpture. Creative placemakers must take a bird's-eye view, since they aim to change the nature of a neighborhood or an entire community — a much-longer-term approach. Leo Vazquez, of the National Consortium for Creative Placemaking, explained that artists make good creative initiators only when they show up on time, know how to motivate other people, and get stuff done.

Nancy was great at most of that. She wasn't trying to gentrify the town or remake it in her own image. She accepted Prattsville as it was. Maybe she saw a better Prattsville, where everyone had a skill to teach and a talent to display. "To categorize people as creative or noncreative is flawed from the beginning," she told me. "People bring their imagination to projects, whether it's repairing a tractor or taking a tractor apart and making it part of a sculpture. It's the same thing."

If she failed at anything, it was recognizing other people's reluctance. Her enthusiasm was so forceful and wide-ranging, she couldn't fathom that someone like Christl might not share it. Usually she managed to lure even the skittish with the art center's warmth as a gathering place.

In the back of the building, the brand-new coffee bar was strung with globe lights. Baristas, some from the local high school, served up a custom local blend. All day people flitted in and out — a passerby who spotted the sandwich board outside advertising $1 coffee, a neighbor who settled into a thrift store chair, saying, "I just wanted to see what was going on."

One woman, a New York City transplant like Nancy, spent the morning frying green tomatoes grown in the tire planters out front. At lunchtime, she gave away the thick, tangy slices to whoever was around. Chairs filled and emptied, conversations began and subsided, all while a documentary about an artist called Llama Man looped endlessly in the background.

Nancy especially loved the misfit teenagers who hung out at the art center. She'd once been a troubled kid herself, who was saved by a similar kind of place in her hometown of Los Angeles. "It was the first place I had ever felt I fit in or been listened to," she said. "I feel like the art center [in Prattsville] is giving me a chance to look back at my life as a teenager and reclaim that period from a different angle." A few of the center's young interns and baristas are gay; one of them had her arm broken at the local high school because of it. Nancy consciously offers sanctuary to every misfit, rebel, and artistic kid for miles. Some girls mustered the confidence to couple up for the high school prom, thanks in part to Nancy's encouragement.

Maggie, a seventeen-year-old serving coffee in the art center, seemed a bit dumbfounded by Nancy's presence in Prattsville. "I never in a million years could imagine somebody like her wanting to live here. People don't usually come here who are like her. They mostly stay with people who are like them."

Nancy was clearly *not* like them. Yet her social network encompassed most of the town, from the pastor's wife who took art classes at the center to the members of the Ladies' Auxiliary of the American Legion who held their meetings there. She excelled on place attachment scale measures like "I know a lot of people here," "The friendships and associations I have with other people in this town mean a lot to me," and "I can rely on people in this town to help me." She valued the differences between her and the townies and knew how to gloss over them when she needed to. By galvanizing residents around the art center, she had created her own little community.

Measuring the success of placemaking projects is notoriously difficult. Data can be hard to collect and evaluate. Jamie Hand, ArtPlace's research director, told me that the organization asks grant recipients, "What are you trying to do? And how will you know when to stop?" When rents in adjacent businesses go up and vacancy rates decline? When teenagers who use the art center start graduating from high school? When there's less crime, more employment, and more economic growth?

Place attachment is seldom used as a measure of success, and yet, anecdotally at least, it's among creative placemaking's most dependable outcomes. In Prattsville, I met twenty-seven-year-old Kate Milo, one of the volunteer teachers at the art center. She'd grown up in the area, so miserable that she had pledged never to return after escaping to art school in New Orleans. Then health problems forced her hand.

This time around, Kate's experience of her town changed for the better — partly due to nostalgia, an adult's fondness for the mental maps forged on childhood bike rides and tramps through the woods. And partly due to the benefits of growing up; the classmates who tormented her have mostly learned to be civil now. A substantial factor in her feeling of contentment, however, is the art center. Having access to a place where her quirks are valued, where she's surrounded by creativity and openness, makes her happy where she lives. It makes her want to stay.

Over dinner one night, I asked Nancy if she thought running the art center made her more attached to Prattsville. In some ways, I knew, it had complicated her once-quiet life, forcing her to grapple with planning, hiring, and the everlasting problem of having more ideas than cash. She was now keenly aware of the many poverty-related needs in Prattsville. With the ArtPlace America grant winding down, she had to scramble to find other grants to install a professional kitchen for a pay-what-you-can restaurant and turn the overgrown backyard into a community garden.

Nancy hedged. She could be happy in any number of cities in the world, she said. She has a soft spot for Wonder Valley, California, outside of Joshua Tree ("It's the Prattsville of the desert").

On the other hand, she and her husband

recently bought a dilapidated farmhouse next to their property, with plans to repurpose it into studio space. She fantasizes about living here full-time. She's invested.

Eleven years after she moved to Prattsville, one of the checkers at the grocery store said to her, "I've always wanted to ask you: Where did you get those glasses?" It was a sign. Nancy had finally become one of them.

PRACTICE LIGHTER, QUICKER, CHEAPER

Further evidence that placemaking had entered the American mainstream: In 2013, Southwest Airlines launched its Heart of the Community program, a multiyear, multimillion-dollar grant program to bring urban public spaces to life.

One of the company's first projects was Campus Martius, a 2.6-acre park beneath the skyscrapers of downtown Detroit. Southwest's grant money paid to build a man-made sand beach on the former traffic island — a madcap idea that produced the desired effect of turning Campus Martius into a gathering place for beleaguered Detroit residents. In the summer, office drones flock to lounge chairs there to eat lunch, listen to live music, and therapeutically wriggle their toes in the sand. Just like that, Detroit got a little happier.

Ethan Kent, senior vice president of the Project for Public Spaces, the nonprofit that partners with Southwest on Heart of the Community, confessed that "definitely a few years ago no corporation was at all interested in this. So we were really surprised when Southwest came to us." There's been a ripple effect, as well. Perhaps inspired by Southwest's work reviving public spaces in Providence, San Antonio, and other cities where the airline flies, in 2014, Redbox sponsored a series of placemaking events at libraries nationwide.

Government agencies like the NEA, corporations like Southwest, and nonprofits like ArtPlace America fund big-idea, big-budget placemaking to the tune of hundreds of thousands of dollars a pop — a daunting amount of money. That may be why I'm so attracted to a catchphrase coined by the Project for Public Spaces: "Lighter, Quicker, Cheaper." The idea is that you can change the way people feel about and interact with a space without bankrupting yourself financially or emotionally. You make interesting things happen in your community, fast.

The artist Edi Rama tells a story of how, as mayor of Tirana, Albania, he set out to transform the depressing physical relics of the city's socialist era with the world's cheapest solution: paint. Blocky apartment houses in shades of sickbed gray were painted indigo or melon orange. Buildings were striped with rainbows. They were slathered in goldenrod stars.

The crowd-gathering colors and designs were not universally beloved. Iridescent orange, one official complained, wasn't up to EU standards. In a poll of residents, however, 63 percent liked the new painting program — and of those who didn't, half agreed it should continue anyway.

Paint feels like something of a Band-Aid solution. And yet the effects can be dramatic for place attachment. "The rehabilitation of public spaces revived the feeling of belonging to a city that people [had] lost," Rama explained to a TEDx crowd in 2011. "When colors came out everywhere, a mood of change started transforming the spirit of people." As the city literally brightened, residents felt safer and happier. In tandem, crime decreased and less litter sullied the streets.

Making cities prettier, more vibrant, or, dare I say, *cooler,* can instill hope. We already know from the Knight Soul of the Community study that the aesthetics of a place matter. According to one survey, living in a beautiful city is a more important predictor of personal happiness than objectively more consequential attributes like clean drinking water or safe streets.

Blacksburg is slathered with murals, and my favorite, painted by the local artist Den Bento on the side of the She-Sha Café and Hookah Lounge, is called *Loving Blacksburg.* I keep a $5 postcard of the picture — a stag superimposed over a bright swirl of color and the word LOVE — on my dresser. Just as in Prattsville, where the mere funkified presence of the art center, with its painted storefront and red Chinese lanterns, drew visitors and gave the town a new sense of itself, certain small placemaking projects make a town like Blacksburg look cared for. That may make it easier for residents to love.

In placemaking, ideas for Lighter, Quicker, Cheaper city makeovers abound. You could roll out sod in a parking space, the way the PARK(ing) Day designers did. You could emulate the Better Block movement by temporarily installing outdoor seating, plants, and pop-up stores to activate a neglected neighborhood.

Or you could copy the work of artist Hunter Franks's League of Creative Interventionists. In 2014, Franks challenged creative types to design on-the-fly place-making projects based on one-word monthly themes like "love," "neighbor," "play," or "music." When the theme was "gratitude," Creative Interventionists in Akron, Ohio, dropped a soapbox and a megaphone on a downtown street corner and urged pass-ersby to shout what they were thankful for. For "fear" month, San Franciscans set up a Fix Your Fears booth, at which visitors could receive a customized typewritten fear pre-scription ("1/4 cup belief, 1/4 cup faith, 1/4 cup confidence").

League members in other cities have cre-ated hopscotch boards, pop-up karaoke stages, and sidewalk "slow lanes" that encouraged dancing and taking photos. Most of the projects didn't cost more than $50, and like Jen Prod's sweet Random Acts of Happiness in Minneapolis, they were weird enough that strangers felt compelled to stop and talk about them with each other.

Really, that's the point of creative place-making projects, from the painted facelift of Tirana, Albania, to the redesign of Campus Martius. When they work well, they pull people together in interactions that build trust and a sense of community. Singing, chatting, drawing, painting, and howling together at a really bad joke are free, but they offer an astounding return on investment in terms of their place attachment dividend. As architect and urban designer Susan Silberberg points out, "The importance of the placemaking process itself is a key factor that has often been overlooked. . . . The most successful placemaking initiatives transcend the 'place' to forefront the 'making.' " The journey of building the Prattsville Art Center, Nancy Barton seemed to know instinctively, mattered more than what it looked like in the end.

My fondness for Lighter, Quicker, Cheaper projects doesn't mean that I think the arts should never cost money. One night in midwinter, Quinn and I bought $25 tickets to a concert in the historic Alexander Black House in downtown Blacksburg. A hundred people were milling around the Black House's Victorian living room, balancing plates of rice and beans from Cabo Fish Taco. There was no stage to take, so the band, David Wax Museum, set up in a corner of the living room and started rocking their Mexicali songs (several of which required a donkey jawbone as an instrument). All of a sudden the floor was packed with swaying bodies. I'm not much of a dancer, but that night I danced. It was the kind of night that leaves you blissed out with place attachment for days.

A few weeks later, I talked to the man who'd organized the concert, a lawyer in town named James Creekmore, who's known in Blacksburg for his artistic patronage as much as for his eponymous law firm. The bottom floor of his law office doubles as an art gallery. The space next door is a gallery store. A house he owns one street over is a studio space for working artists. He's like a one-man NEA.

I figured: Lawyer. He's rich. What about average people? Could they do what he did, sponsoring arts events that made their town come alive? He set me straight at once. "You're looking at an average person who's doing it. The law firm is not funding it at all."

Every penny for arts events like the David Wax Museum concert came from his personal bank account. After the Saturday night show, when his girlfriend, Diana, told him how much money they'd made, he said, "We have four twelve-packs of beer that are unopened. Can you take those back?" He scrounged through the garbage can for receipts, returning $120 in unused items that effectively doubled their take. "We're counting the dollars and cents and the nickels," James said. "We're not riding any bankroll. We're hustling money to make this thing work."

Why do it? Two reasons: He cares about the arts and he cares about Blacksburg. If James won the lottery, he'd buy all the property behind his law office in Blacksburg and turn it into a downtown piazza like Campus Martius. "That parking lot could be no cars, with a fountain in the middle. You could have a porch and an area where bands could play to an outside crowd. There's an alley that connects PK's to us — that could be the art walk. All of those restaurants could have outdoor backyard seating. It would be nothing but pedestrians."

On second thought, his real aim has nothing to do with real estate. "What we're doing is building people. We're creating this warmth. That's what I think is going to last, this warmth."

COLLABORATE WITH PEOPLE

Living in Blacksburg, I'd come to understand that most of what I love about my town is there only because someone at some point raised their hand and said, "I'll do it." At the Blacksburg Citizens Institute I'd learned that the city government was a duck, gliding smoothly across the surface but propelled by fierce paddling under-neath. In truth, there was unacknowledged paddling going on *everywhere* around Blacksburg. Someone had stepped up to restore the Lyric movie theater. Someone had turned Smithfield Plantation into a museum. Someone had carved hiking trails through the mountains and converted an old coal train line into the Huckleberry Trail. Someone had spent tedious, Red Bull–fueled hours coding apps that would help people find a park to take their kids to.

Many of my own Love Where You Live experiments revolved around the fruits of someone else's labors. I'd marched in the town Christmas parade, but who was the one who'd first said, "Blacksburg needs a Christmas parade, and I'll organize it"? I'd paid to join the Glade Road Growing CSA, but my $350 made me only a bottom-feeder in a process that began with Jason Pall and Sally Walker sweating over a row of weedy turnips. None of the delightful and attachment-inducing elements of Blacks-burg were created ex nihilo. The good people of Blacksburg made them happen.

Creative placemakers, I'd learned from Nancy Barton, aren't superheroes. They're usually average citizens — teachers, artists, entrepreneurs, lawyers, designers, activists, moms, dads, friends, neighbors — who decide to take matters into their own hands. They have a sense of what their city could be, and they love their place enough to try to change it, even a little bit.

The world, I realized, is full of people who say, "That would be fun." What it needs is more people who say, "Let's give it a whirl." Like everyone in my city's history who had built each thing I love here, I wanted to create something cool in this town. I wanted to become a doer. And within five minutes of Ella's mentioning it, I decided that organizing the First Annual Blacksburg Chalk Walk might as well be that something.

I envisioned it looking like the one we'd been to in Texas. Blacksburg's streets would glow with chalk drawings by professionals and children like mine. There would be judges, probably cash prizes. All the Soul of the Community elements would be present: beauty, openness, social offerings. Potentially this could be a place attachment bonanza, especially because one of my general theories of place attachment was: What's good for your community is usually good for you.

Wasn't this what the momentum of my Love Where You Live experiments was propelling me toward? Weren't my small actions — walking, buying locally, volunteering — meant to eventually lead to something substantial? Well, *relatively* substantial. Compared to ArtPlace America's megaprojects, a chalk walk was outlandishly small potatoes. That's what made it feel doable.

In a rush of optimism, I said to Ella, "I bet you could make a sidewalk chalk festival happen."

"Really?" she said, glancing up from her Instagram feed. "Like, what would I do?"

"Well, what if you and I organized it? Maybe we could work with one of the art festivals that already happen in Blacksburg. Kind of cooperate with them. But we'd be the ones doing it."

"Are you serious?"

"Yeah. Let's do it."

So that was my rough plan. Organize chalk walk. Make Ella happy. Make Blacksburgians happy. Make myself happy. Increase place attachment all around. The end.

Obviously, we can't interpret every "That would be awesome" that falls from the lips of our children as a divine edict. But sometimes we need to say yes. It's how neighborhoods, towns, and cities are built. The next morning I e-mailed Laureen Blakemore, the director of our local Main Street Association and the woman who runs Blacksburg's cash mobs. Five hours later a response pinged into my in-box: "Melody, this is wonderful. Let's meet and chat about this idea very soon."

Oh crap, I thought. *This is for real now. This is happening.*

It was decided that the logical place to seek help and collaboration would be Artsburg, a collaborative of artists, curators, museum directors, and arts enthusiasts who wanted to spur creativity among Blacksburg kids. At the group's next meeting — during the school day, thus absolving Ella of attending — I babbled nervously. "We've lived here for a couple years, and my daughter Ella had this idea for a sidewalk chalk festival, and I thought, *Hey, why not see if we can pull this off?*"

Everyone was enormously kind. Robin Boucher, the curly-haired art programs director at Virginia Tech, said, "This sounds fantastic. I bet I can get some of my student interns to help out."

"We can use folding tables from the Lyric," offered Susan Mattingly, the executive director of the Lyric. "I'm pretty sure Downtown Blacksburg has a canopy we can borrow, too."

The evolution from *my* project to *our*

project was disconcertingly quick. Everyone's ideas gave form and life to what was previously a nebulous vision. (Creative initiator lesson from Nancy: Incorporate other people's ideas.) We spent a few minutes hashing out details, eventually deciding to hold the chalk walk in July, when we could piggyback it onto an annual festival called Art at the Market. I left with a long to-do list and some e-mail addresses to recruit others to the cause. *This was happening.*

And then I panicked. I shouldn't have, I know. I've been in charge of things before. But once I'd set the balls in motion, the enormity of what I hoped to accomplish frightened me. So many moving parts! So many opportunities for public failure! At night, I lay awake attempting to fend off mishaps by worrying to death about them. What if it was too hot in July? What if kids burned themselves on the pavement? What if we didn't have enough chalk? What if nobody came?

Creative initiators are supposed to let go of desired outcomes and roll with whatever happens. That level of Zen did not appear to be in my skill set. I'd seen how Nancy Barton gracefully maneuvered what amounted to a second full-time job in addition to her teaching responsibilities at NYU. My piled-up responsibilities — the usual drill of meeting work deadlines, cooking dinner, shuttling kids to gymnastics — seemed pathetically minor in comparison. And yet I couldn't seem to get a handle on making my placemaking project as big as it deserved to be *and* keep the other parts of my life afloat. I wanted to believe the chalk walk would work out — I wanted to *make* it work out — and yet I couldn't move past my mini crisis of faith.

So I chickened out. I didn't bail completely, but at the next Artsburg meeting, on the porch of the Alexander Black House, I announced a vastly scaled-back plan. No professional artists. No money. No prizes. "Since this is the very first event and we've never done it before, what if we just have a little sidewalk chalk activity for kids to do?" I suggested in a small voice. "We'll set up a tent, we'll give out little cups of chalk, and the kids can go to town."

No one argued. No one cast me disappointed glances. Everyone leaned back in their rocking chairs and said that sounded fine. "I can still bring the chalk," Robin said.

The Saturday morning of Art at the Market, drizzle was falling like it meant it. Susan from the Lyric and a Tech student named

Michelle helped Ella and me set up the borrowed canopy, then we all dove under it as the drizzle turned to rain. The ominous orange and yellow blobs on Susan's WeatherBug app signified that we were going to be dumped on for the next several hours.

Despite Ella's "Free Sidewalk Chalk" sign, our ombré rows of chalk had no takers in the rain. We made halfhearted come-ons to preschoolers holding their parents' hands — "Draw a picture! It's free!" — but didn't persist when they shied away.

After a few hours, the rain finally broke. Ella helped me set trays of chalk on the ground around our canopy. The sticks glowed fluorescently against the wet-black pavement. Within a few minutes, they proved irresistible. A couple children who had been giving us the side-eye while their parents browsed the farmers' market grabbed colors by the fistful and started drawing smiley faces and writing their names. A toddler scratched at the ground and laughed when a bright yellow snake burst out. One little boy wrote "Butt butt butt butt" on the asphalt, then turned to us gleefully and announced, "I wrote 'butt'!"

In the afternoon, sunshine and foot traffic picked up. Ella helped Michelle, the Tech student, draw oversized Disney princesses

— Ariel with neon-red hair, Elsa from *Frozen.* I looked at Ella fondly, at her long legs splayed behind a chalk picture of Princess Jasmine. I knew my daughter well enough to know that the day she'd mentioned the Round Rock sidewalk chalk festival, she'd had zero thought of *this* happening. She'd gone along with it in the same grudging and graceful way she'd gone along with my other crazy Love Where You Live experiments — hikes and banana muffin deliveries and so on — because *I* wanted it. Because I thought that being a creative initiator was the ultimate big-hearted way to prove my love for my town, apart from getting a Blacksburg tattoo.

What I'd discovered in the process was that I was no Nancy Barton. I'd freaked out and gone too small, and now I was wondering why I had bothered. I could have gotten the same results throwing down a few boxes of chalk for kids to fight over.

Did everyone who truly loved their town need to make something happen in it? Susan, the Lyric director, is an inveterate placemaker and volunteer, and when I asked her this question, she wisely counseled, "If you're not passionate about it that would just be soul-killing to feel the obligation to do those things. I did those things because I wanted to, and as I did them I became more passionate about making a difference in the community I had chosen. But I have a lot of friends who feel really connected to the community who did not do those things, and they were just as happy, thank you very much."

Later, I asked Kate Nevin, the founder of the Charleston, South Carolina, creative placemaking nonprofit Enough Pie (the name references the idea that there are enough resources for everyone), what she thought. Kate's one of those do-it-all mom/nonprofit founder/investment banker types who normally induce existential angst in people like me, but she pointed out that if you didn't want to be a creative initiator, you shouldn't. You could be a facilitator instead — the person who lends a canopy or donates money. Or be a participant. "It's so much fun to be a participant!" Kate said. "That's the beauty of this movement in general. There really is a place for everyone in the project."

So you do the gig that works for you. Sometimes you lead and sometimes, as Susan put it, "You say, 'I will pass out chalk to children between twelve and one, and then I'll go do my own things.' " You do what you can.

All day at the chalk walk (or rather, the scaled-down chalk activity), Ella and I watched people aim their fancy DSLR cameras at the farmers' market's beautiful produce. Then they'd see the children's chalk drawings that had unspooled all over Draper Avenue, and they'd come take equally careful photos of those. Seeing their appreciation made me think, with some pride, *We helped create this beauty here.* In our own imperfect way, Ella and I made something tangible happen in our town. I only hoped that being dragged along for the ride would help her feel like at last she had a hometown where she belonged.

Driving to piano lessons one afternoon, Ella had said, "Mom, do you think if you'd lived in Blacksburg when you were a kid that you would have liked it?"

"Probably," I told her. "It's a small town and I think that would have been cool. Why? Do you not like it?"

"No, I guess I like it. But my friends all sit around the lunch table and say that they can't wait to get out of here. They say that the second they graduate they're gone."

Taking off was what kids did, what they were meant to do. I didn't want Ella to live in Blacksburg forever. I didn't ever want her to feel like she was stuck. Even if she adored it, I wanted her to go away to college and perhaps have her own epiphany about how great Blacksburg was. If she wanted to come back, she'd be doing it because she was rooted. Because she chose here.

LOVE YOUR CITY CHECKLIST

☐ Find out what art events are happening in your neighborhood — concerts, dance shows, festivals, guys with guitars playing at the back of a coffee house on Friday night — and show up to as many as you can afford, even if it's not typically your thing. It might become your thing.

☐ Throw a few bucks in the case whenever you see a busker in your town. Their presence makes your town an interesting place to be.

☐ Gather friends for an adventure and make something silly and creative happen in your neighborhood. Write inspiring quotes in chalk on the sidewalk. Instead of a lemonade stand, set up a good luck stand and pass out homemade fortunes. Mimic the League of Creative Interventionists and encourage impromptu singing, dancing, and befriending.

☐ Write a love letter to your town, explaining all the things you adore about it. Seal it in an envelope and leave it somewhere for a stranger to find. You may help change someone else's mind about your place in the same moment you change your own.

☐ If you have it in you, be a creative initiator and organize a placemaking project in your town. If you don't, be a facilitator, a helper, or a participant instead. They're all valuable contributions that promote place attachment.

☐ Tour all the public art in your town, including murals, statues, and sculptures. If there isn't one already, consider making a digital guide to them with an app like Tour Buddy.

Chapter Eleven:
Stay Loyal

Before April 16, 2007, if you'd heard of Blacksburg it was probably because you were from around here. Maybe you'd watched the Hokies play on TV once or twice. Then one sunny spring morning a student named Seung-Hui Cho killed two people in a dorm at Virginia Tech. A few hours later he chained shut the double doors to Norris Hall, a classroom building on campus, and shot and killed thirty students and faculty members inside. As police stormed the building, Cho turned the gun on himself.

April 16, 2007, marked the deadliest mass shooting in U.S. history. Afterward *everyone* had heard of Blacksburg. I remember sitting on the couch in our duplex in Ames, Iowa, watching the breathless evening news about the tragedy, the footage of ambulances and cop cars surrounding the kelly green Drillfield. I was a thousand miles away, and the shooting was merely the freshest entry in a seemingly endless series of outrages. A momentary kick in the gut, soon forgotten. I watched, then I moved on.

Once Quinn applied for a job at Virginia Tech, in the same English department where Cho had been a student, the shooting forced itself back into my consciousness. Like most acts of random violence, April 16 had been a horrible anomaly. There was nothing intrinsic to the place in it; it could have happened anywhere. Yet I couldn't help wondering whether the shooting had cast a permanent pall over Blacksburg. Had that single day irrevocably changed the town? Could people be happy living there? Or would moving to Blacksburg be like a horror film where outsiders buy the house the locals all know to be haunted, then act surprised when poltergeists bang the china about?

After we broke the news about our move to one friend in Texas, all he said was, "Better start carrying a gun."

In most states, the fame of all but the biggest cities peters out near the border — until, that is, tragedy or disaster sinks in its teeth. Who outside of Missouri knew anything about Joplin before a tornado mowed it down? Or Newtown, Connecticut, before a school shooting freighted it with a singular awful meaning? I'm guessing that if anyone outside West Virginia knows Buffalo Creek, it's because of the coal slurry flood that Gertie Moore survived there forty years ago. Today you can drive up and down that narrow valley with its brightly rippling creek and see not a single sign of the disaster, not a trailer or tree out of place, but in the collective American memory, the stain is there all the same. In the insult added to injury, tragedy destroys a town, then tarnishes its reputation.

From the outside, geographic infamy could be seen as a branding problem, since a disaster affected what people said about your town behind your back. To locals, the aftermath of a disaster was something else entirely. A tragedy could make a town feel unlivable — emotionally, psychologically, and in very real ways, physically. I returned to the same questions I'd asked about Gertie just after I moved to Blacksburg: When a Bad Thing happens where you live, why would you stay?

Chernobyl, Ukraine, is known worldwide for only one thing: a nuclear reactor explosion in April 1986 that sprayed the region with radiation in quantities four hundred times those released by the Hiroshima atomic bomb. Area residents were told to pack for a "three-day temporary evacuation." More than 130,000 people left and never came back. Their abandoned cities and villages decayed into ghost towns.

In Pripyat, the Soviet model city built to house the nuclear plant's highly educated workers, forests eventually reclaimed the apartment buildings and the park with its new Ferris wheel. In Chernobyl proper, the twelfth-century village slowly succumbed to mold, weeds, and wet. Before the explosion, 14,000 people had lived in Chernobyl. Almost thirty years later, the town was still considered one of the most toxic places on earth.

To this forbidding setting a few hundred residents — mostly elderly women, known as babushkas — defied official orders and returned to live as subsistence farmers. Ostensibly, everything in the nineteen-mile exclusion zone around Chernobyl was poison. Government officials warned against eating the carrots and radishes they planted in their own backyards or drinking the milk that came from their goats and cows. The women did it anyway, having decided they'd rather live five happy years near the ancient graves of their ancestors than ten miserable ones in a sterile Kyiv high-rise.

Holly Morris struggled to fathom this kind of bullheaded place attachment. A travel journalist who confessed a deeper connection to her laptop than to any bit of soil, Morris spent several years making a documentary about the babushkas. "If you leave, you die," the babushkas told her. "All those who left died." *Folklore,* she scoffed. Except anecdotes piled up about Chernobyl residents who had agreed to relocate, only to pass away a few months later. Though there's no official study, the people in the exclusion zone seemed to be outliving their uprooted former neighbors by some ten years. As the babushkas explained to Morris, the transplants "are dying of sadness."

That wasn't far from the truth. People who have been forcibly displaced from their neighborhoods and towns — because of war, genocide, famine, disaster, or urban renewal — suffer what the psychiatrist Mindy Thompson Fullilove calls "root shock," a kind of traumatic stress reaction like PTSD. "Root shock, at the level of the individual, is a profound emotional upheaval that destroys the working model of the world that had existed in the individual's head," writes Fullilove in her book *Root Shock.* Without mental maps or an emotional ecosystem of familiar places, routines, and relationships, the displaced suffer anxiety, depression, alcoholism, unemployment, and a propensity for stress-related diseases, including heart attacks. They're left "chronically cranky, barking a distinctive croaky complaint that their world was abruptly taken away."

The trouble with place attachment is that to fall in love with a place is to risk losing it and grieving for it. Morris met a group of transplanted babushkas whose village was so radioactive that it had been plowed under by bulldozers. "They're talking thirty years later about how they still dream about it every night," Morris told me. "They still want to go home. They're crying. You're just thinking, *This is so very real and raw for them.*"

So the babushkas of Chernobyl risked everything to return to a town that's existed since 1193. "They have this deep, soulful connection to a particular place that most of us don't have," Morris said. As a descendant of immigrants who came through Ellis Island, she can barely wrap her head around such loyalty to land. Many Americans can't. We're a nation of immigrants, transplants, and literal trailblazers, people whose DNA appears to carry the code for burning the ships and starting again somewhere else.

And yet for the first time in her life, Morris was inspired to consider staking herself to a piece of land — not an ancestral home, but a spot in the Rocky Mountains, "where my body feels like it's supposed to be. That's as far as it comes for me," she added. "I don't culturally have a place that feels like home, but I have a geographic, physical feeling of home."

Home is nothing more or less than the place where you feel at home and choose to stake yourself — maybe not in that order. When we decide to plant roots, often the feeling of at-homeness follows. The problem is that your town, wherever it is, will in all likelihood fall apart someday. It's not really a question of *if,* more a question of *how.* Tornado? Wildfire? Crime? Blight? Sooner or later, every city struggles. What we locals do next, after the disaster, is a key measure of how place attached we really are. How loyal will we be when things go wrong? Will we stay through the flood, like Nancy Barton did, and become a placemaker? Defend our town as a staunch local loyalist, like Gertie Moore? Or will we cut and run?

My Love Where You Live experiments thus far had tested the hypothesis that actively seeking the good things in Blacksburg, investing my time and energy, and immersing myself in my surroundings would make me feel more like I belonged in Blacksburg. For the most part, they had. The bulk of the walking, shopping, eating, hiking, volunteering, socializing, and exploring I'd done in the name of place attachment had been like starting a new relationship: bouts of fear and failure mixed with overwhelming delight.

What I had never tested was whether I had the mettle to make it through a crisis. Would enduring a disaster with my town increase my attachment to it? Or had all my moving around left me ill equipped to tolerate Bad Things? How could I test that, anyway?

I couldn't manufacture a crisis, nor would I want to. For this experiment, I opted for the next best thing: learning from how and why other people made the choice to stay after their cities' worst-case scenarios. What could tragedies, and the way locals prepared for and responded to them, teach us about place attachment? Could the April sixteenth calamity make me love Blacksburg more?

One could argue, reasonably, that the babushkas shouldn't have gone back to Chernobyl. Some places are so toxic, they demand to be abandoned. But the babushkas seemed pleased that they'd returned. In spite of everything, they believed their life was better in Chernobyl. They loved their place more than anyone else I could think of.

TAKE MICRO-ACTIONS

Bad Things in cities (and in life) come in two primary flavors: shocks and stresses. Shocks are acute — once-and-done disasters like fires, earthquakes, and hurricanes, or sudden outbursts of violence, like the ones that have lit up Littleton, Newtown, and Charleston. Stresses, on the other hand, are the chronic challenges of which almost every city has an assortment. Racial and class tension. Crime. Water and fuel shortages. Public health issues. Unemployment.

Both shocks and stresses seem to be bearing down on cities at ratcheted-up speeds, driven by causes from climate change to socioeconomic ills. In 2013, the Rockefeller Foundation, one of the most well-funded philanthropies in the country, founded the nonprofit 100 Resilient Cities to help cities prepare for, prevent, and mitigate their Bad Things, then quickly recover normalcy afterward. When I spoke with Andrew Salkin, chief operating officer of 100 Resilient Cities, the first thing he told me was that shocks and stresses aren't created equal. "We point out that cities have been facing shocks for years and years, but the only cities that have died, have died because of slow-burning stress."

For an example, he says, look at Detroit. In 1950 the city had the highest income per capita in the United States. In 2000 Detroit almost ceased to exist. "That didn't happen because of a hurricane or a tornado or an Asian beetle infestation. It happened because the city really failed to understand the stresses it was facing."

It's easy for cities to get it wrong. All the planning in the world won't save you if you misidentify your shocks and stresses, if they change midstream, or if they simply pile up too fast. Salkin makes this point about a different city. "When Katrina happened to New Orleans they were planning for a hurricane and they got a flood. When Ike came they were planning for a hurricane and a flood, and they got a blackout. The next big disaster they had was an economic downturn. Then they were recovering from the economic downturn, the flood, and the hurricane, and they got an oil spill."

When Victoria Salinas became the first chief resilience officer in Oakland, a position funded by 100 Resilient Cities in sixty-seven cities around the globe, she assumed that poverty would be at the top of her list of worries. Soon statewide drought in California was more pressing. Surveys of citizens and nonprofit leaders pointed to a host of additional problems, none of which could be roundly ignored without risking future catastrophe. "Resilience is a huge umbrella," Salinas told me. "It's the shocks, like earthquakes or even social unrest. It's the stressors, like lack of affordable housing, air pollution, or economic issues. So the first phase of all our city's work is to home in on what, out of all the challenges, are the five most important ones to deal with and tackle together first. It's a huge range of issues that each city is dealing with." Subtext: Who knows what's coming, but look into your crystal ball and figure it out anyway.

If these are enormous problems for a city government official to tackle, how can an average resident possibly help? Resilience stresses tear at the social structure of a city, but so quietly, like termites gnawing at the woodwork, that you don't notice until your city is falling down around your ears. Stresses make you fearful; over time, they can make you hate where you live.

I found hope in a story told to me by Daniel Aldrich, a professor of political science, public policy, and urban affairs at North-eastern University and author of *Building Resilience*. Aldrich had been studying the tsunami that killed almost sixteen thousand people in Japan in March 2011. In most parts of the country, some forty minutes elapsed between the undersea earthquake and the arrival of thirty-foot waves. Yet the death rates in the 133 affected cities, towns, and villages along the coast varied from zero to almost 10 percent.

To explain the disparity, Aldrich and his fellow researcher Yasuyuki Sawada, a University of Tokyo economics professor, looked at factors like the average age of residents, the presence of seawalls, and the height of the tsunami when it hit land. Surprisingly, those physical elements couldn't account for the varying survival rates. What did? Each town's level of social connection.

Forty minutes was enough time for the able-bodied to travel the two or three kilometers from the lowest houses near the ocean to the highest point in town. It was not always enough time for the sick, elderly, infirm, disabled, or wheelchair bound to do so. Those who survived told Aldrich and his research team that a friend, a neighbor, a caregiver, or a family member helped them. That implied two things: First, someone knew that a disabled person lived in that house and needed help. "If you don't know someone is there you're not going to bother knocking," Aldrich notes.

Second, the helper was willing to endanger his or her own life to save someone else's. No one knew how soon the tsunami would crash into the shore. Ferrying an elderly or disabled person uphill requires time. Most people wouldn't bother unless they had an existing relationship strong enough to merit that kind of consideration. "You can't build that during the disaster," says Aldrich. "You can't say, 'Okay, the tsunami is coming, let's go make friends now.' You have to do this before the disaster strikes."

Aldrich calls this the Mr. Rogers approach to disaster preparedness and recovery — "Won't you be my neighbor?" — and its effects have been visible in other places. After Superstorm Sandy walloped the East Coast, nearly seven in ten storm victims reported receiving help from their neighbors, compared to around 56 percent who said they received help from the local or federal government or FEMA. Regionally, the communities that recovered the fastest in the two years following the storm had the strongest social resources *before* the storm — measured as a combination of place attachment factors like social cohesion, helping behaviors, trust, and social control. More social resources in the neighborhood meant more confidence among residents about their chances of handling future disasters.

Any infrastructure that promotes cohesion among neighbors and community members can enhance resilience: wide front porches that invite casual hanging out; shared gathering spaces like parks; and greenbelts where neighbors cross paths. In Madison, Wisconsin, the nonprofit Center for Resilient Cities built the Badger Rock Neighborhood Center, a combination reading room/computer lab/café, as a model of how casual meeting spaces and programming can build social capital and resilience.

Simple actions like showing up to community festivals, joining a neighborhood knitting club, or attending the same synagogue every Saturday also build cohesion and trust. Aldrich says they're a far better investment than building seawalls or, worse, rebuilding a city after it's destroyed.

Social connections don't quite form a deflector shield against disaster or tragedy. Shocks continue to happen. Cohesion and collective efficacy, however, can alleviate the effects of chronic stresses in practical ways by making people more attached and invested. And as I learned from placemaking and volunteering, when people are attached and invested, they help.

Victoria Salinas, the Oakland chief resilience officer, told me, "We're a city that's very cash strapped, that doesn't have enough money to cut trees, unless it's an emergency and the tree is falling over. We don't even do preventive tree trimming in Oakland because we don't have the staff for it. Instead we have these people who volunteer for nonprofits who follow the city's procedures and trim the trees.

"That kind of activism and engagement is a core of Oakland's resilience. It's something we can use more of always, because there's not enough resources in the city to meet all the needs. But it also means that there's so much space for individuals to contribute."

Cities in crisis are frightening, but they offer one uniquely alluring trade-off: They allow residents more opportunity to create their city in their own image, the very thing that binds placemakers to where they live.

In 2009, the foreclosure crisis was catastrophic for the struggling West Rockland Street neighborhood of Philadelphia. Longtime residents were forced out of their houses. Slumlords took over, bringing in new, poorer renters. Some houses were abandoned altogether. The street, with its school, church, forty-six homes, and seven vacant lots, became a microcosm of poverty, crime, decay, and all the other ills of the inner city.

"What we saw happen immediately was the quality of life degrade," remembers Emaleigh Doley, thirty-one, a bubbly, curly-haired communications consultant who lives in a three-story row house on West Rockland with her older sister, Aine. "It was the little things. There was way more trash on the street. There were way more unsupervised kids. The vacant lots were getting out of control. And just in terms of how people got along, there was more tension and friction."

The Doley sisters realized they had a choice: Move away or do something about West Rockland's problems. Financially, they were in the same sinking boat as everyone else, saddled with a hundred-year-old house that was physically falling apart and financially losing value with each passing day. Moving was a nonstarter. So they began picking up trash and planting flowers in their neighbors' postage-stamp front yards. Betting on the power of "change you could see," they planned a clean-and-green event they called Grow This Block. Theirs was the "broken windows" theory of neighborhood repair. Maybe fixing small, visible problems of litter and decay on West Rockland might galvanize neighbors into caring about each other.

They fixed up two or three neighbors' gardens in advance "as an advertisement of what your garden could be like if you participate in this project." Aine worked with a neighbor to make large sidewalk planters, the kind you saw in the business district. Some residents asked, "On planting day are we going to get to make those? Because I want one." "People are really attracted by little things," Emaleigh told me. "I think that can create a lot of energy."

Grow This Block gave neighbors something cheerful to talk about, which led to regular block meetings among new and older residents. To make it easier to solicit donations and recruit outside volunteers, Aine and Emaleigh built a snappy website and called their efforts the W Rockland Street Project. Other neighborhood problems they approached with a Lighter, Quicker, Cheaper form of tactical urbanism. When they helped plant a community garden in a vacant lot, neighbors loved it so much they started mowing the other vacant lots. "Once people know they can use something," Emaleigh said, "people will also feel responsibility and take care of it." And as with other placemaking projects, places that look cared for become easier to love.

Emaleigh and Aine refer to the W Rockland Street Project as "DIY citizenship," emphasis on the DIY. Everything they do is meant to be copied by other places. For their next project, making an outdoor gathering place in a vacant lot, the Doleys got an architecture firm to design a community message board that could be assembled for $600 — not ArtPlace America money, just car wash/bake sale money. Every step of the makeover would be documented like an Ikea catalog, with photos, price tags, and how-tos. "It's basically what my sister and I have been looking for," Emaleigh said.

The Theodore Roosevelt quote that Emaleigh recited to me — "Do what you can, with what you've got, where you are" — summed up her approach. Renter or homeowner, she said, there are things you should do to improve a stressed-out neighborhood. Over time you can make your community a more satisfying place to live. Residents will want to stay longer, and they won't mind pitching in. That's resilience, and it looks an awful lot like place attachment.

Emaleigh knows that the "Two Selfless Sisters Revamp Their Downtrodden Block" trope makes good copy, so she feels obliged to clarify that, planters and community gardens notwithstanding, West Rockland Street is still beset with overwhelming problems. People who live there are still working poor. Ugly vacant lots still bristle with weeds. There aren't easy solutions for those kinds of chronic resilient stresses, "but I know that if we weren't doing this work, that potentially on our block the scales would have tipped to the point of no return."

ACCEPT THAT BAD THINGS WILL HAPPEN

Worrying about disaster scenarios does *not* make you feel good about where you live. It makes you want to stockpile cans of tuna fish in your underground bunker. There can be a fine line between realistically preparing for your area's most common shocks and stresses — by retrofitting your house for earthquakes or making seventy-two-hour emergency kits — and descending into the kind of crazy doomsday paranoia that leads you to push neighbors away. (*That last gal-*

446

lon of milk belongs to me!)

The paradox of resilience is that while anticipating Bad Things can make you feel antisocial, the aftermath of the actual event tends to increase social capital. After Sandy, 36 percent of residents in ten affected neighborhoods said they'd met neighbors they'd never met before because of the storm. Thirty-three percent said that the storm brought neighbors closer, an effect felt most strongly in places where Sandy's ravages were most devastating. These newfound ties have the added benefit of making residents feel more rooted just at the moment they're waffling between fight and flight.

Four days after Hurricane Katrina, sixty-year-old Beth Riley still hadn't seen her house in Ocean Springs, Mississippi. She and her husband, Jack, had spent the storm holed up in their daughter's house in Alabama, a four-and-a-half-hour drive away. The television news was a steady stream of New Orleans with a dash of Mobile. Relatively little emerged about how Mississippi had fared, and less than nothing about Ocean Springs. The Rileys' house was on the water; they wondered whether it had survived intact.

When they finally made it home — this

time a ten-and-a-half-hour drive, on roads clogged with panicked Gulf Coast residents — the relatively untrammeled state of Ocean Springs' main thoroughfare gave Beth hope. *Oh my gosh, we've been spared,* she thought as she looked over Washington Avenue. Then someone said, "You haven't been down to the beach yet, have you? It's not all like this."

Nearer the water, the streets were so matted with debris they were impassable. Beth and Jack parked their car near the police roadblocks and walked the rest of the way. From a distance, their house on Harbor Drive looked okay — doors and windows blown out, but still standing. As she got closer, Beth saw a cushion lying on the ground across the street. "It looked real familiar," Beth told me, "and I realized it was from our house. I thought, 'What's that doing over there?' " Her high school yearbooks and a heavy Pottery Barn sofa were on the lawn, too. Beth couldn't understand why. As she moved toward the front deck, she realized with a start that the whole front of the house was gone, ripped away like a Halloween mask.

Judging by the mark on the walls inside, the water had reached eight feet. The Rileys' bed had been dashed into a wall, the kitchen table shoved against the sink. Rotting food spilled out of the toppled refrigerator. Everything they owned had been spun into chaos. "Nothing landed where it should have been," Beth said. "Almost everything inside was destroyed or scattered." One of their chairs turned up on the pier. Most of the framed photographs on the walls — Beth's favorites — were washed away like so much flotsam and jetsam.

Other hurricanes had blown through the Spanish moss–draped town of Ocean Springs (population 17,000). Everyone agrees they were nothing like the 120-mile-per-hour winds and twenty-eight-foot storm surge of Katrina. Connie Moran, an Ocean Springs native who was elected mayor just six weeks before Katrina hit in August 2005, told me that no one had any idea how bad it was going to be. "We knew we were going to get hit, and yet I was on TV the day before reminding people to bring in their trash cans and all the stuff in the yard so it didn't get clogged up in the culverts. And there were no homes left," she said, laughing ruefully.

During the storm Moran slept in her mayoral office; afterward, locals straggled in wet, with stories about spending the night in trees. The town's relatively high elevation

— twenty-three feet above sea level — spared them the worst of the damage. In Pascagoula, seventeen miles away, 90 percent of the city flooded. Still, three hundred Ocean Springs residents ended up living at a shelter at the middle school, and four people died, including an elderly couple that refused to evacuate. "It was amazing that we did not have more casualties," Moran said.

Disaster recovery tends to proceed through orderly emotional phases, like the Kübler-Ross stages of grief in reverse. First comes the Heroic Phase. Motivated by equal parts adrenaline and altruism, people surge forward to help and rescue the suffering. Then comes the Honeymoon Phase, when support pours in from around the country. After Katrina, Ocean Springs acquired several self-appointed sister cities — Islamorada, Florida; Parkville, Missouri; Washington Township, New Jersey — that sent truckloads of equipment and workers or sponsored fund-raisers for the city. Residents who found lost photos and belongings set them out in their yards, like the world's saddest garage sale, so the rightful owners could claim them. A woman threw a "household shower" at the community center to replace damaged ironing boards, pots and pans, sheets, mops, and toasters for ten Katrina victims she didn't know. Everyone felt united in a sense of shared experience.

In disaster recovery, as in marriage, the Honeymoon doesn't last. Eventually, the Disillusionment Phase sets in, with its trademark impatience, anxiety, and exhaustion, followed by the Civil War–inflected final phase of Reconstruction, which is as laborious and interminable as it sounds.

Even as friends helped the Rileys dredge their house of ruined belongings, and the neighbors next door to their rental property cooked them dinner every night for a month, Beth and Jack couldn't decide which was scarier: rebuilding in Ocean Springs or starting over elsewhere. They filled one side of a corkboard with to-do lists — call the insurance agent, talk to FEMA — the other side with index cards on which they had written places they could move. Annapolis, Maryland, where they grew up? Auburn, Alabama, where their daughter lived? "It was going to be a big investment to rebuild," said Beth, "and then you're thinking, *We live in an area where you can just lose everything in a matter of hours. Do we want to put ourselves at this risk again? If we don't, what do we do?*"

One in four Americans envision themselves living on the beach someday, basking in the benefits of blue mind, but this periodic destruction seemed a terrible price to pay for a view of the gulf. One of the Rileys' neighbors couldn't even bring himself to mow the grass in front of his house, with the ocean leering at him like that.

Local architect Bruce Tolar remembered that after Katrina, every time he drove back to Ocean Springs from a temporary job in Florida, he saw the curbs piled with other people's swollen books and salt-crusted linens, and he could feel depression lowering like a scrim. He didn't dare confide in anyone about what he was suffering, because they were likely to be suffering worse. If he ran into a friend on the street and asked, "How's your house?" the reply would often be, "I don't have a house."

It took Bruce five years to realize he probably should have called it quits. At a community meeting in 2000, he listened as other Ocean Springs residents one by one acknowledged what they wished they had done differently when the hurricane came. "I'd take my photos with me," said one person. Another confessed, "I'd have gotten out sooner." When it came to Bruce, a bear of a man with a graying goatee, he said, "I wouldn't come back." Everyone in the room, including his mother, gawped.

Explaining his logic to me, Bruce said that Katrina was personally devastating in ways he never imagined at the time. The true problem wasn't just the three feet of flood-water that destroyed the first floor of his house. It was the slow burn of trauma. In the resulting economic slowdown, his business collapsed. He and his wife ended up divorcing, in part because of the terrible pressures the hurricane exerted on their family.

Ocean Springs was safe and clean, the schools were good, and his family and friends all lived there. He knew the town was lovelier and livelier than most places you could go. Bruce thought they were doing the right thing by staying loyal to Ocean Springs, in the manner of the babushkas of Chernobyl. In retrospect, he says, "it would have been a lot easier just to stay in Florida and keep going." He made a pledge to himself: If another Katrina happened, he wouldn't stick around to see how it turned out.

Outcomes aren't necessarily improved for those who stay in place after a disaster. In one study of seven hundred low-income women who moved to new cities after

Katrina, Penn State sociologist Corina Graif found that their new neighborhoods boasted higher median family income, more employed people, and less poverty than the ones they left. Another study found that ex-cons who were released from prison shortly after the hurricane, and who were forced by Katrina to settle in unfamiliar neighborhoods rather than their old haunts, had lower recidivism rates by 15 percent. Katrina had done them the favor of making it impossible to reenter their old lives.

Malcolm Gladwell explains in a 2015 *New Yorker* piece that Katrina victims who abandoned New Orleans for good after the hurricane were largely better off than those who returned. "Katrina was a trauma," he writes. "But so, for some people, was life in New Orleans before Katrina." Given that people raised in New Orleans earn, on average, 14.8 percent less than the rest of America — a serious place penalty — why would any of the 1.1 million residents displaced by Katrina make a herculean effort to return to their hometown?

The answer is place attachment. In a field study of 101 Ninth Ward residents who evacuated to Houston after Katrina, Emily Chamlee-Wright, of Beloit College, and Virgil Henry Storr, of George Mason University, found that more than half preferred to live in New Orleans, despite Houston's better quality of life. Sixty-nine percent simply said, "New Orleans is home." One man, when asked if it had occurred to him to stay in Houston, said, "No, that ain't never crossed my mind [not to come back]. This is my home. . . . Why would I leave? This is my home."

All my research on place attachment had shown me that loyalty to where you live matters. But at what cost? And how do you know when to leave? In the desperate, confusing months after a severe resilience shock like Katrina, no wonder people like Beth Riley struggled to make that call.

Of the large number of Katrina horror stories that Ocean Springs residents had to share, the most wrenching I heard came from a lawyer in town named Alwyn Luckey. As the storm approached, Alwyn packed his wife and children off to Disney World and stayed behind to get the family's beachfront house ready for a political fund-raiser they were hosting the next day. As the storm scudded toward landfall, a colleague urged him to take refuge in his law office a couple miles inland. "That's ridiculous," Alwyn thought. "I've been in this house for three or four hurricanes. I'm not going to leave now." Eventually sense got the better of him, and he threw his dogs, his wife's good jewelry, and a change of clothes in the car.

The storm raged through Ocean Springs. When Alwyn returned, his house was gone, nothing left but a bare slab of concrete. He had to call his wife to break the awful news. They comforted each other that at least no one had been hurt. It was all just stuff.

Three days later, he was the one to get a phone call. On their way home from Florida, his family had been in a car accident. The SUV his wife, Jeanne, had been driving with her mother and children inside had rolled on the highway. Jeanne was paralyzed. She's been in a wheelchair ever since.

When sorrows come not as single spies but in battalions, I've always leaned toward taking off and not leaving a forwarding address. It never occurred to Alwyn to move permanently. "You live in Tornado Alley in Oklahoma and people wonder why you stay," he said, "and it's because it's home. That's the short answer about Ocean Springs. For those of us who've been here forever, it's home. You don't necessarily choose to leave just because it has the attributes of being a hurricane target."

Or a tsunami target. Or a violence target. Or a toxic radiation target. Disasters and threats that make outsiders say, "This must be nature's way of telling you there shouldn't be a city here," have little effect on the truly place attached. We're not quite logical about these things. Consider that New York City has been obliterated on-screen no less than thirty-four times by various apocalyptic agents, including aliens, rats, superhero battles, nuclear weapons, pandemics, and nine monsters (King Kong wrecked it twice), yet 8.4 million Americans are still happy to live there.

"The problem," says Daniel Aldrich, the resilience expert, "is that people are very sticky." Aldrich has seen this firsthand. He and his wife moved to New Orleans for graduate school at Tulane six weeks before Katrina. The storm destroyed their house and car but taught him his first lessons in where resilience comes from — not from the FEMA check ("which by the way never came"), but from "feeling that we weren't alone, that we had connections, that we had a broader place in the community. That really drove the process of resilience there."

Maybe disasters, like any other Bad Thing, are merely incredibly effective vehicles for focusing your thoughts about what matters in your life, the way a cancer diagnosis or an accident does. As Aldrich says, "When something bad happens, what do you really want? A bigger car, a bigger home, more money? Or the belief that we'll get through this together, with our sense of community intact?"

Beth and Jack Riley took six months to recommit to Ocean Springs. In the end, after they made the pros and cons lists, Ocean Springs had more pros than anyplace else. "Friendship and community are very hard to duplicate or start all over again — at our point in life, too," Beth said. With the insurance money from their home, they moved a few miles inland, but "we're happy enough that this is where we'll stay until we die probably." She calls Ocean Springs a great place that just has a very bad day once in a while.

In the paradox of resilience, the moment you might profitably consider abandoning your hometown is the moment social connectedness surges. With your grief and loss, you turn to your friends and neighbors. You commiserate. You help and receive help. And eventually, as happened with the Rileys, the strength of your network reels you back, making you want to stay despite everything.

FEEL THE PAIN

Visiting Ocean Springs, ten years after Katrina, I'd passed the remains of a few graying, buckling houses, their windows boarded and their FEMA case numbers spray-painted on the plywood. Ten years and the houses had been neither rebuilt nor demolished. They were left to creep into disrepair, a disturbing memorial to the hurricane's passage.

Even on swanky Beach Drive, where the newish mansions loomed ten feet higher than their predecessors, telltale grassy gaps marked the sites where no one had yet found the courage or foolhardiness to rebuild. In the midst of Ocean Springs' almost complete recovery, a few niggly little reminders remained, if you knew to look for them.

That there were no visible scars from the April sixteenth shootings in Blacksburg made it that much harder to fathom. Once, at a PTO meeting, someone mentioned "security measures since April sixteenth," and I thought, *April sixteenth? What's that?* The perplexity of the memory jolted me every time. *Oh yeah. That happened here.*

April 16 was my town's personal 9/11, and I hadn't bothered to learn more about it than the condensed version I'd heard on the nightly news. I couldn't even keep the date straight. Probably I should have been happy to leave it that way. If by dint of luck, distance, or disinterest I could keep one iota of extraneous sadness at arm's length, why shouldn't I?

And I would have, except for a stray thought prompted by Jeff Coates, of the National Conference on Citizenship. He'd been living in New Orleans before Hurricane Katrina, and afterward he'd noticed that, along with the water in the bay, empathy in the city surged. Compassion for neighbors was the Honeymoon Phase at work, yes, but it paved the way for stronger social ties, civic engagement, neighborhood cohesion, and collective efficacy — the behaviors that help locals get things done. Empathy, in short, was a harbinger of place attachment, or at least some of the behaviors linked to place attachment. "I think you can't have anything without building empathy," Coates said to me. "I think it's the foundational building block" for towns.

For my Love Where You Live experiments, I'd worked at being kind to my neighbors, volunteering and donating money to good causes in my town, and placemaking my city into happiness. I'd tried to really see the humans behind the stores and restaurants and farms in my town, to hold out a hand to them. It seemed like my experiments *had* made me more compassionate. After so many months of trying to fall in love with where I lived, I looked at my town and saw people that I liked and whose lives I wanted to help improve in some small way. In a city of 43,000 people you can't know everyone — I'd maybe met 1 percent of who lived here — but my Love Where You Live efforts had made me feel a sense of community anyway. In place attachment scale terms, I could say, "My town isn't perfect, but there are a lot of things that make me love it."

We were closer, Blacksburg and I. We'd become good friends. But for good friends to become best friends requires some depth of intimacy, some revealing of the inner self. We'd arrived at the stage of our relationship where, if Blacksburg were a girlfriend, we'd be ugly-crying to each other about our tough childhoods. Truly knowing Blacksburg meant understanding its Bad Thing. That was April 16.

Not every town has a tragedy in its past, thankfully, nor is one a prerequisite for empathy. You can feel compassion and understanding for any shock or stress, for whatever history left your town racially divided or poorer than it should be, killed its once-thriving industry, made it less than you wish it were. You should feel empathy for all the things that drive you crazy about your city. Accept them or work to change them, but first, feel empathy.

My city happened to have a preexisting tragedy, and my hypothesis was that if I could muster more empathy for my town's heavy history, I'd love it more. The way I thought I could do that was by learning what had happened. Making it more real for myself. For my final Love Where You Live experiment, I wanted to experience an iota of the empathy that disasters produce. I wanted to *get* it.

One Sunday at church, my friend Joyce handed me an enormous scrapbook she'd compiled about the April sixteenth shooting. Knowing that she and her husband, Scott, had lived in Blacksburg for thirty-six years, I'd asked them to talk to me about their experiences that day. This was the study guide, apparently.

For a week I hesitated to look at it. It had made perfect sense in my head when I had arranged to speak with them. Joyce assured me that they had talked about April 16 with other newcomers. But I still worried that this new line of inquiry was both self-serving and self-flagellating. Was I crossing the line between empathy and voyeurism? I couldn't tell. The scrapbook sat there for a while, looking intimidating, until one afternoon, in the dim of my bedroom, I spread the binder open and began leafing through the plastic sleeves stuffed with family letters, newspaper clippings, and journal entries.

This was their story: On Monday, April 16, Scott, a Virginia Tech mechanical engineering professor, was in his office in Norris Hall when Seung-Hui Cho began firing into classrooms one floor below. A colleague across the hall ran downstairs to see what was happening. He was killed. Scott called 911, and the operator told him to barricade himself behind his desk. He stayed there until police banged their way inside, guns drawn, and escorted him out the door. In a daze, he wandered home.

Joyce and Scott had lived in Blacksburg so long that when the identities of the thirty-two dead were released, they knew a quarter of them personally as colleagues, friends, acquaintances, or friends of their children. What to me were names in a list, to Scott and Joyce were real people who had families and loved their work and ran carpools and sat in meetings and played on the volleyball team. I spent a couple hours reading Joyce's scrapbook, crying, then feeling terrible about crying. *Why am I crying? I don't deserve to cry!*

The strange thing, said Scott, when I later sat with him and Joyce in their living room, was that his current students didn't know much about the shootings. Incoming freshmen had been just ten years old when April 16 happened, and if they remembered the day at all, it was hazily. For Scott and Joyce, it's like hardly any time has passed. To this day, Joyce panics a bit when she hears more than one police siren at a time. Scott still has a hard time walking through the second floor of Norris Hall, even though the classrooms where Seung-Hui Cho rampaged have been converted into a Center for Peace Studies and Violence Prevention. He seemed surprised to find out that the eighth anniversary of the shootings was coming up. "Has it really been eight years? I guess it has."

Bursts of man-made violence could understandably make locals skittish or suspicious. In Blacksburg, April 16 made residents more tender with each other. Southerners are inclined to say hi to strangers anyway, but after the shooting, "you could be at the grocery store and somebody would burst into tears, and everyone understood why they were crying, and somebody would give them a hug," Joyce said. "There was just a community feeling." Not Virginians by birth, Scott and Joyce had long ago fallen in love with Blacksburg. April 16 cemented their loyalty into a fierce protectiveness.

"Is there a difference," I asked them, "between people who were here in Blacksburg for April sixteenth and people like me who weren't?"

Joyce paused, then said, "Yes, but I don't think it's one where we say, 'This is our tragedy; you can't take part of it.' But if they weren't here, they certainly don't have the same feelings, the same connection. It's just something that happened here, rather than something that happened *to them* here."

There was that eternal line separating me from them, no matter what efforts I made to cross it. And yet in mid-April, I felt newly alert to the anniversary of the shooting. I found myself tearing up in parking lots and restaurants for no good reason other than that there were people around me who had weathered an enormous storm. The saying "Be kind, for everyone you meet is fighting a hard battle" came to mind. After talking to Scott and Joyce, I had a better understanding of what the hard battles were. That made me more inclined to be generous and gentle.

Each year Virginia Tech organizes memorial events the week of April 16, including a 3.2-mile Run in Remembrance in honor of the thirty-two dead. At lunch one day, my friend Megan asked me if I planned to sign up. "I don't know," I said. "I feel a little weird about it. Are newcomers allowed?"

"I think so," said Megan, who's newer to Blacksburg than I am. "My whole family's going to run it. Well, 'run' may not exactly be the right word. I run about as fast as my kids walk."

For an avid nonrunner like me, signing up for the "3.2 for 32" was a chance to test myself. Did I genuinely mean to remember what had happened in Blacksburg? Or was it all just words? My empathy felt real enough, but maybe the race would provide the experiment that proved the results to myself. "Maybe there was a time when the run was mostly for families and survivors, but not anymore," Joyce confirmed. "Now anyone can do it." I signed up.

The bright morning of the run, the Drill-field was choked with people. Someone yelled the Hokie battle call of "Let's go!" and immediately the chatter ceased and the involuntary response cry rose up: "Hokies!"

With Quinn and Ruby — Ella had gone ahead with some friends — I found a spot in the back of the pack among the walkers. White flags were raised to signal the moment of silence. Ten thousand people hushed.

For an eerie minute, I didn't hear a child whisper or a baby cry. Around me were students in tank tops, parents gripping baby strollers, gray-haired faculty members fumbling with their iPods. I couldn't tell who'd actually been present in Blacksburg for April 16. In the quiet, we all remembered the day in our own way. Then the balloon arches lifted and we collectively began slow-motion shuffling down Drillfield Drive toward the campus duck pond.

I'd be lying if I described the run as a solemn march of grief. Once the moment of silence ended, the route erupted in sound. Laughter and a cappella singing and shouts of "Keep it up! You're beautiful!" faded in and out as I trotted along. The marching band was playing near the football stadium, where a bottleneck had formed, hundreds of us pressing forward like we were waiting for a ride at Disneyland, then at last shooting into the tunnel the football players used to enter the field on game day. In a fever of team spirit, someone shouted,

"Let's go!"

"Hokies!" I called back, like I knew what I was doing.

There's nothing more egotistical than telling the world how someone else's tragedy makes you feel. I'm still conscious of the fact that I'll never truly understand Blacksburg's resilience shock. After the 5K, a line of visitors filed past the horseshoe of thirty-two Hokie Stones, one for each of the lives lost, that form the April 16 memorial. I had no inclination to join in. That space still felt too sacred for outsiders.

Still, I'd seen that as I invested emotional energy into considering my town's shocks and stresses, my empathy had increased. Like battle buddies, Blacksburg and I were tighter because I knew what the city had been through.

Growing up in Southern California, a child of earthquake drills and occasional tremors that knocked knickknacks off the fireplace mantel, I felt a grim pride in being a person who lived through earthquakes. Other people would say, "Oh, no, no, no, I could never live in a place that had earthquakes," and I'd shrug and say, "You get used to it." Undertext: No big deal to us hardy souls.

I suppose that's what I mean by resilience.

You know some of the Bad Things your city is dealing with, and you love your city anyway. In a perverse way, you love it *because* of the Bad Things. You start to wear your resilience like a badge of honor: "I made it through a six-point-oh!" or "I survived Katrina." You start to see yourself as someone who endures.

Of course, you can always move away. Sometimes that's the better (or only) option. But when we let them, shocks and stresses bind us to our town. At least some of the placemakers I'd learned about through my Love Where You Live experiments — Nancy Barton creating the Prattsville Art Center after a flood, Belva Davis working with neighbors after Detroit's economic collapse, Brian Mogren starting St. Jane House as a reaction to chronic stresses in North Minneapolis — were inspired by their community's hardships.

In that sense, disaster is a loyalty proving ground, the thing that changes your town but doesn't define it. Although if it does define your town, that's okay, too. As Joyce told me, she doesn't mind if when people think of Blacksburg, they think of April 16, "because there's some sympathy there. Maybe they're thinking kind thoughts. At least they know where it is."

LOVE YOUR CITY CHECKLIST

☐ Create an emergency contact list for your neighbors. You'll be one another's first line of defense in case of a disaster, with the added benefit that now you have their numbers to invite them to your Sunday Night Dinner.

☐ Take a broken windows approach to your own street. Are there small signs of chronic stress, like trash in the street — or, for that matter, literal broken windows? Start a cleaning and greening program like the Doley sisters did, or work with your neighbors on other solutions. (It'll have the place attachment benefit of building collective efficacy.)

☐ Read about your town's history so you have a better sense of what it's been through. Even small towns tend to carry local history books in the library.

☐ Treat people in your community with kindness. Make your town a more gentle place to live. When you're tempted to blow up at a neighbor or a slow-moving store clerk, invoke some empathy by imagining what hard battles the person might be fighting in his or her life.

☐ Make your own personal resilience plan. Identify the most common shocks in your region — earthquakes, floods, wildfires — and figure out what you need to do to deal with them. Do you need a weather radio? A supply of water? Make an evacuation plan and assemble seventy-two-hour kits for each member of your family. You'll feel less stressed if you know what to do when a Bad Thing happens.

☐ Learn to be more self-sufficient by picking up helpful practical skills — gardening, hunting, canning, clothing repair. They'll be super handy when the zombie apocalypse occurs.

☐ Find out what your city is doing to prepare for resilience shocks. Read about, for instance, new plans to prevent flooding. It will tamp down your anxiety and perhaps present ways to become civically engaged — if only by cheerfully paying the new stormwater abatement tax.

CHAPTER TWELVE: SETTLE DOWN

Summertime is moving season — more than 40 percent of long-distance moves in America happen between May and August — and in a college town like Blacksburg it takes on a particularly manic quality. One day the students are there, the next Blacksburg is awash in U-Hauls and pickup trucks, and the day after that half the population has left en masse and you can get a table in Cabo Fish Taco anytime you want.

A bit more slowly, the townies scatter to the winds. This year, Quinn had colleagues take new jobs in Buffalo, Charlotte, and West Lafayette, Indiana. People we'd seen at church every Sunday for three years one by one left for Omaha or Austin. My friend Brittany burst into tears announcing that her family was leaving for Las Vegas. My walking buddy Laura, the one with whom I'd been rained on hiking the Blue Ridge, decamped for Laramie, Wyoming. For two years we'd paced past the municipal golf course and the new houses on Willard Drive, hashing out our anxieties about job searches and real estate. Then one June day, she, too, was gone.

Like a virus, the idea of moving began infecting everyone else. People had fever dreams of starting over. My friend Nicki, who'd lived her whole life in nearby Radford, confessed, "Sometimes I think it would be fun just to try living somewhere else for a while." My friend Jen agreed. Wistfully, she said, "I think about how it would be to move to a new town and just chop off this commitment and that commitment till there's nothing left."

Listening to them talk was like hearing a recording of my Texas self in the full throes of my starting-over fantasy. I'd been there. I'd said versions of those things. So it was weird that, for the first time in a while, I didn't feel the urge to uproot. Things had changed for me in Blacksburg. I actually wanted to stay put.

I had begun my Love Where You Live experiments with a few theories about what would happen to me if I consciously and effortfully attempted to become attached to where I lived. I suspected that I might recognize more people in the grocery store.

That I'd make a few new friends. That I'd become more involved in the goings-on of my town. I figured that the more place attachment and placemaking behaviors I mimicked, the more settled I'd feel.

At first I couldn't tell if the experiments were working. Every so often I'd grab a stick and poke at myself: *Do I like it here? Huh? Do I?* The pace of my emotional evolution was so glacial that for a long time I wasn't sure it was happening at all.

Only at the end of all my Love Where You Live experiments did I get a clear picture of the Before and After. Before, that awful first drive into town made me feel as if I'd been stranded in a foreign country whose language I barely spoke — forlorn and lonely and awful. Before, when people asked me how I liked Blacksburg, I could barely muster a "meh." Before, I wasted hours on Realtor.com trying to find a new life for myself in a different city.

After, I said hi to my neighbors. After, I took pure pleasure in my morning walk past the golf course, in the crisp loaves of sourdough at Our Daily Bread, in the way the leaves turned yellow in the fall. After, I realized I felt homesick for Blacksburg when I left to visit other cities. The homesickness was a revelation in itself. That meant Blacksburg was familiar now, which it hadn't always been.

Evidence for my change of heart kept piling up. When people asked me how I liked Blacksburg now, I blurted, "I love it!" without feeling like I was selling something. The sight of Blacksburg's green hills filled me with tender affection. I'd become possessive and defensive of Blacksburg's honor. I'd turned into the woman who posted annoying articles on Facebook about Blacksburg's ranking in a new "best places" list.

Precisely how had this all happened? When and where had my narrative of my town changed? According to Katherine Loflin, the place guru who'd led the Knight Soul of the Community study, place attachment peaks three to five years after one moves to a new city, and I was rapidly hurtling toward my third anniversary in Blacksburg. Surely time had healed some of my moving-truck-inflicted wounds. Had I simply acclimated to my new environment in a way that would have happened regardless of my Love Where You Live experiments?

Possibly. Then again, emotion follows action, and my experiments had driven me to actions in Blacksburg that I likely never would have dared otherwise, like joining the

Blacksburg Citizens Institute, running the 3.2 for 32, volunteering at the Lyric, and buying into the Glade Road Growing CSA. In the library not long ago, I walked past some volunteers trying to get passersby to write e-mails protesting a proposed gas pipeline through the county. I actually climbed into my car before doubling back to talk with them, thinking, *This is what a person who loves it here would do.*

Asking myself, *What would someone who loves Blacksburg do?* had become a regular mental refrain. *Would a person who loves their town go to the concert in the park? Would a person who loves their town pick up the nasty piece of trash in the road?* Yes. Yes, they would.

Learning about placemaking, too, had reframed the way I viewed Blacksburg's deficiencies. Toward the end of my Love Where You Live experiments, I took a trip to Lynchburg, Virginia. A city park there had a freshly built splash pad, the kind that sprays small beings into an ecstatic frenzy. I watched a little longingly as car-sized buckets of water doused a dozen joyful, screaming kids. Nothing like a splash pad existed in Blacksburg, and a few years ago, I would have taken this as a sign that my family lived in the wrong place. Look, here was the evidence! Better cities existed. Time to move.

At some point, however, I'd accepted that I would never find my Platonic ideal of a town. No matter how freakishly low the cost of living or how joyous the splash pads, any place would be aggravating in its own special way. I had two choices: Deal with it or change it. So I tweeted a photo of the splash pad to @Blacksburg_Gov, the town's official Twitter feed. "Seriously," I wrote, "we need one of these splash pads in Blacksburg. How can we make it happen?"

Within a half hour someone tweeted back. "That seems cool! Contact Parks and Recreation. They can share with you what it would take." I felt both accomplished and heard. Certainly Nancy Barton would have already written a grant or convened a community meeting about it, but if I was ill equipped to be a powerful placemaker myself, at least it had become a habit to consider and feel responsible for Blacksburg's improvement.

So time had changed me, but so had effort and will. After three years in Blacksburg, when I looked at the place attachment scale statements researchers used, I found I could agree with almost all of them:

I feel rooted here.

I know a lot of people here.

I know my way around.

I feel comfortable here.

I like to tell people about where I live.

I rely on where I live to do the stuff I care about most.

If I could live anywhere in the world, I would live here.

I can rely on people in this town to help me.

My town isn't perfect, but there are a lot of things that make me love it.

Things were going so well that I started thinking about buying a house. Quinn and I had been renting since we moved to town, in deference to our unceasing mobility, but having worked so hard to fall in love with Blacksburg, I had no interest in pressing the reset button — in which case, didn't it make sense to buy? Giddily, I began to do drive-bys of For Sale signs. I populated an entire Pinterest board with bungalow floor plans.

Then, sitting in Lefty's one night, Quinn swirled his fork in the pan sauce from his steak au poivre and dropped a bomb. The holy grail English professor job we'd moved for? It wasn't feeling like the holy grail anymore. Maybe he wasn't the right fit in his department. Maybe he wouldn't earn tenure. Maybe he was just feeling that familiar itch to try something different. Maybe in a different place.

I froze. "Don't tell me we're moving again."

"I don't know. I hope not. I really don't want to uproot our kids again. But if I don't spend the next thirty years as a professor, I'm not sure how to keep us here. Blacksburg isn't exactly a big city." He glanced at me nervously. "Look, I'm not talking about packing up our stuff next week. I'm just not sure where we'll be in a few years."

If that was on the table, why was I bothering with Love Where You Live experiments at all? Rooting was the point, right? You chose a town, you settled down, and you became a Stayer, like Gertie Moore. The line on the place attachment scale about "I don't want to move anytime soon" spoke to the heart of the matter. When you loved where you lived, you stayed. You tried to, at least.

Katherine Loflin explained it to me with this story. Back when she was heading up the Knight Soul of the Community study, she was like a faith healer who'd lost her religion — preaching the gospel of place love at town halls across America, then flying back to Miami, a city where she'd never really felt at home. On the openness, aesthetics, and social offerings that Soul of the Community said mattered most, Miami did well. It was the person-environment fit that felt off. "You have to find your heart match," Loflin tells me. "It's not just about having the amenities, but how they show up in your life. Even though on paper Miami is perfect, its manifestation of its perfection was not working for my narrative."

Eventually, Loflin moved. She sold her Miami condo. She rented a house in Cary, North Carolina, near her hometown. One morning as she was reading the paper there over coffee, her daughter walked into the room and said, "We have lived in a lot of different places that I've liked. This is the first place I never want to leave."

"And that is the difference," Loflin told me, "between place satisfaction and place attachment. Liking where you live is satisfaction. Never wanting to leave is attachment."

I hadn't expected forever. I'd always known that Quinn's job might not last. In the beginning I didn't care. The best I could hope was wanting to stay in Blacksburg right now, getting through another day or month or year. It wasn't until I observed my own visceral reaction to the specter of moving again — disbelief, depression, generalized anxiety — that I understood what Katherine Loflin meant. I didn't want to leave. Not now. Possibly not ever.

So there it was. I was place attached. I'd done it.

Which made the idea of leaving even more ironic, like getting divorced a week after you finally learn to love the guy. Heartbreaking. Pointless. I started wondering why I'd tried so hard to fall in love with my town at all.

Then I remembered Greg Tehven.

PAINT ANOTHER PICTURE

Greg Tehven grew up in Fargo, North Dakota, one of the most sneered-at regions of America's flyover, and early on he absorbed a general sense of geography-related unworthiness. He recalls a teen at the Mall of America in Minneapolis jeering, "Do you live in a teepee?" At a summer camp he attended in Colorado, the joke was "Have you heard of the Internet?"

As a child, Greg implicitly understood one of Fargo's foundational truths — that those who could get out did. "Inside the community, I remember a lot of headlines and politicians talking about brain drain," he says. "I never wanted to stay there because if I stayed that meant I wasn't smart. If you were going to make anything of your life, you wouldn't want to be one of those kids who wasn't able to leave or couldn't cut it outside." To escape, he got a business degree at the University of Minnesota, then traveled for almost a year through Europe and Asia.

After a while, he had an aha moment: No matter where in Europe he went, nobody knew his name. Whereas in his hometown, which had been settled by his great-great-grandfather, he'd been the fifth generation of his family to attend the same church. "I missed feeling part of a community," he told me.

So in 2011 he went home. Within a few months Greg had pulled together the first-ever TEDx Fargo, then two more in quick succession, one with the theme of City 2.0. He began an event called Startup Drinks, which morphed into Startup Weekend, a fifty-four-hour entrepreneurial competition that attracted participants from as far as San Francisco and Washington, D.C. Grad school plans were forgotten as Greg realized, "Hey, I love it here. I want to make a great city." He became a placemaker.

Greg saw artists and entrepreneurs as the

two primary patrons and producers of Fargo's renaissance, and he liked to combine the groups in unexpected, magical ways. Midnight Brunch, which Greg conceived in 2013, did this perfectly. Fifty people gathered at a downtown art gallery at ten p.m. on a Thursday night for a mix-and-mingle cocktail party, followed at eleven p.m. by a white-tablecloth vegan meal catered by husband-and-wife chefs who'd moved to Fargo from Colorado. Creative types and businesspeople, Movers and Stayers, settled on both sides of a long table for what Greg described rhapsodically as the closest thing Fargo had ever seen to a nineteenth-century European salon. At one Midnight Brunch, a violinist from the Fargo-Moorhead Symphony provided a soulful accompaniment to the stylings of international yo-yo champion John Narum, who lives in town. At midnight, there was a toast.

In other cities, ideas could float around for a few months before dying from bureaucratic paper cuts or neglect. In Fargo, the start-up mentality fostered by people like Greg Tehven effectively shortened the lag time between idea and iteration. Hipster businesses began opening — a craft store and arts market called Unglued, a food truck turned wood-fired pizza restaurant. A man named Rory Beil organized Streets Alive, a local version of Open Streets that for two afternoons a summer let loose a flood of bikers, walkers, skateboarders, Rollerbladers, wheelchair riders, stroller pushers, and Segways into a three-mile loop of closed downtown streets.

One day, a friend told Greg that he wanted to plan an alley fair. A few months later, a fully realized street festival, with bands, food, and art, was happening in a derelict downtown alleyway. All someone had to do was mention a good idea and people clamored to bring it to life. Communal living for entrepreneurs? Sure. Free dinners for city visitors? Why not? People in Fargo weren't necessarily calling those efforts placemaking, but they had the effect of genuinely making Fargo a better place to live.

That's not to understate Fargo's geography-related challenges. The city is isolated, and brutally cold; in January, the average high temperature hovers around 15.9 degrees Fahrenheit. One man who moved to North Dakota from England told me that when he first arrived, he walked to a convenience store in January. By the time he got back to his office the bottle of water he'd bought had frozen solid in his pocket.

Several transplants impressed upon me the absolute necessity of a midwinter tropical vacation.

Despite all that, the revamped Fargo was fielding so many new arrivals — often under-thirties from Oregon, Washington, Colorado, and Arizona — that the city's annual growth rate doubled to 2 percent. Mike Williams, one of Fargo's city commissioners, told me that in surveys of local high schoolers, "it used to be that if you asked the students where they were going to live once they graduated, 65 percent said, 'I'm moving.' Now 65 percent say that they're staying here, and another 10 percent are staying in the region. That's a hundred-and-eighty-degree change, and it just happened in the last ten years."

On the surface, maybe what was happening in Fargo resembled gentrification or a Brooklyn-style hipster takeover. The real change was that people felt empowered to make where they lived better without waiting for a forward-thinking mayor or a well-endowed foundation to do it for them. As Ethan Kent of the Project for Public Spaces pointed out to me, the "maker" ethos is infusing towns; people want to feel like they have a hand in creating the city where they live. The kind of change that was happening in Fargo was starting to happen in cities all over the country where people were actively starting art centers, clubs, conferences, and festivals, painting murals, volunteering, breaking trails, and writing letters to the mayor. Fargo had one of the purest manifestations of the spirit of placemaking I'd seen. With people like Greg Tehven in the vanguard, everyone else said, "Hey, I can change my town, too."

I figured that leading a placemaking movement in one's ancestral homeplace might seal the deal on geographic permanence. Greg would stay in North Dakota forever, I assumed. But when I said this to him, he seemed taken aback. "I will always be committed to this community, and it will always be part of me," he said. "But I've always dreamed of living in multiple cities and being engaged in multiple communities. I'm not a person who thinks of one place as home."

I was pretty much laboring under the impression that thinking of one place as home was *exactly* what Stayers did. If you went all in and invested big-time in your city, you'd eventually experience a kind of religious conversion from Mover to Stayer. You'd be magically shielded from wanting to move ever again. That's what the Love

Where You Live experiments were all about.

Except Greg Tehven was doing all the things that placemakers and place-attached people do, and he still kept an eye on the exit sign. He told me he had a twenty-year plan to stay and fix up Fargo before moving on, so it was a long-term strategy. But still.

As I researched placemaking, I heard similarly disconcerting stories. I'd learned about Nick Arnett because he was a weirdly anomalous eighteen-year-old who had no intention of leaving the town where he grew up, Fort Wayne, Indiana. He loved his city so precociously that at age nine he had his mom take him downtown almost every day so he could study the high-rise buildings. At eleven he founded his own nonprofit to get kids to weigh in on a downtown planning process. "While all my friends were out playing football," he said, "they would make fun of me. 'Are you going to some city thing tonight?' I was the weird kid among my friends."

When his fellow high school graduates were abandoning Fort Wayne for Indianapolis or Chicago, Arnett launched the Twelve Cities Project, to learn what other great cities were doing to attract Millennials. Roadtripping to Chattanooga, Tucson, San Jose, and Portland, Oregon, Arnett met with business leaders and residents about what made them love their towns, then returned to Fort Wayne to import those other cities' tips and tricks and make his hometown better than ever. A more die-hard place fan would be hard to find.

And then at the end of 2014, I looked him up and he'd moved. To Chattanooga, one of those great cities he'd visited.

I'd never even met Arnett, yet I felt betrayed. Stayers were meant to stay! But in fact, Stayers were moving in disturbing numbers. Tonya Beeler, the woman who helped start Sunday Night Dinners in the Fountain Square neighborhood of Indianapolis, e-mailed me one day to confess that her husband had an opportunity "too good to pass up" in Atlanta. "I get the ugly cry every time I even think about it," she said, but they moved anyway. Emaleigh Doley admitted that in a few years she'd probably move on from West Rockland Street, the Pennsylvania neighborhood she and her sister were transforming with block cleanups and vacant lot makeovers.

Even Susan Mattingly, the Lyric director who'd lived in Blacksburg since 1991, told me that she thought she had another urban experience left in her. As much as she'd adored Blacksburg all these years, she'd sacrificed career growth to live here. "There are little pangs of regret that if we had been open to moving and leaving, maybe things would have turned out differently, but the reality is that to get something you have to give up something, and you have to make sure what you're giving up is worth what you're getting," she said. With small children and a strong circle of friends, "I never thought the equation was worth it." Now that her kids were grown, she was willing to put rootedness on the altar for personal growth.

Scott and Helen Nearing were well-known back-to-the-landers who'd homesteaded a piece of land in Vermont — an intense process that necessarily built place dependence and attachment. In 1951, they began considering a move to Maine. Scott wrote Helen a note about it: "You thought you might have some trouble in detaching from the Vermont house. You said that the step to Maine would be a bit of a plunge. I expected you'd feel that way. . . . We have done a nice job there. We can be proud of it. But having done the job, if we still have time, energy and creativity, why not move on and do another nice job? We've painted that picture. Why not try another?"

HAVE JOY NOW

One day not long ago my friend Leslie announced that her family was moving from Blacksburg to Austin, where a new job had turned up. "Austin! It's such a great city! You'll love it!" I exclaimed, eerily echoing everything Quinn and I had been told back in 2010. "I'm going to make you a list of all the places you absolutely have to go in Austin." With not much effort, I came up with twenty-nine, among them: Home Slice for pizza. Fresh tortillas from HEB grocery store. Zilker Park, with its miniature train whizzing around. The Nature and Science Center, where Ella had traded a hornets' nest for a beetle carapace at the naturalist bartering station. The swimming hole at Barton Springs. Alamo Drafthouse for movies. Deep Eddy Pool.

The wave of homesickness I felt thinking about Austin bewildered me. Was it possible to pine for a place I'd been perfectly happy to leave?

For a long time, while I worked on my Love Where You Live experiments, I had thought of place attachment as an either-or proposition. Either you adored your city and stayed there forever in connubial bliss or you didn't. Moving was a failure of commitment and love.

Except here's the thing: I *had* loved Austin. Silver Spring, Maryland; St. George, Utah; and Ames, Iowa, too, not to mention Fullerton, California, where I'd grown up. It was not clear whether any of these towns qualified as what Katherine Loflin would call a "heart match" — the place in my heart I truly considered home. Yet my mental maps of each of these cities were pinned with memories of transcendent happiness. My Facebook list brimmed with friends I'd made in six different states. Each of the places I'd lived, however briefly, had changed me and enriched me, and it's possible that in at least a couple of those places, I'd changed my city for the better, too.

As I completed each Love Where You Live experiment and took stock of what I had learned and how I felt, I realized that no matter how much I liked the idea of staying, no matter how beneficial studies showed it to be, for many Americans it just wasn't possible. In one of the most mobile nations on the planet, people move, sometimes over and over, for all kinds of reasons. Nick Arnett called it fluidity. "I don't know if that's a Millennial thing or more of an entrepreneurial trait," he said. "I've always hated the idea of being locked into one place."

Nick had learned on his Twelve Cities tour that one way cities like Louisville and Nashville cultivated an entrepreneur-friendly culture was by welcoming a steady influx of Movers. "For every person I've met here who is a Chattanooga native, I've met seven or eight people that are transplants," he said. Movers infused places with new ideas. That was one of the reasons cross-roads cities like New York buzzed with energy.

Careers ebb and flow, children are born, parents age. We chase after our desires, and then our desires change and we chase them somewhere else. Sometimes we move because our person-environment fit has experienced tectonic shifts over time. The city you would have sold everything you owned to live in at age twenty-three might feel fundamentally mismatched with who you've become at forty-three. That's not to say you never loved each other, just that one morning it hits you: It's time to move on. No acrimony. Just a lot of fond memories.

Maybe that's okay. We can't always control where we live, how long we stay there, or when we'll need to move next. My friend Jen's husband is in the army, and early in their marriage, his grandmother gave her some advice. "She told me this thing in

Spanish that basically translates to 'Unpack your life wherever you are,' " Jen says. "And I have taken it to heart. I even unpack at hotels. When you live out of a suitcase you are only marking time, and you will be miserable because you can only think of what was or what might have been, or fear what is to come."

Sometimes our paths surprise us. Honestly, at this point I'm not sure what will happen in Blacksburg. Will Quinn find a job he likes better locally? Will he start casting around in other states? Will we leave in a year? In ten? Never?

Who knows?

What I can say definitively is that I will never let mobility stop me from loving wherever I live right now. Americans are mobile because we see geography's power to make us happier, which it can. Even when our stops in places are dogged with uncertainty, we can still unpack the suitcase — and by that I mean be open to the pleasures of place. We can dive deeply, engage, invest, and create happy memories where we live. We can become place attached.

Because I was constantly trying to measure the success of my Love Where You Live experiments in Blacksburg, I'd trained myself to watch for sporadic moments of pure bliss. Every so often I'd be riding my bike on the Huckleberry Trail and I'd suddenly think, *It's beautiful here.* Or on a hike I'd sigh with satisfaction, *Look at this crazy-blue sky.* Out of nowhere, the happy thoughts would wash over me: *I love these people. I love this park. I love this restaurant. I love this hamburger.* My Love Where You Live experiments acted as an extended exercise in positive thinking. Eager to see good in my town, I found it over and over again. Almost without realizing it, I fell in love.

Here's what I learned from that: Wherever you are, experience joy. Milk your city for all it's worth, for as long as you're there. Whether or not I stay in Blacksburg forever, I can reap all the emotional, psychological, and physical benefits of place attachment while I'm here. I can soak up every last drop of pleasure to be had in my town. I can choose to make myself belong.

I would do that in Blacksburg for as long as I was able. If I had to, I could do it all over again somewhere else.

LOVE WHERE YOU LIVE PRINCIPLES

1. Our towns are what we think they are.
2. Emotion follows behavior; feelings follow action.
3. If you want to love your town, act like someone who loves your town would act.
4. When you're happy (and healthy), then you're happy (and healthy) where you live.
5. If you love your city, you should do what's good for it. (Corollary: What's good for your community is usually good for you.)
6. Relationships with people are what make you feel most at home.
7. Every town is good at something. Do what your town is good at.
8. Put pins in the map. Happy memories create place attachment.
9. When you invest, you feel invested.
10. There is no right town for everyone, just the right town for you right now.

11. Experience joy for as long as you're there.

ACKNOWLEDGMENTS

Really, every writer needs an agent as steady and wise as Lisa Grubka to talk her off all the ledges, and an editor as clear-eyed and thoughtful as Melanie Tortoroli to make things better. Many thanks as well to Tara Singh Carlson, Georgia Bodnar, Sheila Moody, Meredith Burks, Lindsay Prevette, Kate Stark, Andrea Schulz, Brian Tart, and the rest of the wonderful team at Viking.

People who love where they live happen to be some of the most delightful folks on the planet. I'm indebted to the friends and strangers who told me their stories and to the researchers who illuminated my thinking. Katherine Loflin's work in particular laid the foundation for this one. Special thanks to Gertie Moore, Holly Doggett, Jessica Esch, Kate McCarty, Sean Hagan, Sarah Sutton, Alisha Niswander, Nancy Barton, Kate Milo, Betsy Birmingham, Kevin Brooks, Rory Beil, Tom Smith, Mike

Williams, Melissa Sobolik, Matt Tomasulo, Kelley Brackett, Rupa DeLoach, Alwyn Luckey, Ken and Vanessa Vanhille, and Brian Mogren. Good souls, all.

In Blacksburg, Jane Aronson, Laureen Blakemore, Robin Boucher, James Creekmore, Neal Feierabend, Diana Francis, Scott and Joyce Hendricks, Kristy Hudson, Laura Krisch, Susan Mattingly, Ben Schoenfeld, Betty Watts, my neighbors, and everyone from the Blacksburg Citizens Institute informed, participated in, or unwittingly aided my Love Where You Live experiments. I'm grateful to them.

Beta readers Neal and Jolene Henshaw, Megan Rust, Rhonda Burch, Amber Daines, and Jacob Rawlins offered encouragement, advice, and a shot of confidence when I needed it. Other friends and family members who cheered me on or provided key insights include Stan and Linda Warnick, Jon and Heather Coombs, Laura Oler, Adrienne Penrod, Erika Layland, Jessie Charles, Jen Galán, Chris and Marin Riegger, Nate and Lucynthia Rockwood, Jon and Cami Felt, Danille Christensen, Brittany Cornelsen, Michelle Lucas, Nicki Watson, Jen Averett, Althea Aschmann, Shirley Andersen, Rita Rowe, and others too numerous to mention.

My writing group has (digitally) had my back for years. Thanks to Teri Cettina, Denise DiFulco, Meagan Francis, Heather Greenwood Davis, Kate Hanley, Sandra Hume, Jeannette Moninger, Gwen Moran, Leslie Pepper, Kate Reilly, Gretchen Roberts, Emily Rogan, Denise Schipani, and Caroline Tiger.

None of this would have happened without the early faith and enthusiasm of my parents, Richard McGrath and Judi Fox, and gifted teachers over the years, including Beverly Maeda, Jean Lahey, Carol Hallenbeck, Patrick Lampman, and Jeff Driggs.

Most of all, thanks to my family. Quinn, Ella, and Ruby give the places I live meaning. They are home for me.

NOTES

Chapter One: The Lost Art of Staying Put

move long distances: a job: In 2013, 4.2 million Americans completed long-distance moves of more than two hundred miles; 2.1 million, or just more than half, attributed their move to an "employment-related reason." The other major reasons were family (cited by 1.1 million) and housing (cited by 874,000). See U.S. Census Bureau, "Table 27: Distance of Intercounty Move, by Sex, Age, Race and Hispanic Origin, Relationship to Householder, Educational Attainment, Marital Status, Nativity, Tenure, Poverty Status, Reason for Move, and State of Residence 1 Year Ago: 2013 to 2014," in "Geographical Mobility: 2013 to 2014," https://www.census.gov/hhes/migration/data/cps/cps2014.html.

11.7 times before he or she dies: U.S.

Census Bureau, "Calculating Migration Expectancy Using ACS Data," https://www.census.gov/hhes/migration/about/cal-mig-exp.html.

"a move to a new place": Gretchen Rubin, *Better Than Before* (New York: Crown, 2015).

"care if I died": Anne Gadwa Nicodemus, in conversation with the author, February 2015.

with 36 million players: U.S. Census data indicates that in 2013, 30,960,000 Americans moved. See U.S. Census Bureau, "Table 1: General Mobility, by Race and Hispanic Origin, Region, Sex, Age, Relationship to Householder, Educational Attainment, Marital Status, Nativity, Tenure, and Poverty Status: 2013 to 2014," in "Geographical Mobility: 2013 to 2014," https://www.census.gov/hhes/migration/data/cps/cps2014.html. For information on average annual migration rates — a moving target — see Alison Fields and Robert Kominski, "America: A Nation on the Move," *Random Samplings: The Official Blog of the U.S. Census Bureau,* December 10, 2012, http://blogs.census.gov/2012/12/10/america-a-nation-on-the-move/.

pulling up stakes: National League of Cities, "The 30 Most Populous Cities," http://

www.nlc.org/build-skills-and-networks/ resources/ cities-101/city-factoids/the-30-most-populous-cities.

the past five years: Neli Esipova, Anita Pugliese, and Julie Ray, "The Demographics of Global Internal Migration," *Migration Policy Practice* 3, no. 2 (April–May 2013), http://publications.iom.int/book store/free/ MigrationPolicyPracticeJournal10_15May 2013.pdf.

35 percent of us have: Fields and Kominski, "America: A Nation on the Move," http://blogs.census.gov/2012/12/10/ america-a-nation-on-the-move/.

gigs around the country: U.S. Department of Labor, Bureau of Labor Statistics, "Employee Tenure Summary," September 18, 2014, http://www.bls.gov/news.release/ tenure.nr0.htm.

or Omaha, Nebraska: Sam Roberts, "Slump Creates Lack of Mobility for Americans," *New York Times,* April 22, 2009, http://www.nytimes.com/2009/04/ 23/us/23census.html?_r=0, and Annalyn Censky, "America's Most Recession-Proof Cities," CNN.com, September 16, 2010, http://money.cnn.com/2010/09/15/news/ economy/recession_proof_cities/.

to get them there: The Segmentation

Company/Yankelovich, "Attracting College-Educated, Young Adults to Cities," report prepared for CEOs for Cities, May 8, 2006, http://www.centerfor houstonsfuture.org/cmsFiles/Files/ Attracting%20College-Educated%20 Adults%20to%20Cities.pdf. Cited in Ania Wieckowski, "Back to the City," *Harvard Business Review,* May 2010, https:// hbr.org/2010/05/ back-to-the-city/sb1, and explained well by Matt Carmichael, "Do People Really Move for Better Cities?" *Livability,* January 7, 2015, http://www .livability.com/blog/demographics/do-people-really-move-better-cities.

still in Portland: Holly Doggett, in conversation with the author, September 2014. You can find out more about Holly and Daryl's cross-country road trip at their website, Cheese Deluxe, http://www .cheesedeluxe.com/roadtrip/index1.html.

In 2012, he did: Ben Bristoll, in conversation with the author, March 2015.

"knows what I mean": Eric Weiner, *The Geography of Bliss* (New York: Twelve, 2009).

seven hundred thousand of us do: National Association of Realtors, "Vacation Home Sales Surge in 2013, Investment Property Declines," press release, April 2,

2014, http://www.realtor.org/news-releases/2014/04/vacation-home-sales-surge-in-2013-investment-property-declines.

crowing about America's cities: City-Data's self-reported monthly visitors via http://www.city-data.com/contacts.html. For comparison, the statistic about TED .com's monthly visitors comes from Alexa rankings, accessed April 3, 2015, Alexa .com.

viewed 1.2 million times: "Houston vs. Dallas," Texas forum, City-Data, http://www.city-data.com/forum/texas/39529-houston-vs-dallas.html, accessed March 2015.

from San Jose, California, did: Raj Chetty et al., "Where is the Land of Opportunity? The Geography of Intergenerational Mobility in the United States," *Quarterly Journal of Economics* 129, no. 4 (2014): 1553–623. See also Raj Chetty and Nathaniel Hendren, "The Causal Effects of Growing Up in Different Counties on Earnings in Adulthood," Equality of Opportunity Project, http://www.equality-of-opportunity.org. Why do outcomes differ so vastly from place to place? Chetty points to five factors: residential segregation, income inequality, school quality, social capital, and family structure. Only the last has little to do with where you live.

to help struggling communities: Tara McGuinness, senior advisor White House Office of Management and Budget, speaking at the White House Convening on Rural Placemaking, November 2015.

"zip code shouldn't decide their destiny": CBS News, "Obama: 'A Person's Zip Code Shouldn't Decide Their Destiny,' " July 11, 2015, http://www.cbs news.com/videos/obama-a-persons-zip-code-shouldnt-decide-their-destiny/.

like New York or Chicago: David Leonhardt and Kevin Quealy, "How Your Hometown Affects Your Chances of Marriage," *New York Times,* May 15, 2015, http://www.nytimes.com/interactive/2015/05/15/upshot/ the-places-that-discourage-marriage-most.html.

say, Youngstown, Ohio: Gallup-Healthways, "State of American Well-Being: 2014 Community Well-Being Rankings," http://www.well-beingindex .com/.

just sixty-four years old: Haidong Wang, Austin E. Schumacher, Carly E. Levitz, Ali H. Mokdad, and Christopher J. L. Murray, "Left Behind: Widening Disparities for Males and Females in US County Life Expectancy, 1985–2010," *Population Health Metrics* 11, no. 8 (2013), http://www.pophealthmetrics.com/content/11/1/8.

like cancer and asthma: For more on how this works, watch Bill Davenhall's excellent TED Talk. Bill Davenhall, "Your Health Depends on Where You Live," talk given at TEDMED conference, October 2009, http://www.ted.com/talks/bill_daven hall_your_health_depends_on_where_ you_live? language=en. Also see Harvard School of Public Health, *The Public Health Disparities Geocoding Project Monograph,* http://www.hsph.harvard.edu/thegeo codingproject/, and Ed Hess, "The Role of 'Place' in Patient Care," *Health IT Outcomes,* December 2, 2014, http://www .healthitoutcomes.com/doc/the-role-of-place-in-patient-care-0001.

follow-up appointment: Shigehiro Oishi and Ulrich Schimmack, "Residential Mobility, Well-Being, and Mortality," *Journal of Personality and Social Psychology* 98, no. 6 (2010): 980–94.

than "Stayers": J. Patrick Seder and Shigehiro Oishi, "Friendculture: Predictors of Diversity in the Social Networks of

College Students," poster session presented at the annual meeting of the Society for Personality and Social Psychology, Albuquerque, N.M., February 2008, as described in Shigehiro Oishi, "The Psychology of Residential Mobility: Implications for the Self, Social Relationships, and Well-Being," *Perspectives on Psychological Science* 5, no. 1 (2010): 5–21.

"give him confidence, rootedness, and stability": Victoria Derr, "Children's Sense of Place in Northern New Mexico," *Journal of Environmental Psychology* 22 (2002): 125–37.

statewide well-being levels: Dan Witters, "Alaska Leads U.S. States in Well-Being for First Time," Gallup, February 19, 2015, http://www.gallup.com/poll/181547/alaska-leads-states-first-time.aspx.

never left their hometown: Paul Taylor, Rich Morin, D'Vera Cohn, and Wendy Wang, "American Mobility: Who Moves? Who Stays Put? Where's Home?" Pew Research Center, December 29, 2008.

headline from the *Onion*: "Unambitious Loser with Happy, Fulfilling Life Still Lives in Hometown," *The Onion,* July 23, 2013, http://www.theonion.com/article/unambitious-loser-with-happy-fulfilling-life-still-33233.

content where they are: Richard Florida, *Who's Your City?: How the Creative Economy Is Making Where to Live the Most Important Decision of Your Life* (New York: Basic, 2009), and "Why People Stay Where They Are," *CityLab,* September 22, 2014, http://www.citylab.com/housing/2014/09/why-people-stay-where-they-are/380583/.

"need of the human soul": Simone Weil, *The Need for Roots: Prelude to a Declaration of Duties Towards Mankind* (New York: Harper Torchbooks, 1971).

connected to one's environment: Peter H. Kahn, Jr., and Patricia H. Hasbach, eds., *Ecopsychology: Science, Totems, and the Technological Species* (Cambridge, Mass.: MIT Press, 2012), 256.

or "at-homeness": For a nice summary of different ways to describe person-place relationships, see Mark S. Rosenbaum, James Ward, Beth A. Walker, and Amy L. Ostrom, "A Cup of Coffee with a Dash of Love: An Investigation of Commercial Social Support and Third-Place Attachment," *Journal of Service Research* 10 (August 2007): 43–59.

whose neighbors didn't move away, either, had more friends: Daniel Tumminelli O'Brien, Andrew C. Gallup, and

509

David Sloan Wilson, "Residential Mobility and Prosocial Development within a Single City," *American Journal of Community Psychology* 50 (2012): 26–36.

less likely to complain about ailments: Cari Jo Clark, et al., "Neighborhood Cohesion Is Associated with Reduced Risk of Stroke Mortality," *Stroke* (May 2011): 1212–17; Eric S. Kim, Nansook Park, and Christopher Peterson, "Perceived Neighborhood Social Cohesion and Stroke," *Social Science and Medicine* 97 (2013) 49–55; A. M. Ziersch, et al., "Neighborhood Life and Social Capital: The Implications for Health," *Social Science and Medicine* 60 (2005): 71–86; Lisa Wood and Billie Giles-Corti, "Is There a Place for Social Capital in the Psychology of Health and Place?" *Journal of Environmental Psychology* 28 (2008): 154–63; Jennifer W. Robinette, Susan T. Charles, Jacqueline A. Mogle, and David M. Almeida, "Neighborhood Cohesion and Daily Well-Being: Results from a Diary Study," *Social Science and Medicine* 96 (2013): 174–82.

shot up by an additional 6 percent: Ayako Morita, et al., "Contribution of Interaction with Family, Friends and Neighbours, and Sense of Neighbourhood

Attachment to Survival in Senior Citizens: 5-Year Follow-Up Study," *Social Science and Medicine* 70 (2010) 543–49.

a general sense of well-being: Gene L. Theodori, "Examining the Effects of Community Satisfaction and Attachment on Individual Well-Being," *Rural Sociology* 66, no. 4 (2001): 618–28. See also R. Araya, et al., "Perceptions of Social Capital and the Built Environment and Mental Health," *Social Science and Medicine* 62, no. 12 (2006): 3072–83.

the town prospered economically: John S. and James L. Knight Foundation, "Knight Communities Overall," *Knight Soul of the Community 2010. Why People Love Where They Live and Why It Matters: A National Perspective* (Miami: John S. and James L. Knight Foundation, 2010), http://knightfoundation.org/sotc/overall-findings/. I'll explain more about the Knight Foundation study in chapter 5, including its finding that GDP increased in well-loved cities.

how we fit in with our cities: Eva Kahana, Loren Lovegreen, Boaz Kahana, and Michael Kahana, "Person, Environment, and Person-Environment Fit as Influences on Residential Satisfaction of Elders," *En-*

vironment and Behavior 35 (2003): 434–53; and David R. Phillips, et al., "Person-Environment (P-E) Fit Models and Psychological Well-Being Among Older Persons in Hong Kong," *Environment and Behavior* 42, no. 2 (2010): 221–42.

"as a personal relationship": Katherine Loflin, in conversation with the author, November 2014.

three to five years after moving: Ibid.

with action or behavior: Setha M. Low and Irwin Altman, "Place Attachment: A Conceptual Inquiry," in *Place Attachment,* ed. Setha M. Low and Irwin Altman (New York: Plenum Press, 1992).

(ultimately makes you happier): Tara L. Kraft and Sarah D. Pressman, "Grin and Bear It: The Influence of Manipulated Facial Expression on the Stress Response," *Psychological Science* 23, no. 11 (2012): 1372–78.

communities more livable: The nonprofit Project for Public Spaces is credited with originally popularizing the term "placemaking" in the 1970s to describe its efforts at revitalizing towns' public squares, plazas, parks, and streets. Ethan Kent, in conversation with the author, April 2015.

as return on investment: To learn more about Hsieh's project, visit http://www

.downtownproject.com/ or read Sara Corbett, "How Zappos' CEO Turned Las Vegas into a Startup Fantasyland," *Wired,* January 2014, http://www.wired.com/ 2014/01/zappos-tony-hsieh-las-vegas/.

"I enjoy being around": Susan Berfield, "Tony Hsieh Is Building a Startup Paradise in Vegas," *Bloomberg Business,* December 30, 2014, http://www.bloomberg .com/bw/articles/ 2014-12-30/zappos-ceo-tony-hsiehs-las-vegas-startup-paradise.

into downtown revitalization: Joann Muller, "Gilbertville: A Billionaire's Drive to Rebuild the Motor City," *Forbes,* October 20, 2014, http://www.forbes.com/ sites/joannmuller/2014/09/29/ gilbertville-a-billionaires-drive-to-rebuild-the-motor-city/.

"an extension of themselves": Ethan Kent, in conversation with the author, April 2015.

"where the magic is": Carol Coletta, in conversation with the author, May 2015.

Chapter Two: Lace Up Your Sneakers

10 percent happened on foot: U.S. Department of Transportation, *Summary of Travel Trends: 2009 National Household Travel Survey,* by Adelia Santos, et al.

(Washington, D.C.: Department of Transportation, 2011), 19.

to only 35 percent: National Center for Safe Routes to School, *How Children Get to School: School Travel Patterns from 1969 to 2009,* November 2011, http://saferoutes info.org/sites/default/files/resources/NHTS _school_travel_report_2011_0.pdf.

walkable, bikeable neighborhoods: National Association of Realtors, "National Community Preference Survey," October 2013, http://www.realtor.org/sites/default/ files/reports/2013/2013-community-preference-analysis-slides.pdf.

ones in Copenhagen and Paris: Andrew Simmons, "In Indianapolis, a Bike Path to Progress," *New York Times,* March 4, 2014, http://www.nytimes.com/2014/03/ 09/travel/ in-indianapolis-a-bike-path-to-progress.html.

number of bike lanes since 2006: Transportation Alternatives, "Bike Lanes," http://transalt.org/issues/bike/network/ bikelanes.

"Cyclists have more sex": VÉLO North Loop brochure, http://issuu.com/alpha theory/docs/velo_residential_book_102 913_ebook?e=6978238/7358267.

scamper through it later: "Tolman, Edward," *International Encyclopedia of the*

Social Sciences, vol. 8, ed. William A. Darity, Jr. (Detroit: Macmillan Reference USA, 2008), 386–87.

in advance wandered, lost: Emil W. Menzel, "Chimpanzee Spatial Memory Organization," *Science* 182, no. 4115 (1973): 943–45.

get directions almost daily: Larry Shannon-Missal, "Different Priorities in Smartphone vs. Computer Use, but Some Common Ground," *Harris Poll,* no. 1 (January 3, 2013), http://www.harrisinter active.com/NewsRoom/HarrisPolls/tabid/ 447/ctl/ ReadCustom%20Default/mid/ 1508/ArticleId/1132/Default.aspx; and Salesforce Marketing Cloud, "2014 Mobile Behavior Report," http://www.exact target.com/sites/exacttarget/files/deliver ables/etmc-2014mobilebehaviorreport .pdf. See also Marcello Mari, "Top Global Smartphone Apps: Who's in the Top 10," *GlobalWebIndex,* August 2, 2013, https:// www.globalwebindex.net/blog/top-global- smartphone-apps.

"pick them back up later": Julia Frankenstein, "Is GPS All in Our Heads?" *New York Times,* February 2, 2012, http:// www.nytimes.com/2012/02/05/opinion/ sunday/is-gps-all-in-our-head.html.

a sense of local geography: Sarah Goodyear, "Kids Who Get Driven Everywhere Don't Know Where They're Going," *City-Lab,* May 7, 2012, http://www.citylab.com/commute/2012/05/kids-who-get-driven-everywhere-dont-know-where-theyre-going/1943/.

who rode public transit: Andrew Mondschein, Evelyn Blumenberg, and Brian D. Taylor, "Going Mental: Everyday Travel and the Cognitive Map," *Access* 43 (Fall 2013).

"rather a new way of looking at things": Henry Miller, *Big Sur and the Oranges of Hieronymus Bosch* (New York: New Directions, 1957).

"other animals around you": E-mail to the author, dated January 27, 2015, from Jeff Speck, author, *Walkable City* (New York: North Point Press, 2012).

"that is where I met my love": Alexander McCall Smith, *Love over Scotland* (New York: Anchor, 2007).

"unique visitors on the site": Eric Meltzer, "Matt Lerner and Walk Score: Put a Number on It," *Creative Live,* August 7, 2014, http://blog.creativelive.com/matt-lerner-walk-score-put-number/.

" 'the most important criterion' ": Josh Herst, "Over 8,000 Sites Now Using Walk Score Professional," *Walk Score Blog,*

April 18, 2011, http://blog.walkscore.com/ 2011/04/over-8000-sites-now-using-walk-score-professional/ #.VcQZCZNVikp.

"does not pay off": Alois Stutzer and Bruno S. Frey, "Stress That Doesn't Pay: The Commuting Paradox," *Scandinavian Journal of Economics* 110, no. 2 (June 2008): 339–66.

are less freaked out: Andrew Clark, "Want to Feel Less Stress? Become a Fighter Pilot, Not a Commuter," *Guardian,* November 29, 2004, http://www.theguardian .com/uk/2004/nov/30/research.transport.

fallen in love: Adam Martin, Yevgeniy Goryakin, and Marc Suhrcke, "Does Active Commuting Improve Psychological Wellbeing? Longitudinal Evidence from Eighteen Waves of the British Household Panel Survey," *Preventive Medicine* 69 (December 2014): 296–303.

better at creative thinking: Marily Oppezzo and Daniel L. Schwartz, "Give Your Ideas Some Legs: The Positive Effect of Walking on Creative Thinking," *Journal of Experimental Psychology: Learning, Memory, and Cognition* 40, no. 4 (2014): 1142–52; and Ferris Jabr, "Why Walking Helps Us Think," *New Yorker,* September 3, 2014, http://www.newyorker.com/tech/ elements/walking-helps-us-think.

trust their neighbors: Shannon H. Rogers, John M. Halstead, Kevin H. Gardner, and Cynthia H. Carlson, "Examining Walkability and Social Capital as Indicators of Quality of Life at the Municipal and Neighborhood Scales," *Applied Research in Quality of Life* 6 (2011): 201–13.

diabetes or high blood pressure: Alliance for Biking and Walking, *Bicycling and Walking in the United States: 2014 Benchmarking Report,* 69–72, http://www.bike walkalliance.org/resources/benchmarking.

every last one of its neighborhoods by 2025: City of Vancouver, "Environments to Thrive In," Vancouver, Canada, city website, http://vancouver.ca/people-programs/environments-to-thrive-in.aspx.

by launching Open Streets initiatives: Open Streets Project, http://openstreets project.org/.

up to seventy-five thousand pedestrians: Aaron Bialick, "After 50 Events, Sunday Streets Director Departs to Spread the Word," *Streetsblog SF,* August 25, 2014, http://sf.streetsblog.org/2014/08/25/after-50-events-sunday-streets-director-departs-to-spread-the-word/.

and thus more expensive: Josh Herst, "A Look Back and a Look Ahead," *Walk Score Blog,* October 22, 2014, http://blog

.walkscore.com/2014/10/look-back-look-ahead/.

"one way to do so": Joe Cortright, *Walking the Walk: How Walkability Raises Home Values in U.S. Cities,* CEOs for Cities, August 2009.

"closer to your place of work": "How to 'Thrive': Short Commutes, More Happy Hours," interview with Dan Buettner conducted by Neal Conan, *Talk of the Nation,* NPR, October 19, 2011, http://www.npr.org/2011/10/19/141514467/small-changes-can-help-you-thrive-happily.

to cross those tracks: Matt Tomasulo in discussion with the author, August 2014.

"you get people and places": Fred Kent, "Streets Are People Places," Project for Public Spaces, June 1, 2005, http://www.pps.org/blog/transportationasplace/.

Walks must be interesting: Speck, *Walkable City,* 71–72.

(to increase its walkability and bikeability): New York has doubled its number of bike lanes since 2006, according to the nonprofit Transportation Alternatives, "Bike Lanes," http://transalt.org/issues/bike/network/bikelanes.

eighteen hours a day: Cole E. Judge, "The Experiment of American Pedestrian Malls," Fresno Future, October 11, 2013,

http://downtowndevelopment.com/pdf/
americanpedmallexperiment.pdf.

Great American Cities: Jane Jacobs, *The Death and Life of Great American Cities* (New York: Vintage, 1961). The book is a readable, nonacademic classic of urban planning. I recommend reading it for more ideas on what makes cities thrive — and people thrive in cities.

South of Market district: Emily Peckenham, "Talking Public Space and Urban Intervention with San Francisco's Rebar Studio," *Inhabit,* June 10, 2014, http://inhabitat.com/talking-public-space-and-urban-intervention-with-san-franciscos-rebar-studio.

dozens more around the world: Pavement to Parks program, http://pavementtoparks.sfplanning.org/map-sf.html.

until the meters expired: PARK(ing) Day, http://parkingday.org/about-parking-day/.

I sometimes forget they exist: You can see photos of my Walk [Your City] signs at MelodyWarnick.com.

not starving enough?: Peter Wallenstein, "Early Blacksburg, 1740s–1840s," in *A Special Place for 200 Years: A History of Blacksburg, Virginia,* ed. Clara B. Cox

(Blacksburg, Va.: Town of Blacksburg, 1998).

making the journey, alone and on foot: Joan Vannorsdall Schroeder, "Mary Draper Ingles' Return to Virginia's New River Valley," *Blue Ridge Country,* March 1, 1998, http://blueridgecountry.com/archive/favorites/mary-draper-ingles/.

errands under a mile: For ideas on how to do this, see Andrew R. Cline, "The 1-Mile Solution," *Carbon Trace* (blog), http://isocrates.us/bike/the-1-mile-solution/.

Chapter Three: Buy Local

"activity generated by moves": Sam Roberts, "Slump Creates Lack of Mobility for Americans," *New York Times,* April 22, 2009, http://www.nytimes.com/2009/04/23/us/23census.html?_r=0.

move cost $12,230: Worldwide ERC, "2011 U.S. Transfer Volume and Cost Survey," http://www.worldwideerc.org/Resources/Research/Documents/TVCS_2011.pdf.

"stay out of their stores": Richard C. Schragger, "The Anti-Chain Store Movement, Localist Ideology, and the Remnants of the Progressive Constitution, 1920–1940," University of Virginia Law

School Public Law and Legal Theory Working Paper Series, Paper 21, 2005.

JCPenney, and Sears: Philip Bump, "The Parts of America Big Box Stores Haven't Devoured Yet," *The Wire: News from the Atlantic,* December 9, 2013, http://www.thewire.com/politics/2013/12/where-small-business-really-thrives-america-mapped/355927/.

eliminates 1.4 jobs locally: David Neumark, Junfu Zhang, and Stephen Ciccarella, "The Effects of Wal-Mart on Local Labor Markets," *Journal of Urban Economics* 63 (2008): 405–30.

drives down wages citywide: Arindrajit Dube, T. William Lester, and Barry Eidlin, "A Downward Push: The Impact of Wal-Mart Stores on Retail Wages and Benefits," Research Brief, UC Berkeley Center for Labor Research and Education, December 2007, http://laborcenter.berkeley.edu/pdf/2007/walmart_downward_push07.pdf.

business district into ruin: Kenneth E. Stone and Georgeanne M. Artz, "Revisiting Wal-Mart's Impact on Iowa Small Town Retail: Twenty-Five Years Later," Working Paper No. 12010, Iowa State University Department of Economics, May 2012, https://www.econ.iastate.edu/

sites/default/files/publications/papers/p15202-2012-05-31.pdf.

only $3.50 did: Civic Economics, "Indie Impact Study Series: A National Comparative Survey with the American Booksellers Association," Summer 2012.

communities where they work: The American Independent Business Alliance has a helpful primer on the local multiplier effect at its website, http://www.amiba.net/resources/multiplier-effect/.

works in town, not at headquarters: Civic Economics, "The San Francisco Retail Diversity Study," May 2007, http://ilsr.org/wp-content/uploads/2011/12/SFRDS-May07-2.pdf.

from a nearby farmer: Civic Economics, "Indie Impact Study Series: A National Comparative Survey with the American Booksellers Association," Summer 2012.

extra $500 million in revenue: Civic Economics, "Indie Impact Study Series: A National Comparative Survey with the American Booksellers Association," Summer 2012.

thirty-seven-year-old King's English Bookshop: David Grogan, "Study Finds Shopping Local Generates Almost Four Times the Economic Benefit," *Bookselling This Week,* American Booksellers Associa-

tion, September 6, 2012, http://
www.bookweb.org/news/study-finds-
shopping-local-generates-almost-four-
times-economic-benefit.

"prevent that from happening": Jeff
Milchen, in conversation with the author,
May 2014.

a higher regional GDP: David A. Fleming
and Stephan J. Goetz, "Does Local Firm
Ownership Matter?" *Economic Development Quarterly* 25, no. 3 (August 2011):
277–81.

"what creates community fabric": Jeff
Milchen, in conversation with the author,
May 2014.

It's now a Foot Locker: Jeremiah Moss,
"2014 Vanishings," *Jeremiah's Vanishing
New York* (blog), December 30, 2014,
http://vanishingnewyork.blogspot.com/
2014/12/2014-vanishings.html.

each month in New York City: Kate
Rogers, "#SaveNYC: A Push to Keep
New York's Character," CNBC.com,
March 12, 2015, http://www.cnbc.com/
2015/03/11/savenyc-a-push-to-keep-new-
yorks-character.html.

**"people won't want to go there any-
more":** Anonymous comment on Jeremiah Moss, "Shakespeare & Co.," *Jeremiah's Vanishing New York* (blog),

September 4, 2014, http://vanishingnew
york.blogspot.com/2014/09/shakespeare-
co.html.

refusing to renew a lease: You can read
about the Small Business Jobs Survival
Act, sign the petition, or volunteer at the
website of TakeBackNYC, the political
lobbying group that is pushing the bill:
http://takebacknyc.nyc/sbjsa/.

in certain parts of the city: East Village
Community Coalition, "Preserving Local,
Independent Retail: Recommendations for
Formula Retail Zoning in the East Vil-
lage," May 2015, http://evccnyc.org/wp-
content/uploads/2015/06/2015_Preserving
_LocalInd_Retail.pdf.

**"strong protections for the city's small
businesses":** Jeremiah Moss, "Master
List, 2001–2013," *Jeremiah's Vanishing
New York* (blog), December 30, 2013,
http://vanishingnewyork.blogspot.com/
2013/12/master-list-2001-2013.html.

Strands of Sunshine jewelry shop: Judy
Hill, "Calendar Features 'Shop Dogs' of
St. Pete," *St. Petersburg Tribune,* October
27, 2013.

maple-glazed apple bacon donut: San
Franciscans can buy the card at http://
livelocalcard.com/.

Dirty Bastard beer: Michiganders can

525

learn more at the Local First website, www.localfirst.com.

lauding their favorite endangered retailers: You can add your own photo or video at #SaveNYC, http://www.savenyc.nyc/.

campaign boosted their business: Stacy Mitchell, "2013 Independent Business Survey," Institute for Local Self-Reliance, February 2013, http://ilsr.org/wp-content/uploads/2013/02/2013-Survey.pdf.

"it takes grassroots engagement": Jeff Milchen, in conversation with the author, May 2014.

make property more affordable for small-business owners: Rebecca Melançon and the Local Business Conference Leadership Circle, "2014 Local Business Conference: Austin Independent Business Alliance Presentation of Goals and Proposals," August 24, 2015, http://www.ibuy austin.com/indie-biz/documents-and-files/advocacy/23-conference-goals-presenta tion-to-eoc/file.html.

it went viral: Andrew Samtoy, in conversation with the author, January 2015.

under an hour: Campbell County Chamber of Commerce, "Cash Mob: FCA Country Store," Flickr, https://www.flickr .com/photos/ccccwyo/sets/72157633

402945186.

oldest five-and-dime store: " 'Cash Mobs': Flash Mobs Go to Bat for Small Local Businesses," NBCNews.com, February 14, 2012, http://usnews.nbcnews.com/_news/2012/02/14/10400367-cash-mobs-flash-mobs-go-to-bat-for-small-local-businesses.

on six continents: Andrew Samtoy, in conversation with the author, January 2015.

"she's already read it": Stacy Mitchell, "Why We Can't Shop Our Way to a Better Economy," talk given at TEDxDirigo, Lewiston, Maine, October 20, 2012, https://www.youtube.com/watch?v=b6rAgHcuYtE.

"solving problems and innovating": Stacy Mitchell, in conversation with the author, August 2014.

local grocery store, Fitch's IGA: Jay Leeson, in conversation with the author, January 2015.

one dismal February alone: Valarie Honeycutt Spears, "Wilmore's Residents Work to Save Its Grocery Store," *Lexington Herald-Leader,* May 3, 2011, http://www.kentucky.com/2011/05/03/1728346/wilmores-residents-work-to-save.html.

"he's still offering neighborliness": Jay

Leeson, "Letter to the Editor: Wilmore's Identity Rests on IGA's Future," *Central Kentucky News,* March 2, 2011, http://articles.centralkynews.com/2011-03-02/jessaminejournal/28648358_1_wilmore-fitches-neighborliness.

store's operations and pricing: Jonathan Kleppinger, "Wilmore Group Fitch's Neighbors Turns Out to Help Longtime Grocer," *Central Kentucky News,* May 11, 2011, http://articles.centralkynews.com/2011-05-11/jessaminejournal/29534610_1_wilmore-community-fitchs-iga-paint.

service to Fitch's: Leonard Fitch, in conversation with the author, May 2014. Also, Jonathan Kleppinger, "Wilmore Group Turns Out to Help Longtime Grocer," *Jessamine Journal,* May 12, 2011, http://www.kypress.com/excellence2011results/tearsheets/w3-c04-3.pdf.

"change this town forever": "Fitch's IGA Documentary," YouTube, July 19, 2011, https://www.youtube.com/watch?v=CzJr75p1yzI.

"make your town stronger": Jay Leeson, in conversation with the author, January 2015.

above eighty thousand square feet: Blacksburg Town Ordinance 1450, passed May 29, 2007.

in favor of the town: *Edward Hale, et al., v. Board of Zoning Appealings for the Town of Blacksburg, et al.,* Record No. 081000, Virginia State Supreme Court, February 27, 2009, http://www.courts.state.va.us/opinions/opnscvwp/1081000.pdf.

unfriendly to business: Mike Gangloff, "First & Main Moving Past the Pain, New Ownership Team Says," *Roanoke Times,* April 6, 2014, http://www.roanoke.com/news/local/blacksburg/first-main-moving-past-the-pain-new-ownership-team-says/article_5aea3b84-bb64-11e3-890e-0017a43b2370.html.

"keeps those businesses around": "The 3/50 Project: Saving the Brick and Mortars Our Nation Is Built On," http://www.the350project.net/look_local_home.html.

generate $42.6 billion in revenue: Ibid.

15 percent of their total budget: Jay Leeson, "Letter to the Editor: Wilmore's Identity Rests on IGA's Future," *Central Kentucky News,* March 2, 2011, http://articles.centralkynews.com/2011-03-02/jessaminejournal/28648358_1_wilmore-fitches-neighborliness.

a multimillion-dollar impact: Civic Economics, "Indie Impact Study Series: A National Comparative Survey with the American Booksellers Association," Summer 2012.

on that day alone: National Federation of Independent Business and American Express, "First Annual Small Business Saturday Consumer Insights," November 26, 2012, https://www.americanexpress .com/us/content/small-business/shop-small/about/.

"our community to support us": Laureen Blakemore, in conversation with the author, May 2015.

than chain stores: Institute for Local Self-Reliance, "The Economic Impact of Locally Owned Businesses vs. Chains: A Case Study in Midcoast Maine," September 2003, http://ilsr.org/wp-content/uploads/files/midcoaststudy.pdf.

and Madison, Wisconsin: Amy Cortese, in conversation with the author, June 2012.

Chapter Four: Say Hi to Your Neighbors

never quite felt like home: Sloan Mandler, in conversation with the author, March 2015.

"about to start kindergarten": David Ihrke, "Reason for Moving: 2012 to 2013 — Population Characteristics," U.S. Census Bureau, June 2014, https://www.census

.gov/prod/2014pubs/p20-574.pdf.

"even in a farming community": Lynita Delaney, in conversation with the author, January 2014.

members of their extended family: D'Vera Cohn and Rich Morin, "Who Moves? Who Stays Put? Where's Home?" Pew Research Center, December 17, 2008, http://www.pewsocialtrends.org/2008/12/17/who-moves-who-stays-put-wheres-home/.

go where the jobs are: E. G. Ravenstein, "The Laws of Migration," *Journal of the Statistical Society of London* 48, no. 2 (June 1885): 167–235.

better for you financially: Alden Speare, Jr., Frances Kobrin, and Ward Kingkade, "The Influence of Socioeconomic Bonds and Satisfaction on Interstate Migration," *Social Forces* 61, no. 2 (December 1982): 551–74.

to make the move worthwhile: Michael S. Dahl and Olav Sorenson, "The Social Attachment to Place," *Social Forces* 89, no. 2 (2010): 633–58.

getting an £85,000 raise: Nattavudh Powdthavee, "Putting a Price Tag on Friends, Relatives and Neighbours: Using Surveys of Life Satisfaction to Value Social Relationships," *Journal of Socio-Economics* 37, no. 4 (2008): 1459–80.

just fourteen years earlier: Robert D. Putnam, *Bowling Alone: The Collapse and Revival of American Community* (New York: Simon & Schuster, 2000), 106.

too occupied for extracurricular socializing: Jena McGregor, "Average Work Week Is Now 47 Hours," *Washington Post,* September 2, 2014, http://www.washingtonpost.com/news/on-leadership/wp/2014/09/02/the-average-work-week-is-now-47-hours/.

"replaced by a kind of detachment": Marc J. Dunkelman, *The Vanishing Neighbor: The Transformation of American Community* (New York: W. W. Norton, 2014), 130. Dunkelman's comment echoes the work of Harvard Medical School psychiatrists Jacqueline Olds and Richard S. Schwartz, in *The Lonely American: Drifting Apart in the Twenty-first Century* (Boston: Beacon Press, 2009), 21.

28 percent know no one at all: Aaron Smith, "Neighbors Online," Pew Research Center, June 9, 2010, http://www.pewinternet.org/2010/06/09/neighbors-online/.

"The End of Neighbours" in 2014: Brian Bethune, "The End of Neighbours: How Our Increasingly Closed-Off Lives Are

Poisoning Our Politics and Endangering Our Health," *Maclean's,* August 8, 2014, http://www.macleans.ca/society/the-end-of-neighbours/.

"bothered to speak to them": Rosa Silverman and Agencies, "Snub Thy Neighbour: Millions Are Feuding with People on Their Street," *Telegraph* (London), August 5, 2013, http://www.telegraph.co.uk/news/newstopics/howaboutthat/10223144/Snub-thy-neighbour-millions-are-feuding-with-people-on-their-street.html; "The Neighbourhood," Swinton Insurance, January 3, 2014, http://www.swinton.co.uk/home-insurance/guides/britains-greatest-neighbour; SKV Communications, "Neighbours Survey Reveals Surprising Results," press release, August 6, 2013, http://www.skvcommunications.co.uk/press-releases/neighbours-survey-reveals-surprising-results/.

"his wife put the paper back": Misfit Rebel, Twitter post, September 4, 2014, 6:28 p.m., https://twitter.com/MisfitRebel1/status/507671459678785536.

"saying 'I hate kids' ": Desiree stinyard, Twitter post, May 14, 2014, 4:32 p.m., https://twitter.com/Desiree_Stin/status/466692662695718912.

"knowing my name anyway": "Do people in your neighborhood socialize? (adults, college, neighbors, business)," Non-Romantic Relationships Forum, City-Data.com, January 26, 2013, http://www.city-data.com/forum/non-romantic-relationships/1781470-do-people-your-neighborhood-socialize-adults-4.html.

less likely to suffer a heart attack: Eric S. Kim, Armani M. Hawes, and Jacqui Smith, "Perceived Neighbourhood Social Cohesion and Myocardial Infarction," *Journal of Epidemiology and Community Health* 68, no. 11 (November 2014); also James Hamblin, "Always Talk to Strangers," *Atlantic,* August 19, 2014, http://www.theatlantic.com/health/archive/2014/08/social-cohesion-heart-attack-prevention/378694/.

less likely to suffer a stroke: Eric S. Kim, Nansook Park, and Christopher Peterson, "Perceived Neighborhood Social Cohesion and Stroke," *Social Science and Medicine* 97, no. C (2013): 49–55.

survival chances went up significantly: Cari Jo Clark, et al., "Neighborhood Cohesion Is Associated with Reduced Risk of Stroke Mortality," *Stroke* 42 (2011): 1212–17.

in tight-knit neighborhoods: Louisa M. Holmes, "Behavioral, Physiological and

Psychological Stress Among Legal and Unauthorized Brazilian Immigrants: The Moderating Influence of Neighborhood Environments," dissertation, University of Southern California, 2014, UMI: 3609902; Hiroshi Murayama, Yoshinori Fujiwara, and Ichiro Kawachi, "Social Capital and Health: A Review of Prospective Multilevel Studies," *Journal of Epidemiology* 22, no. 3 (2012): 179–87.

less connected part of the city: Fran E. Baum, Anna M. Ziersch, Guangyu Zhang, and Katy Osborne, "Do Perceived Neighbourhood Cohesion and Safety Contribute to Neighbourhood Differences in Health?" *Health and Place* 15 (2009) 925–34.

play with neighbor kids: James Garbarino and Deborah Sherman, "High-Risk Neighborhoods and High-Risk Families: The Human Ecology of Child Maltreatment," *Child Development* 51, no. 1 (March 1980): 188–98.

act out in class: Jennifer S. Silk, et al., "Neighborhood Cohesion as a Buffer against Hostile Maternal Parenting," *Journal of Family Psychology* 18, no. 1 (March 2004): 135–46.

less negatively to them: Jennifer W. Robinette, Susan T. Charles, Jacqueline A.

Mogle, and David M. Almeida, "Neighborhood Cohesion and Daily Well-Being: Results from a Diary Study," *Social Science and Medicine* 96 (2013): 174–82.

spouse or a good friend: Ibid.

"appropriate ceremonies and activities": Jimmy Carter, "National Good Neighbor Day, 1978," U.S. Presidential Proclamation 4601, September 22, 1978, http://www.presidency.ucsb.edu/ws/?pid=23733.

live among people who are like us: Kyle Crowder, Jeremy Pais, and Scott J. South, "Neighborhood Diversity, Metropolitan Constraints, and Household Migration," *American Sociological Review* 77, no. 3 (2012): 325–53. See also Stephanie Pappas, "Blacks and Whites Favor Same-Race Neighborhoods," *Live Science,* May 31, 2012, http://www.livescience.com/20663-black-white-segregated-neighborhoods.html.

"Pretty warm for May": Jay Walljasper, in conversation with the author, July 2011.

painfully old-fashioned: Robert D. Putnam, *Bowling Alone: The Collapse and Revival of American Community* (New York: Simon & Schuster, 2000).

is its Block Party Trailer: Jeff Martin, in conversation with the author, November

2014. For more information about the Block Party Trailer, see its website at http://www.surpriseaz.gov/index.aspx?NID=869.

like Rock Hill, South Carolina: "Rock Hill Council of Neighborhoods," City of Rock Hill website, http://www.cityofrockhill.com/departments/housing-neighborhood-services/more/housing-neighborhood-services/neighborhood-empowerment/rhcn.

ward off crime: For more information on how to organize or attend a National Night Out, visit https://natw.org/.

playgrounds, festivals, and tournaments: "Neighborhood Matching Fund," Seattle Department of Neighborhoods, City of Seattle website, http://www.seattle.gov/neighborhoods/neighborhood-matching-fund.

"better crime prevention strategy": Saguaro Seminar, "About Social Capital: Factoids," Harvard Kennedy School of Government, http://www.hks.harvard.edu/programs/saguaro/about-social-capital/factoids.

were all in Detroit: Kate Abbey-Lambertz, "Most Dangerous Neighborhoods: Detroit Home to 3 Most Violent Areas in America," *Huffington Post,* May 2, 2013, http://

www.huffingtonpost.com/2013/05/02/
most-dangerous-neighborhoods-america-
detroit_n_3187931.html.

claimed only #8, #9, and #11: "Neighborhoodscout's Most Dangerous Neighborhoods: Top 25 Most Dangerous Neighborhoods in America," Neighborhood Scout, http://www.neighborhoodscout .com/neighborhoods/crime-rates/25-most-dangerous-neighborhoods/.

the palliative effects: Lauren E. Johns, et al., "Neighborhood Social Cohesion and Posttraumatic Stress Disorder in a Community-Based Sample: Findings from the Detroit Neighborhood Health Study," *Social Psychiatry and Psychiatric Epidemiology* 47 (2012): 1899–1906.

become less stressful: Barbara Brown, Douglas D. Perkins, and Graham Brown, "Place Attachment in a Revitalizing Neighborhood: Individual and Block Levels of Analysis," *Journal of Environmental Psychology* 23 (2003): 259–71.

invest in their community: Ronald O. Pitner, Mansoo Yu, and Edna Brown, "Which Factor Has More Impact?: An Examination of the Effects of Income Level, Perceived Neighborhood Disorder, and Crime on Community Care and Vigilance among Low-Income African

American Residents," *Race and Social Problems* 5 (2013): 57–64.

invest where they are: Jesslyn Chew, "Neighborhood Residents with Lowest Incomes Most Likely to Care About Their Communities, MU Researcher Finds," University of Missouri News Bureau, July 1, 2013, http://munews.missouri.edu/news-releases/2013/0701-neighborhood-residents-with-lowest-incomes-most-likely-to-care-about-their-communities-mu-researcher-finds/.

to solve problems: "Every Neighborhood Has a Future: Mike Duggan's Neighborhood Plan," Duggan for Detroit Campaign, http://www.dugganfordetroit.com/wp-content/themes/duggan/Duggan NeighborhoodPlan.pdf.

struggled to find steady work: Belva Davis, in conversation with the author, July 2011.

allowed Belva to stay in her home: Nancy Brigham, in conversation with the author, July 2011.

"get a new stoplight put in": Marc Dunkelman, in conversation with the author, November 2014.

violence in the neighborhood went down: Robert J. Sampson, Stephen W. Raudenbush, and Felton Earls, "Neighborhoods and Violent Crime: A Multilevel Study of Collective Efficacy," *Science* 277 (August 15, 1997).

less likely to be depressed, use drugs, or be victimized by violence: Jennifer Ahern and Sandro Galea, "Collective Efficacy and Major Depression in Urban Neighborhoods," *American Journal of Epidemiology* 173, no. 12 (2011); Christopher Browning and Kathleen Cagney, "Neighborhood Structural Disadvantage, Collective Efficacy, and Self-Rated Physical Health in an Urban Setting," *Journal of Health and Social Behavior* 43 (December 2002): 383–99; Abigail Fagan, Emily Wright, and Gillian Pinchevsky, "The Protective Effects of Neighborhood Collective Efficacy on Adolescent Substance Abuse and Violence following Exposure to Violence," *Journal of Youth Adolescence* 43 (2014): 1498–1512.

attached to where they live: Nicole Comstock, et al., "Neighborhood Attachment and Its Correlates: Exploring Neighborhood Conditions, Collective Efficacy, and Gardening," *Journal of Environmental Psychology* 30 (2010): 435–42.

"unofficial mayor of the street": Marc Dunkelman, in conversation with the author, November 2014.

"Heaven will look like": Tonya Beeler, e-mail to the author, December 2014.

Chapter Five: Do Something Fun

"first thing that comes to mind": North Star Destination Strategies, "Sierra Vista Understanding and Insights," presentation, April 23, 2015.

"communities is all we do": Kelley Brackett, in conversation with the author, January 2015.

"the freedom we all crave": Samantha Shankman, "A Brief History of 'What Happens in Vegas Stays in Vegas,' *The Week,* October 1, 2013, http://theweek .com/articles/459434/brief-history-what-happens-vegas-stays-vegas.

wonderland of excess and anonymity: Ed Komenda, "How One Ad Campaign Changed the Face of Las Vegas," *Vegas Inc,* April 6, 2014, http://vegasinc.com/ news/2014/apr/06/how-one-ad-campaign-changed-face-las-vegas/.

the vanilla to hipper neighbor Pasadena's chocolate: Brittany Levine, "Glendale to Get 'Animated' in Image Makeover," *Glendale News-Press,* November 30, 2011, http://articles.glendalenews press.com/2011-11-30/news/tn-gnp-1130-

glendale-to-get-animated-in-image-makeover_1_brand-boulevard-north-star-destination-strategies-new-logo; and Xavier Sibaja, "Glendale Struggles for Attention: City Aims to Become a More Hip Location," *Examiner: Glendale Community Issues,* July 30, 2012, http://www.examiner.com/article/glendale-struggles-for-attention-city-aims-to-become-a-more-hip-location.

studios in town: Don McEachern, in conversation with the author, December 2014; and North Star Destination Strategies, "Glendale, California, City Branding Study," North Star website, http://www.northstarideas.com/case-studies/glendale-california.

" **'Less Ghetto Than You Think' ":** Scot Lowe, Twitter, March 5, 2013, 7:11 p.m., https://twitter.com/tropicostation/status/309108925901443073.

"There's an art to it": North Star Destination Strategies, "Petersburg, Alaska, Case Study," North Star website, http://www.northstarideas.com/sites/default/files/petersburg.pdf, and "Green County, Wisconsin, County Branding Case Study," North Star website, http://www.northstarideas.com/case-studies/green-county-wisconsin.

"the way residents feel about the town": Don McEachern, in conversation with the author, December 2014.

the writer Emily St. John Mandel: Emily St. John Mandel, "Long Trains Leaving," in *Good-bye to All That: Writers on Loving and Leaving New York,* ed. Sari Botton (Berkeley, Cal.: Seal Press, 2013), 177.

"of human perception, use and response": Quoted in Philip L. Fradkin, *Wallace Stegner and the American West* (Oakland: University of California Press, 2009), 189.

map the change over time: Katherine Loflin, in conversation with the author, November 2014.

effectiveness of local police: Gallup and John S. and James L. Knight Foundation, "Knight Foundation Questionnaire 2010," Soul of the Community study, 2010.

"on a global scale," she told me: Katherine Loflin, in conversation with the author, November 2014.

showed the same result: John S. and James L. Knight Foundation, *Knight Soul of the Community 2010: Why People Love Where They Live and Why It Matters: A National Perspective* (Miami, Fla.: John S. and James L. Knight Foundation, 2010), http://knightfoundation.org/sotc/overall-findings/.

GDP growth per capita than cities that weren't: Ibid.

"feel, think, and act about something": Katherine Loflin, in conversation with the author, November 2014.

"that is the paradigm shift": Carol Coletta, in conversation with the author, May 2015.

"can't see our employees living [in Oklahoma City]": Ryan Holywell, "OKC Mayor Urges Cities to Have 'High Standards,' " *The Urban Edge,* blog of the Kinder Institute for Urban Research, July 1, 2015, http://urbanedge.blogs.rice.edu/2015/07/01/okc-mayor-urges-cities-to-have-high-standards/#.VdNya1NViko.

"on why place matters": Katherine Loflin, "Place Matters: The Emerging Role of Place in the Success of Communities," presentation given to Nova Scotia Planning Directors Annual Conference, 2012, http://www.nspda.ca/component/option.com_docman/Itemid,/gid,612/task.doc_download/.

among cities its size: Bureau of Labor Statistics, U.S. Department of Labor, "Metropolitan Area Employment and Unemployment — June 2015," news release, July 29, 2015, http://www.bls.gov/

544

news.release/pdf/metro.pdf.

"than vice versa," says Cornett: Mick Cornett, "Oklahoma City Invests in New Urban Infrastructure," *American Infrastructure,* Summer 2012, http://american infrastructuremag.com/summer-2012-24.php.

"need to invest in themselves": Ibid.

bigger, more amenity-rich cities: John S. and James L. Knight Foundation, *Knight Soul of the Community 2010.*

strongest neighborhood ties and rootedness: Maria Lewicka, "Ways to Make People Active: The Role of Place Attachment, Cultural Capital, and Neighborhood Ties," *Journal of Environmental Psychology* 25 (2005): 381–95.

Asset-Based Community Development Institute at Northwestern University: Mary Nelson, in conversation with the author, May 2015.

bike the Huckleberry Trail: NextThreeDays, Twitter, November 21, 2014, 3:18 p.m, https://twitter.com/Next3Days/status/535905030537510912, and Blacksburg Stuff, Twitter, November 21, 2014, 3:35 p.m., https://twitter.com/BlacksburgStuff/status/535909386452209664.

#1 attraction in Blacksburg: "Lane Stadium reviews," TripAdvisor.com, http://

www.tripadvisor.com/Attraction_Review
-g57513-d7195060-Reviews-Lane_Stad
ium-Blacksburg_Virginia.html.

graduate to insider status: For an example, see Miyoun Lim, Angela Calabrese Barton, "Exploring Insideness in Urban Children's Sense of Place," *Journal of Environmental Psychology* 30 (2010): 328–37.

You say, "*We* won": Nyla R. Branscombe and Daniel L. Wann, "The Positive Social and Self Concept Consequences of Sports Team Identification," *Journal of Sport and Social Issues* 15, no. 2 (1991): 115–27.

an old-school arcade: Suban Nir Cooley, in conversation with the author, May 2014.

"at Chicago's Millennium Park": Anthony Flint, "Wait Your Turn for the Swings at Boston's Adult Playground," *CityLab,* September 17, 2014, http://www .citylab.com/design/2014/09/wait-your -turn-for-the-swings-at-bostons-adult -playground/380355/.

stop and play chess: Barrett Lawliss, "Game On! Game Boards, Free Wi-Fi Added to Zane Square," *Lancester Eagle-Gazette,* June 28, 2014, http://archive .lancastereaglegazette.com/article/201406

27/NEWS01/306270015/Game-Game
-boards-free-Wi-Fi-added-Zane-Square.

on her street in Hutto, Texas: Christine
Bolaños, "Little Free Library Coming to
Hutto," *Hutto News,* April 16, 2014, http://
www.thehuttonews.com/news/article_
187e4f8c-c565-11e3-a830-0019bb2963f4
.html.

best part is that they're cheap: Emily
Munroe, panel discussion at National
Main Street America Conference, Detroit,
Michigan, May 2015.

hammocks became an event: Hammock
Initiative, http://hammockinitiative
.tumblr.com/; Camille Forlano, "Hammock Initiative Wants Public to Hangout,"
North Dakota State University Spectrum,
October 2, 2014, http://ndsuspectrum
.com/hammock-initiative-wants-public-to-
hangout/; and Becky Parker, "Hanging
Out: Hammock Initiative Fargo," WDAY
6 News, July 22, 2014, http://www.wday
.com/content/hanging-out-hammock-
initiative-fargo.

have meaning to you: To learn more
about the Power of 10+, read "The Power
of 10+: Applying Placemaking at Every
Scale" at http://www.pps.org/reference/
the-power-of-10.

then share it with others: Any future Blacksburg tourists can find my Google map of Blacksburg assets at my website, MelodyWarnick.com.

Chapter Six: Commune with Nature

best city to find a job: Richie Bernardo, "2015's Best and Worst Cities to Find a Job," WalletHub.com, http://wallethub .com/edu/best-cities-for-jobs/2173/.

to raise a family: Daniel D'Addario, "The Best Places to Raise Kids 2013," *Bloomberg Business,* December 18, 2012, http://www.bloomberg.com/bw/slideshows /2012-12-17/the-best-places-to-raise-kids- 2013#slide2.

"the greatest city on the planet": Jessica Misener and Arielle Calderon, "37 Reasons Miami Is the Best (and Weirdest) City in the U.S.," *BuzzFeed,* April 29, 2013, http://www.buzzfeed.com/jessica misener/37-reasons-miami-is-the-best- and-weirdest-city-in-the-us#.jnlV0p3OV; CLEally, "25 Reasons Why Cleveland Is the Best," *BuzzFeed,* August 6, 2013, http://www.buzzfeed.com/itslynnotline/25- reasons-why-cleveland-is-the-best-dfpl; Zoe Tsiris, "16 Reasons Why Pittsburgh Is the Greatest City on the Planet," *Buzz-*

Feed, August 3, 2013, http://www .buzzfeed.com/zoetsiris/18-reasons-why -pittsburgh-is-the-greatest-city-on-d56b# .iuVWdyKVW; Tanner Greenring, "24 Reasons Fort Collins, Colorado Is the Greatest City on Earth," *BuzzFeed*, June 12, 2014, http://www.buzzfeed.com/awe somer/24-reasons-fort-collins-colorado-is -the-greatest-city-on-ear#.ap J6rRQj6.

declaring a top one hundred: "Top 100 Best Places to Live," Livability, http:// www.livability.com/best-places/top-100- best-places-to-live/2015.

fifty best places to live in America: "Best Places to Live 2015," *Money,* October 2015, http://time.com/money/collection/ best-places-to-live-2015/.

"all random anyway, right?": Jeremy Singer-Vine, "Generate Your Own Definitive List of America's Best Cities," *Buzz-Feed,* August 6, 2014, http://www.buzz feed.com/jsvine/generate-your-own -definitive-list-of-americas-best-cities#.sl nNPWlKb. I hit refresh three times. Denton, Texas, Carmel, Indiana, and Vallejo, California, all came up winners. It was like a slot machine.

in the country to retire: William P. Barrett, "The 25 Best Places to Retire in

2014," Forbes.com, January 16, 2014, http://www.forbes.com/sites/williampbarrett /2014/01/16/the-best-places-to-retire-in-2014.

"started poking around": Jonah Ogles, in conversation with the author, December 2014.

"this is where I want to be": Larry Burke, "Where the Outsiders Belong," *New Mexico Magazine,* January 2014, http://www.nmmagazine.com/article/?aid=84440#.VdSlKlNViko.

twenty thousand votes on Facebook: Jonah Ogles, in conversation with the author, December 2014.

(readership is around seven hundred thousand): "Circulation," Outside Media Kit, http://www.outsidemediakit.com/audience_circulation.php.

made it a hard sell: John Myers, "2013–14 Is Duluth's Second-Coldest Winter on Record," *Duluth News-Tribune,* February 28, 2014, http://www.duluthnewstribune.com/content/2013-14-duluths-second-coldest-winter-record.

tweets poured in from Minnesota's senators: Al Franken, Twitter, June 17, 2014, 8:39 a.m., https://twitter.com/alfranken/status/478894615848685568; Amy Klobuchar, Twitter, June 16, 2014, 9:43

a.m., https://twitter.com/amyklobuchar/status/478548380772093953.

"won this contest 20 years ago": Don Ness, Facebook, June 15, 2014, https://www.facebook.com/ness.duluth/posts/10203620817175048.

Wilson calls "biophilia": Edward O. Wilson, *Biophilia* (Cambridge, Mass.: Harvard University Press, 1984).

New York, or Buenos Aires: United Nations Department of Economic and Social Affairs, Population Division, "World Urbanization Prospects: 2014 Revision, Highlights," http://esa.un.org/unpd/wup/Highlights/WUP2014-Highlights.pdf.

bear a higher price tag: Jake Mooney, "New York's Tiny Squares Offer Breathing Room," *New York Times,* October 15, 2010, http://www.nytimes.com/2010/10/17/realestate/17cov.html.

"choose one city over another": Amanda Burden, "How Public Spaces Make Cities Work," talk given at TED conference, March 2014, https://www.ted.com/talks/amanda_burden_how_public_spaces_make_cities_work?language=en.

park per capita in America: Joseph Clancy, "What Makes a Biophilic City?" Landscape Architects Network website, July 4, 2014, http://landarchs.com/

biophilic-city/.

for every one thousand residents: Ibid.

"to roadways to riverfronts": Timothy Beatley, "Biophilic Cities: What Are They?" Biophilic Cities website, http://biophiliccities.org/biophiliccities.html.

urban trails, as in Minneapolis: "The 16 Best Places to Live in the U.S.: 2014," *Outside* website, August 12, 2014, http://www.outsideonline.com/1928016/16-best-places-live-us-2014.

improves immune system function: Qing Li, "Effect of Forest Bathing Trips on Human Immune Function," *Environmental Health and Preventive Medicine* 15, no. 1 (January 2010): 9–17.

lowers blood glucose levels in diabetics: Yau Ohtsuka, Noriyuki Yabunaka, and Shigeru Takayama, "Shinrin-yoku (Forest-Air Bathing and Walking) Effectively Decreases Blood Glucose Levels in Diabetic Patients," *International Journal of Biometeorology* 41, no. 3 (1998): 125–27.

cognitive functioning and concentration: Patrik Grahn and Johan Ottosson, "A Comparison of Leisure Time Spent in a Garden with Leisure Time Spent Indoors: On Measures of Restoration in Residents in Geriatric Care," *Landscape Research* 30 (2005): 23–55.

strengthens impulse control: Frances E. Kuo and Andrea Faber Taylor, "A Potential Natural Treatment for Attention-Deficit/Hyperactivity Disorder: Evidence from a National Study," *American Journal of Public Health* 94, no. 9 (2004): 1580–86.

tend to be thinner: Ramesh Ghimire, et al., "Green Space and Adult Obesity Prevalence in the United States," paper presented at the Southern Agricultural Economics Association Annual Meeting, Atlanta, Georgia, January 31–February 3, 2015.

more likely to be clinically depressed: J. Maas, et al., "Morbidity Is Related to a Green Living Environment," *Journal of Epidemiology and Community Health* 63, no. 12 (December 2009): 967–73.

a view of a brick wall: Roger S. Ulrich, "View Through a Window May Influence Recovery from Surgery," *Science* 224, no. 4647 (April 27, 1984): 420–21.

made people less stressed: Roger S. Ulrich, et al., "Stress Recovery during Exposure to Natural and Urban Environments," *Journal of Environmental Psychology* 11 (1991): 201–30.

to want to spend it on others: Netta Weinstein, Andrew K. Przybylski, and

Richard M. Ryan, "Can Nature Make Us More Caring? Effects of Immersion in Nature on Intrinsic Aspirations and Generosity," *Personality and Social Psychology Bulletin* 35, no. 10 (2009): 1315–29.

develop in tight-knit neighborhoods: Jolanda Maas, Sonja M. E. van Dillen, Robert A. Verheij, and Peter P. Groenewegen, "Social Contacts as a Possible Mechanism Behind the Relation Between Green Space and Health," *Health and Place* 15 (2009): 586–95.

better sense of community: Frances E. Kuo, William C. Sullivan, Rebekah Levine Coley, and Liesette Brunson, "Fertile Ground for Community: Inner-City Neighborhood Common Spaces," *American Journal of Community Psychology* 26, no. 6 (December 1998): 823–51.

who live farther away: Deborah A. Cohen, Sanae Inagami, and Brian Finch, "The Built Environment and Collective Efficacy," *Health and Place* 14, no. 2 (June 2008): 198–208.

with the sparest vegetation: Frances E. Kuo and William C. Sullivan, "Environment and Crime in the Inner City: Does Vegetation Reduce Crime?" *Environment and Behavior* 33, no. 3 (May 2001): 343–67.

between greenery and human health:
"Green Environments Essential for Human Health," press release, College of Agricultural, Consumer, and Environmental Sciences, University of Illinois at Urbana-Champaign, April 19, 2011, http://news.aces.illinois.edu/news/green-environments-essential-human-health.

who can afford to live there: "Park City Home Prices and Values," Zillow, http://www.zillow.com/park-city-ut/home-values/.

"open spaces and access to them": Cheryl Fox, in conversation with the author, December 2014.

likely to protect it: For studies that connect environmentalism with place attachment in some form, see: Leila Scannell and Robert Gifford, "The Relations Between Natural and Civic Place Attachment and Pro-Environmental Behavior," *Journal of Environmental Psychology* 30 (2010): 289–97; Sarah Schweizer, Shawn Davis, and Jessica Leigh Thompson, "Changing the Conversation About Climate Change: A Theoretical Framework for Place-Based Climate Change Engagement," *Environmental Communication* 7, no. 1 (2013): 42–62; and Nicole M. Ardoin, "Exploring Sense of Place and

Environmental Behavior at an Ecoregional Scale in Three Sites," *Human Ecology* 42 (2014): 425–41.

that helped preserve it: Michelle A. Payton, David C. Fulton, and Dorothy H. Anderson, "Influence of Place Attachment and Trust on Civic Action: A Study at Sherburne National Wildlife Refuge," *Society and Natural Resources* 18, no. 6 (2005): 511–28.

washing dishes to conserve water: Jerry J. Vaske and Katherine C. Kobrin, "Place Attachment and Environmentally Responsible Behavior," *Journal of Environmental Education* 32, no. 4 (2001): 16–21.

major environmental impacts there: Marit Vorkinn and Hanne Riese, "Environmental Concern in a Local Context: The Significance of Place Attachment," *Environment and Behavior* 33, no. 2 (March 2001): 249–63. Another study on a similar subject is Patrick Devine-Wright, "Explaining 'NIMBY' Objections to a Power Line: The Role of Personal, Place Attachment and Project-Related Factors," *Environment and Behavior* 45, no. 6 (2013): 761–81.

"when one is still at 'home' ": Daniel B. Smith, "Is There an Ecological Unconscious?" *New York Times Magazine,* January 27, 2010, http://www.nytimes.com/2010/01/31/magazine/31ecopsych-t.html.

the motivation to fight: Ibid.

"a total celebration of place": Liam Barrington-Bush, "Naomi Klein: 'We're Not Who We Were Told We Were,' " *Contributoria,* October 2014, https://contributoria.com/issue/2014-10/53ee2ec2dadce9eb43000043.

"understanding a sense of place": U.S. Environmental Protection Agency, Office of Water, *Community Culture and the Environment: A Guide to Understanding a Sense of Place* (Washington, D.C.: Environmental Protection Agency, 2002).

Denver Botanic Gardens: Cara Marie DiEnno and Jessica Leigh Thompson, "For the Love of the Land: How Emotions Motivate Volunteerism in Ecological Restoration," *Emotion, Space and Society* 6 (2013): 63–72.

"climate change wherever they are": Jessica Thompson, in conversation with the author, December 2014.

"did that we'd be fine": Liam Barrington-Bush, "Naomi Klein: 'We're Not Who We Were Told We Were.' "

" 'to visit, but not to live' ": Jon Montgomery, in conversation with the author,

December 2014.

"the water around you": Abe Streep, "How Water Makes Us Healthier, Happier, and More Successful," *Outside* website, July 22, 2014, http://www.outside online.com/1926656/how-water-makes-us-healthier-happier-and-more-successful.

happiness bump near water: George MacKerron and Susana Mourato, "Happiness Is Greater in Natural Environments," *Global Environmental Change* 23, no. 5 (2013): 992–1000.

of the University of Sussex: Zachary Slobig, "Mind Your Body: The Brain Aquatic," *Psychology Today* website, July 1, 2014, https://www.psychologytoday.com/articles/201408/mind-your-body-the-brain-aquatic.

compared to 14.4 in Kentucky: David G. Moriarty, et al., "Geographic Patterns of Frequent Mental Distress: U.S. Adults, 1993–2001 and 2003–2006," *American Journal of Preventive Medicine* 36, no. 6 (2009): 497–505.

occasional vantage points: The first to propose this theory was the ecologist and ornithologist Gordon Orians; see Gordon H. Orians, "Habitat Selection: General Theory and Applications to Human Behavior," in *The Evolution of Human*

Social Behavior, ed. Joan S. Lockard (Amsterdam: Elsevier, 1980), 49–66, and "An Ecological and Evolutionary Approach to Landscape Esthetics," in *Landscape Meanings and Values,* ed. Edmund Penning-Rowsell and David Lowenthal (London: Allen and Unwin, 1986), 3–22. For more recent work on the subject, see John H. Falk and John D. Balling, "Evolutionary Influence on Human Landscape Preference," *Environment and Behavior* 42, no. 4 (2010): 479–93.

parks, backyards, and even shopping malls: Edward O. Wilson, *Biophilia.*

photos of England's Lake District: Andrew Lothian, "Lake District Landscape Quality Project Summary," 2013.

results emerged time and again: Andrew Lothian catalogs dozens of these studies and their outcomes in an unpublished paper called "Findings of Landscape Preference Studies," but for a few examples, see G. Fry, et al., "The Ecology of Visual Landscapes: Exploring the Conceptual Common Ground of Visual and Ecological Landscape Indicators," *Ecological Indicators* 9, no. 5 (2009): 933–47; Melvin D. Williams, "Water, Power and Human Nature: In Search of Humans Evolving," *Journal of Social and Evolutionary*

Systems 21, no. 1 (1998): 7–18; Yvonne de Kort and Femke Beute, "Let the Sun Shine!: Measuring Explicit and Implicit Preference for Environments Differing in Naturalness, Weather Type and Brightness," *Journal of Environmental Psychology* 36 (2013): 162–78; Shmuel Burmil, Terry C. Daniel, and John D. Hetherington, "Human Values and Perceptions of Water in Arid Landscapes," *Landscape and Urban Planning* 44 (1999): 99–109; Ian D. Bishop and David W. Hulse, "Prediction of Scenic Beauty Using Mapped Data and Geographic Information Systems," *Landscape and Urban Planning* 30, no. 1 (1994): 59–70; and JoAnna Ruth Wherrett, "Natural Landscape Scenic Preference: Techniques for Evaluation and Simulation," dissertation, Robert Gordon University, Aberdeen, Scotland, 1999.

prospect and refuge: Andrew Lothian, in conversation with the author, December 2014.

a similar landscape later on: Anna A. Adevi and Patrik Grahn, "Attachment to Certain Natural Environments: A Basis for Choice of Recreational Settings, Activities and Restoration from Stress?" *Environment and Natural Resources Research* 1, no. 1 (December 2011): 36–52.

"where you're supposed to be": Susan Auten, in conversation with the author, March 2015.

high was below thirty-five degrees: Neil Irwin, "The Giant Retirement Community That Explains Where Americans Are Moving," *New York Times,* March 26, 2015, http://www.nytimes.com/2015/03/27/upshot/the-giant-retirement-community-that-explains-where-americans-are-moving.html.

"at home again on the mountain": Johanna Spyri, *Heidi* (Philadelphia: David McKay Company, 1922), 215.

or a pond in Massachusetts: L. M. Montgomery's *Anne of Green Gables* and Henry David Thoreau's *Walden.* Go read them right now.

"And the peach trees stitched across the land": Both lovely songs, one by James Taylor and the other by the Indigo Girls.

who grew up in Colorado: James Sullivan, "National Seashore Marks Milestone: Cape Cod Preserve Created 50 Years Ago," *Boston Globe,* August 7, 2011, http://www.boston.com/news/local/massachusetts/articles/2011/08/07/cape_cods_national_seashore_celebrates_a_half_century_mark/.

"the smell of the sea": Jenna Sammartino, "Place Where You Live: Cape Cod, Massachusetts," *Orion Magazine,* January 19, 2015, https://orionmagazine.org/place/cape-cod-massachusetts/.

"the Scenic Seven this year": New River Valley Economic Development Alliance, "New River Valley Scenic Seven," http://www.scenicseven.com/.

"often become embedded in the place": Gerard Kyle, in conversation with the author, December 2014.

Chapter Seven: Volunteer

something to brighten their day: Robyn Bomar, in conversation with the author, May 2012.

written about for a women's magazine: You can read about the delightful Birthday Project and about Robyn Bomar's day of birthday kindness at her website, The BDayProject.com: http://www.thebdayproject.com/the-original-38-random-acts-of-birthday-kindess-post.html.

propitious for a July seventeenth birthday: Now that everyone knows my birthday, I have a feeling the next one is going to be really, *really* good.

made them feel better: United Health-

Group, "Doing Good Is Good for You," 2013 Health and Volunteering study, http://www.unitedhealthgroup.com/SocialResponsibility/Volunteering.aspx.

better social skills: Abby S. Letcher and Kathy M. Perlow, "Community-Based Participatory Research Shows How a Community Initiative Creates Networks to Improve Well-Being," *American Journal of Preventive Medicine* 37, no. 6S1 (2009): S292–99.

less anxious and depressed: David Mellor, et al., "Volunteering and Its Relationship with Personal and Neighborhood Well-Being," *Nonprofit and Voluntary Sector Quarterly* 38 (2009): 144–59.

lower blood pressure: Rodlescia S. Sneed and Sheldon Cohen, "A Prospective Study of Volunteerism and Hypertension Risk in Older Adults," *Psychology and Aging* 28, no. 2 (June 2013): 578–86.

healthier hearts: Hannah M. C. Schreier, Kimberly A. Schonert-Reichl, and Edith Chen, "Effect of Volunteering on Risk Factors for Cardiovascular Disease in Adolescents: A Randomized Controlled Trial," *JAMA Pediatrics* 167, no. 4 (2013) 327–32.

less likely to die . . . than non-volunteers: Sara Konrath, et al., "Motives for Volunteering Are Associated with Mortality Risk in Older Adults," *Health Psychology* 31, no. 1 (2012): 87–96.

"creates mood elevation": Meredith Maran, "The Activism Cure," *MORE,* March 2009, http://www.more.com/health/wellness/activism-cure.

"invest, spend, and hire there": National Conference on Citizenship, "Civic Health and Unemployment II: The Case Builds," 2012 issue brief, http://ncoc.net/unemployment2.

an estimated $173 billion: Corporation for National and Community Service, "Dollar Value of Volunteering for States," http://www.volunteeringinamerica.gov/pressroom/value_states.cfm.

"most pressing local challenges": New York City Office of the Mayor, "Mayor Bloomberg, Nashville Mayor Dean and Rockefeller Foundation President Judith Rodin Announce the Next Ten Cities to Receive Cities of Service Leadership Grants," press release, June 30, 2009.

"that has increased dramatically": Laurel Creech, in conversation with the author, May 2015.

"take care of our home": Cities of Service, "Flint Community Toolshed and Blue Badge Volunteer," video, May 8,

2015, https://www.youtube.com/watch?v=
GT6EePTPxP0&feature=youtu.be.

"will be proud of him": This is one of those quotes that is widely attributed to Abraham Lincoln but has never been traced back to the source. Still, it's nice to think that he *would* have said it. See Thomas F. Schwartz, "Lincoln Never Said That," Illinois Historic Preservation Agency, https://www.illinois.gov/ihpa/Research/Pages/Facsimile.aspx.

twenty-second place for volunteering: Corporation for National and Community Service, "Volunteering and Civic Engagement in Nashville, TN," http://www.volunteeringinamerica.gov/TN/Nashville.

quarter of Americans volunteered: U.S. Department of Labor, Bureau of Labor Statistics, "Volunteering in the United States, 2014," February 25, 2015, http://www.bls.gov/news.release/volun.nr0.htm.

less philanthropic than Stayers: Douglas Perkins, Barbara Brown, and Ralph Taylor, "The Ecology of Empowerment: Predicting Participation in Community Organizations," *Journal of Social Issues* 52 (1996): 85–110, and Robert Wuthnow, *Saving America? Faith-Based Services and the Future of Civil Society* (Princeton, N.J.: Princeton University Press, 2004).

tend to have more volunteers: Anil Rupasingha, Stephan J. Goetz, and David Freshwater, "The Production of Social Capital in U.S. Counties," *Journal of Socio-Economics* 35, no. 1 (2006): 83–101. Lili Wang and Elizabeth Graddy, "Social Capital, Volunteering, and Charitable Giving," *Voluntas* 19 (2008): 23–42.

another animal shelter after you move: Becky Nesbit, in conversation with the author, May 2015.

"reconnecting to volunteering": Rebecca Nesbit, "Packing and Unpacking Philanthropy: How Moving Affects Volunteering," unpublished paper, May 2015.

more new move-ins than move-outs: Debra O'Connor, "St. Paul, Minneapolis See Population Gains, Say Met Council Estimates," *Twin Cities Pioneer Press,* May 22, 2014, http://www.twincities.com/local news/ci_25818482/St.-paul-minneapolis-see-population-gains-say-met; U.S. Census, "U.S. and World Population Clock," http://www.census.gov/popclock/.

in 2013, 35.8 percent did: Corporation for National and Community Service, "Volunteering and Civic Engagement in Minneapolis-St Paul, MN," http://www.volunteeringinamerica.gov/mn/minneapolis-st-paul.

Gallup-Healthways' well-being poll: Dan Witters, "Provo-Orem, Utah, Leads U.S. Communities in Well-Being," Gallup, March 25, 2014, http://www .gallup.com/poll/167984/provo-orem- utah-leads-communities.aspx.

more physically active than most of the nation: American College of Sports Medicine, "Actively Moving America to Better Health: Health and Community Fitness Status of the 50 Largest Metropolitan Areas," 2012 report, http://americanfitness index.org/docs/reports/ 2012_afi_report_ final.pdf.

more well-read: John W. Miller, "America's Most Literate Cities, 2013," Central Connecticut State University, http:// web.ccsu.edu/americasmostliteratecities/ 2013/.

more likely to feel safe: Jeffrey M. Jones, "Minneapolis–St. Paul Area Residents Most Likely to Feel Safe," Gallup, April 5, 2013, http://www.gallup.com/poll/ 161648/minneapolis-paul-area-residents- likely-feel-safe.aspx.

kits for the children's hospital: KARE11, "Speed Volunteering at the Great Minnesota Get Together," December 10, 2013, http://www.kare11.com/story/life/ family/eleven-who-care/2013/08/19/speed-volunteering-at-the-great-minnesota-get-together/3846579/.

"a close-knit community": Patricia Garcia, in conversation with the author, August 2014.

the center's special projects director: Meghan Morse, in conversation with the author, August 2014.

"Have you driven on our roads?": Kristin Schurrer, in conversation with the author, August 2014.

"distance to the Canadian border": Robert Putnam, "Social Capital: Measurement and Consequences," Organization for Economic Co-operation and Development, http://www.oecd.org/innovation/research/1825848.pdf.

three blocks from Minnehaha Creek: Jenny Friedman, in conversation with the author, August 2014.

crime is not uncommon: Minneapolis Police Department, "Neighborhood Statistics, January–August 2015," http://www.ci.minneapolis.mn.us/www/groups/public/@mpd/documents/webcontent/wcms1p-148628.pdf.

cajoling them about their grades: Brian Mogren, in conversation with the author, August 2014.

bought a place in Jordan anyway: Don

Samuels, in conversation with the author, August 2014.

where Davies grew up: Louisa Addiscott, "Glyncoch Community Center," Space-hive, http://spacehive.com/glyncochcc.

"something transformative is going on": Rodrigo Davies, in conversation with the author, March 2015.

started in Liberty, Missouri: Fran Bussey, in conversation with the author, March 2015.

whether they were homeowners: Angela M. Eikenberry and Jessica Bearman, "The Impact of Giving Together: Giving Circles' Influence on Members' Philanthropic and Civic Behaviors, Knowledge and Attitudes," published by the Forum of Regional Associations of Grantmakers, the Center on Philanthropy at Indiana University, and the University of Nebraska Omaha (May 2009), available at giving forum.org.

they attend school here: Becky Nesbit, in conversation with the author, September 2015.

(Educated people volunteer more often): Danielle Kurtzleben, "New Data Show Women, More Educated Doing Most Volunteering," *U.S. News and World Report,* February 27, 2013, http://www

.usnews.com/news/articles/2013/02/27/ charts-new-data-show-women-more-educated-doing-most-volunteering.

makes a difference in the world: United HealthGroup, "Doing Good Is Good for You: 2013 Health and Volunteering Study," http://www.unitedhealthgroup .com/SocialResponsibility/Volunteering .aspx.

but wackier and more creative: Jennifer Prod, in conversation with the author, August 2014.

to read the next one: You can see the full, delightful list of Jennifer Prod's Random Acts of Happiness at her blog, *Studio Kindred.* See http://www.studiokindred.com/ random-acts-of-happiness/.

as urban activist Majora Carter has said: Majora Carter, as quoted in Joanna Gangi, "You Don't Have to Move Out of Your Neighborhood to Live in a Better One," *Yes! Magazine,* May 11, 2011, http://www.yesmagazine.org/happiness/ majora-carter-how-to-bring-environment al-justice-to-your-neighborhood.

to guide your contributions: Kathy LeMay, in conversation with the author, September 2014.

high-end camera store in Minneapolis: Sarah Sutton, in conversation with the author, September 2014.

revolves around eating and drinking: Christopher Muther, "Culinary Boom in Portland, Maine," *Boston Globe,* October 4, 2014, https://www.bostonglobe.com/lifestyle/travel/2014/10/04/portland-culinary-boom/vihcaqFHkeQM3BAZegxCGM/story.html; and Suzanne MacNeille, "Portland, Me.: Locavore in Menu and Décor," *New York Times,* August 29, 2013, http://www.nytimes.com/2013/09/01/travel/portland-me-locavore-in-menu-and-decor.html.

head start on the local food trend: Kate McCarty, in conversation with the author, September 2014. See also Kate McCarty, *Portland Food: The Culinary Capital of Maine* (Charleston, S.C.: American Palate, 2014). Sam Hayward was the first Maine chef to win a James Beard Award for best chef, in 2004, for his farm-to-tablerestaurant Fore Street.

than San Francisco: Whit Richardson, "Does Portland Have More Restaurants per Capita Than San Francisco?" *Mainebiz,* August 18, 2009, http://

www.mainebiz.biz/article/20090818/
NEWS02/308189995/does-portland-
have-more-restaurants-per-capita-than-
san-francisco?

"foodiest small town": Andrew Knowl-
ton, "Portland, Maine — America's Foodi-
est Small Town 2009," *Bon Appétit,* August
31, 2009, http://www.bonappetit.com/
columns/the-foodist/article/portland-
maine-america-s-foodiest-small-town-
2009.

one in ten jobs in the United States is
in a restaurant: National Restaurant Association, "Facts at a Glance," 2015,
http://www.restaurant.org/News-Research/
Research/Facts-at-a-Glance.

"rank locations for livability": Ray
Routhier, "Portland Excels at Making the
List," *Portland Press Herald,* August 13,
2012, http://www.pressherald.com/2012/
08/13/portland-excels-at-making-the-
list_2012-08-13/.

mentions by Gourmet.com: "Food Truck
Favorites from Coast to Coast," *Gourmet
Live,* August 8, 2012, http://www.gourmet
.com/food/gourmetlive/2012/080812/best-
US-food-trucks.html.

Food and Wine: "America's Best Lobster
Rolls," *Food and Wine* website, http://
www.foodandwine.com/slideshows/

americas-best-lobster-rolls.

Yelp's top one hundred in America: Dan Frank, "Yelp's Top 100 Places to Eat in the U.S. for 2015," *Yelp Official Blog,* January 22, 2015, http://officialblog .yelp.com/2015/01/yelps-top-100-places-to-eat-in-the-us-for-2015.html.

where her family lived later: Bonny Wolf, in conversation with the author, February 2015.

for Baltimore schoolchildren: Bonny Wolf, "Baltimore Coddies," American Food Roots, December 14, 2012, http:// www.americanfoodroots.com/recipes/ baltimore-coddies/.

local foods were their favorites: Luis L. Cantarero, "Human Food Preferences and Cultural Identity: The Case of Aragón (Spain)," *International Journal of Psychology* 48, no. 5 (2013): 881–90.

"wide open spaces": Gwendolyn Blue, "If It Ain't Alberta, It Ain't Beef: Local Food, Regional Identity, (Inter)National Politics," *Food, Culture and Society* 11, no. 1 (March 2008): 69–85.

"the land has to offer": Rowan Jacobsen, *American Terroir: Savoring the Flavors of Our Woods, Waters, and Fields* (New York: Bloomsbury, 2012).

word of the year: Oxford University Press,

"Oxford Word of the Year 2007: Locavore," *OUPblog,* November 12, 2007, http://blog.oup.com/2007/11/locavore/.

to land on our plate: Sarah DeWeerdt, "Is Local Food Better?," *World Watch Magazine* 22, no. 3 (May–June 2009), http://www.worldwatch.org/node/6064.

milk, sugar, and strawberries: Rich Pirog and Andrew Benjamin, "Calculating Food Miles for a Multiple Ingredient Food Product," Leopold Center for Sustainable Agriculture, Iowa State University, March 2005.

greenhouse gas emissions: Sarah DeWeerdt, "Is Local Food Better?" See also Christopher L. Weber and H. Scott Matthews, "Food-Miles and the Relative Climate Impacts of Food Choices in the United States," *Environmental Science and Technology* 42, no. 10 (2008): 3508–13.

and (horror of horrors) withering flavor: One of my favorite books about how long-distance shipping is altering the taste of foods we eat for the worse is David Mas Masumoto's *Epitaph for a Peach: Four Seasons on My Family Farm* (New York: HarperOne, 1996).

$6.1 billion local food market: Stephen Vogel and Sarah A. Low, "The Size and Scope of Locally Marketed Food Production," U.S. Department of Agriculture, February 2, 2015, http://www.ers.usda .gov/amber-waves/2015-januaryfebruary/ the-size-and-scope-of-locally-marketed-food-production.aspx#.VgmZaY9Viko.

"where human sustenance is concerned": Barbara Kingsolver, *Animal, Vegetable, Miracle* (New York: Harper Perennial, 2008).

pay attention to where you are: Ibid., 36–39.

"I'd never felt so at home": Vicki Robin, "Perspectives: The 10-Mile Diet," *Nourish,* December 2012. See also her book *Blessing the Hands That Feed Us: What Eating Closer to Home Can Teach Us About Food, Community, and Our Place on Earth* (New York: Viking, 2014).

almost 500 percent increase: U.S. Department of Agriculture Economic Research Service, "Number of U.S. Farmers' Markets Continues to Rise," August 4, 2014, http://ers.usda.gov/data-products/ chart-gallery/detail.aspx?chartId=48561 &ref=collection&embed=True&widget ID=37373.

and the store itself: Tracie McMillan, "Where Does Your Grocery Money Go? Mostly Not to the Farmers," CNN.com, August 8, 2012, http://eatocracy.cnn.com/

2012/08/08/where-does-your-grocery-money-go-mostly-not-to-the-farmer/.

"at the Community Farmers Market": Diane Holtaway and Carol Coren, "Assessing the Costs and Benefits of Participation in Community Farmers Markets," Rutgers University study, 2010.

spend their earnings in town: Robert P. King et al., "Comparing the Structure, Size, and Performance of Local and Mainstream Food Supply Chains," USDA Economic Research Report ERR-99, June 2010, www.ers.usda.gov/publications/err-economic-research-report/err99.aspx.

new income for area farms: Eric S. Bendfeldt, et al., "A Community-Based Food System: Building Health, Wealth, Connection, and Capacity as the Foundation of Our Economic Future," Virginia Cooperative Extension, May 2011.

the farmers' market as an event: Ted R. Sommer, Robert Sommer, and John Herrick, "The Behavioral Ecology of Supermarkets and Farmers' Markets," *Journal of Environmental Psychology* 1, no. 1 (1981): 13–19.

as they did in supermarkets: This was quoted in Bill McKibben's wonderful book *Deep Economy: The Wealth of Communities and the Durable Future* (New

York: Times Books, 2007).

"sense of shared learning": Richard McCarthy, in conversation with the author, February 2015.

" 'fit in in this town' ": Ibid.

more conventional supermarkets: Brian K. Obach and Kathleen Tobin, "Civic Agriculture and Community Engagement," *Agriculture and Human Values* 31 (2014): 307–22.

Under the Green Umbrella: Learn more about the delightful people who sell food at the Blacksburg Farmers Market at the market's website, http://www.blacksburg farmersmarket.com/vendors.

higher levels of neighborhood attachment: Nicole Comstock, et al., "Neighborhood Attachment and Its Correlates: Exploring Neighborhood Conditions, Collective Efficacy, and Gardening," *Journal of Environmental Psychology* 30 (2010): 435–42. See also Rachel Kaplan and Stephen Kaplan, "Preference, Restoration, and Meaningful Action in the Context of Nearby Nature," in *Urban Place: Reconnecting with the Natural World,* ed. Peggy F. Barlett (Cambridge, Mass.: MIT Press, 2005), 271–98.

telling me about his CSA: Sean Hagan, in conversation with the author, September 2014. In the off-season, Sean's a graphic designer; find his beautiful website at http://leftfieldmaine.com/.

60 farms nationwide operated CSA programs: Steven McFadden, "The History of Community Supported Agriculture, Part II: CSA's World of Possibilities," *New Farm,* Rodale Institute, http://www.new farm.org/features/0204/csa2/part2.shtml.

more than 12,600 farms did: U.S. Department of Agriculture, "Table 43 — Selected Practices: 2012," in *2012 Census of Agriculture — State Data* (Washington, D.C., National Agricultural Statistics Service, 2014), 558. http://www.agcensus .usda.gov/Publications/2012/Full_Report/ Volume_1,_Chapter_ 2_US_ State_Level/ st99_2_043_043.pdf.

who won't leave the yard: Steven M. Schnell, "Food Miles, Local Eating, and Community Supported Agriculture: Putting Local Food in Its Place," *Agriculture and Human Values* 30 (2013): 615–28.

I want you to succeed here: Ibid.

"happen to have a house that you live in": Steven Schnell, in conversation with the author, September 2015.

when he studied microbreweries: Steven M. Schnell and Joseph F. Reese, "Microbreweries, Place, and Identity in the

United States," in *The Geography of Beer: Regions, Environment, and Societies,* ed. Mark Patterson and Nancy Hoalst-Pullen (Dordrecht, Netherlands: Springer, 2014).

purchase his greenhouses: Katherine Cutko, in conversation with the author, February 2015.

waved off our payment: Jason Pall, in conversation with the author, April 2015.

"wanted to give us half": Molly Wizenberg, *Delancey* (New York: Simon & Schuster, 2014), 177, 223–24.

Bite into Maine's success: Sarah Sutton, in conversation with the author, September 2014.

terms a "third place": Ray Oldenburg, *The Great Good Place: Cafés, Coffee Shops, Bookstores, Bars, Hair Salons, and Other Hangouts at the Heart of a Community* (Boston: Da Capo, 1999).

" 'membership' in a third place": Ibid., xxiii.

chicken chipotle salad: Mark Rosenbaum, in conversation with the author, February 2015.

nameplates on "their" table: Mark Rosenbaum, "Exploring the Social Supportive Role of Third Places in Consumers' Lives," *Journal of Service Research* 9, no. 1 (August 2006): 59–72.

"So I did": Ibid., 59.

increased by 10 to 15 percent: Nickey Friedman, "McDonald's and Burger King Want You to Come In and Stay Awhile," Motley Fool, April 20, 2014, http:// www.fool.com/investing/general/2014/04/ 20/mcdonalds-and-burger-king-want-you-to-come-in-and.aspx.

affection toward a place: Edward T. MacMahon, "The Place Making Dividend," Planetizen, December 22, 2010, http:// www.planetizen.com/node/47402.

"the more it is theirs": Ray Oldenburg, *The Great Good Place.*

called Within One Mile: Helms Jarrell, in conversation with the author, April 2015.

"community [to be] confirmed": Lisa Waxman, "The Coffee Shop: Social and Physical Factors Influencing Place Attachment," *Journal of Interior Design* 31, no. 3 (2006): 35–53.

social eatery: I got the term "strEATing" from the Charleston-based placemaking organization Enough Pie. You can read more about it at its website, http://enough pie.org/streatweekly/.

with his 500 Plates project: Learn more about 500 Plates and download a free tool kit at 500plates.com.

a positive review on Yelp: Jessica Esch, in

conversation with the author, September 2015.

Chapter Nine: Get More Political

cities that host such courses: Rick Morse, in conversation with the author, April 2015.

gear works of their town government: Ibid.

"see how hard they work": Heather Browning, in conversation with the author, March 2015.

the same of the federal government: Justin McCarthy, "Americans Still Trust Local Government More Than State," Gallup, September 22, 2014, http://www.gallup.com/poll/176846/americans-trust-local-government-state.aspx.

who studies citizens academies: Rick Morse, "Citizens Academies Database," University of North Carolina at Chapel Hill School of Government.

famously surveyed its citizens about their happiness in 2011: A nice article about it is John Tierney, "How Happy Are You? A Census Wants to Know," *New York Times,* April 30, 2011, http://www.nytimes.com/2011/05/01/us/01happiness.html.

"making people happier": City of

Somerville, "Somerville, Massachusetts: A Report on Well-Being," August 2011, http://www.somervillema.gov/sites/default/files/documents/Somerville_Well_Being_Report.pdf.

the more civically involved they were: Gene Theodori, "Community Attachment, Satisfaction, and Action," *Journal of the Community Development Society* 35, no. 2 (2004): 73.

thrive on that involvement: A great study about the ways place attachment and place identity foster civic engagement is by Lynne C. Manzo and Douglas D. Perkins, environmental psychologists at the University of Washington, Seattle, and Vanderbilt University, respectively, who write, "Affective bonds to places can help inspire action because people are motivated to seek, stay in, protect, and improve places that are meaningful to them. Consequently, place attachment, place identity, and sense of community can provide a greater understanding of how neighborhood spaces can motivate ordinary residents to act collectively to preserve, protect, or improve their community and participate in local planning processes." Lynne C. Manzo and Douglas D. Perkins, "Finding Common Ground: The Importance of Place Attachment to Community Participation and Planning," *Journal of Planning Literature* 20, no. 4 (May 2006): 335–50.

good ol' boy network: Mike Maciag, "The Citizens Most Vocal in Local Government," *Governing,* July 2014, http://www.governing.com/topics/politics/gov-national-survey-shows-citizens-most-vocal-active-in-local-government.html#data.

"really enjoying its assets": Sam Colville, in conversation with the author, March 2015.

(*Family Circle,* and *Kiplinger* best places lists): Dick Goodman, in conversation with the author, March 2015.

"but in general our town": Emily Rogan, in conversation with the author, March 2015.

going to college: Jeff Coates, in conversation with the author, March 2015.

prioritizing close-knit, walkable neighborhoods: "Vision and Perspective," Matt Tomasulo, Raleigh City Council 2015, http://www.mattforraleigh.com/perspective_vision.

O'Charley's and Cracker Barrel by conservatives: Reid J. Epstein, "Liberals

Eat Here. Conservatives Eat There," *Wall Street Journal,* May 2, 2014, http://blogs.wsj.com/washwire/2014/05/02/liberals-eat-here-conservatives-eat-there/.

drive Ford Mustang convertibles: Mary M. Chapman, "Party Affiliations in Car-Buying Choices: A Thorny Patch of Consumer Analysis," *Wheels* (blog), *New York Times,* March 30, 2012, http://wheels.blogs.nytimes.com/2012/03/30/party-affiliations-in-car-buying-choices-a-thorny-patch-of-consumer-analysis/.

"both geographic and social": Michael Dimock, Jocelyn Kiley, Scott Keeter, and Carroll Doherty, "Political Polarization in the American Public: How Increasing Ideological Uniformity and Partisan Antipathy Affect Politics, Compromise and Everyday Life," Pew Research Center, June 12, 2014, http://www.people-press.org/files/2014/06/6-12-2014-Political-Polarization-Release.pdf.

place attachment in the Soul of the Community study: John S. and James L. Knight Foundation, "Overall Findings," *Knight Soul of the Community 2010. Why People Love Where They Live and Why It Matters: A National Perspective* (Miami: John S. and James L. Knight Foundation, 2010), http://knightfoundation.org/sotc/

overall-findings/.

Democrat living in Hoboken, New Jersey: "Best Cities for Liberals, 2014," Livability.com, http://www.livability.com/top-10/political-cities/best-cities-liberals/2014.

Republican living in Benton, Arkansas: "Best Cities for Conservatives, 2014," Livability.com, http://www.livability.com/top-10/political-cities/best-cities-conserva tives/2014.

Was "maybe" good enough?: You can take an abbreviated version of the Big Five personality test yourself; find a link on my website, MelodyWarnick.com.

from his or her zip code: Jason Rentfrow, in conversation with the author, February 2015.

in certain regions of the United States: Richard Florida, *Rise of the Creative Class — Revisited* (New York: Basic Books, 2014).

clustered geographically: Peter J. Rentfrow, et al., "Divided We Stand: Three Psychological Regions of the United States and Their Political, Economic, Social, and Health Correlates," *Journal of Personality and Social Psychology* 105, no. 6 (2013): 996–1012.

increases by 25 percent: Nicholas A. Christakis and James H. Fowler, "Social

Contagion Theory: Examining Dynamic Social Networks and Human Behavior," *Statistics in Medicine* 32 (2013): 556–77.

"on your daily experiences": Jason Rentfrow, in conversation with the author, February 2015.

what makes us happy: Dan Gilbert, *Stumbling on Happiness* (New York: Vintage, 2007).

seemed more legit: You can find a link to this test at my website, MelodyWarnick.com, or at http://www.claritycampaigns.com/townrank/.

"they're out of a job": Benjamin Barber, "Why Mayors Should Rule the World," TEDGlobal conference, June 2013, http://www.ted.com/talks/benjamin_barber_why_mayors_should_rule_the_world?language=en.

a "steward of place": American Association of State Colleges and Universities, *Stepping Forward as Stewards of Place* (Washington, D.C.: AASCU, 2002). See http://www.aascu.org/programs/ADP/ for more about the American Democracy Project.

a good civic engagement gut check: National Conference on Citizenship, "Civic Health Questions Collected by Census Bureau." For more about the

NCOC's Civic Health Index project, see http://ncoc.net/45.

feel rooted where you live: Michael C. Grillo, Miguel A. Teixeira, and David C. Wilson, "Residential Satisfaction and Civic Engagement: Understanding the Causes of Community Participation," *Social Indicators Research* 97, no. 3 (2010): 451–66.

eligible voters cast a ballot: "2012 Voter Turnout Report," Bipartisan Policy Center, November 8, 2012, http://bipartisanpolicy.org/library/2012-voter-turnout/.

turnout was in the single digits: Devin McCarthy and Rob Richie, "FairVote Report: Low Turnout Plagues U.S. Mayoral Elections, but San Francisco Is Highest," FairVote: The Center for Voting and Democracy, October 24, 2012, http://www.fairvote.org/research-and-analysis/blog/fairvote-report-low-turnout-plagues-u-s-mayoral-elections-but-san-francisco-is-highest/.

operate in an "equilibrium state": Mike Maciag, "Voter Turnout Plummeting in Local Elections," *Governing,* October 2014, http://www.governing.com/topics/politics/gov-voter-turnout-municipal-elections.html.

in the city in real time: Code for America, "New Orleans," https://www.codefor america.org/governments/neworleans/.

offer incarceration alternatives: Code for America, "Louisville," https://www .codeforamerica.org/governments/louis ville/, and Code for America, "Jail Population Management Dashboard," https:// www.codeforamerica.org/apps/jail-popu lation.-management-dashboard/.

help users map public art: Code for America, "Public Art Finder/ArtAround," https://www.codeforamerica.org/apps/ public-art-finder/.

locate social services: Erine Gray, "Aunt Bertha: Why We're Coding for America," Code for America, October 26, 2012, http://www.codeforamerica.org/blog/2012/ 10/26/aunt-bertha-why-were-coding-for-america/.

where to get a flu shot: Code for America, "Flu Shot Finder," https://www.codefor america.org/apps/flu-shot-finder/.

Google Maps images of their street: See the website http://blockee.org.

name your city's neighborhoods: See the website http://click-that-hood.com.

National Day of Civic Hacking: Find events at HackforChange.org.

(now MySidewalk): Emily Olinger, vice

president of client experience, MySidewalk, in conversation with the author,
April 2015.

without leaving the house: "Nick Bow-
den," National Conference on Citizenship,
August 8, 2013, http://ncoc.net/Nick
Bowden.

to express an opinion: Mike Maciag,
"The Citizens Most Vocal in Local Government."

"typically younger and wealthier": Ben
Armstrong, in conversation with the author, April 2015.

" 'and it's happening' ": Emily Olinger,
in conversation with the author, April
2015.

pizza, soda, and beer: Ben Schoenfeld, in
conversation with the author, May 2015.

private, hyperlocal Facebook pages:
Sarah Leary, vice president of Nextdoor,
in conversation with the author, November 2014.

Does anyone know a carpenter?: Anne
Clauss, in conversation with the author,
December 2014.

collective efficacy towns need: Marc
Dunkelman, in conversation with the
author, November 2014.

crime dropped by 15 percent: Bob Mof-
fitt, "Sacramento Police Chief Says Crime

Down 15 Percent," Capital Public Radio News, June 26, 2014, http://www.cap radio.org/articles/2014/06/26/sacramento-police-chief-says-crime-down-15-percent/.

neighborhood emergency response team: Sarah Leary, in conversation with the author, November 2014.

more transparent and welcoming: Code for America, "Digital Front Door," https://www.codeforamerica.org/our-work/initiatives/digitalfrontdoor/.

Chapter Ten: Create Something

Cobbling together resources was what he did best: Rip Rapson, "Creative Place-making: The Next Phase for ArtPlace," address to the ArtPlace Summit in Los Angeles, published at Kresge Foundation, President's Corner blog, March 4, 2014, http://kresge.org/about-us/presidents-corner/creative-placemaking-next-phase-for-artplace. Also helpful were Anne Gadwa Nicodemus, in conversation with the author, February 2015, and Aidan Flax-Clark, "Creative Placemaking: What It Is and Why It's Important for Communities," *Aspen Idea* (blog), October 31, 2014, www.aspeninstitute.org/about/blog/creative-placemaking-what-it-why-its-important-communities.

"how they change over time": Peter R. Orszag, et al., to Heads of Executive Departments and Agencies, "Developing Effective Place-Based Policies for the FY 2011 Budget," White House memorandum M-09-28, August 11, 2009, https://www.whitehouse.gov/sites/default/files/omb/assets/memoranda_fy2009/m09-28.pdf.

"the arts at the community development table": Jason Schupbach, in conversation with the author, December 2015.

in cities all over the country: Tara McGuinness and Victoria Collin, White House Office of Management and Budget, in conversation with the author, December 2015.

your tax dollars are at work: Shaun Donovan, "Here's How the Federal Government Is Working with Local Communities to Create Change, in One Map," White House blog, August 26, 2015, https://www.whitehouse.gov/blog/2015/08/25/heres-how-federal-government-working-local-communities-create-change-one-map.

writing curriculum in Missoula, Montana: The National Endowment for the

Arts has a stunning website where you can read about Our Town recipients. Go to https://www.arts.gov/exploring-our-town/showcase.

in all fifty states and Puerto Rico: Jason Schupbach, in conversation with the author, December 2015.

white paper that inspired the program: Anne Gadwa Nicodemus, in conversation with the author, February 2015.

stage operas based on local oral histories: Those particular projects took place in New York City, Cincinnati, and Houston, respectively. ArtPlace America posts descriptions of all its placemaking projects at its website. Go to www.artplaceamerica.org/grantees?search_api_views_fulltext.

outdoor performance space and urban farm: Lincoln Park Coast Cultural District, "The Facade," http://lpccd.org/featured/church-facade-conceptual-plan/.

" 'Take all my money' ": Lyz Crane, in conversation with the author, July 2014.

tie-dyed, hand-lettered banner: Prattsville Art Center and Residency, "About Us," *Prattsville Art* (blog), August 6, 2012, http://prattsvilleart.blogspot.com/2012/08/about-us.html.

"and everything would stop": Nancy Barton, in conversation with the author,

September 2014.

"people who are like them": Maggie Bernadette, in conversation with the author, September 2014.

"how will you know when to stop?": Jamie Hand, in conversation with the author, March 2015.

health problems forced her hand: Kate Milo, in conversation with the author, September 2014.

bring urban public spaces to life: Southwest Airlines, "Southwest Airlines Introduces Heart of the Community," press release, PR Newswire, April 3, 2014, www.prnewswire.com/news-releases/ southwest-airlines-introduces-heart-of-the-community-253757211.html.

wriggle their toes in the sand: Project for Public Spaces, "Heart of the Community," www.pps.org/heart-of-the-community, and Philip Winn, "Placemaking's Ripple Effect: How a Beach Downtown Is Making Waves in Detroit," Project for Public Spaces, September 26, 2014, www.pps.org/blog/placemakings-ripple-effect-how-a-beach-downtown-is-making-waves-in-detroit.

"when Southwest came to us": Ethan Kent, in conversation with the author, April 2015.

placemaking events at libraries nation-wide: Redbox, "Outside the Box," www.redbox.com/outside-the-box, and Elena Madison, "Placemaking: Coming Soon to a Library Near You!" Project for Public Spaces, June 30, 2014, www.pps .org/blog/placemaking-coming-soon-to-a-library-near-you.

"Lighter, Quicker, Cheaper": Project for Public Spaces, "The Lighter, Quicker, Cheaper Transformation of Public Spaces," www.pps.org/reference/lighter-quicker-cheaper.

less litter sullied the streets: Edi Rama, "Take Back Your City with Paint," TEDx Thessaloniki, May 2012, https://www .ted.com/talks/edi_rama_take_back_your_ city_with_paint?language=en.

clean drinking water or safe streets: Kevin M. Leyden, Abraham Goldberg, and Philip Michelbach, "Understanding the Pursuit of Happiness in Ten Major Cities," *Urban Affairs Review* 47, no. 6 (2011): 861–88; and Ariel Schwartz, "Forget the Suburbs: Living in Beautiful, Well-Designed Cities Makes People Happy," *Co.Exist,* February 8, 2012, http://www.fastcoexist.com/1679263/ forget-the-suburbs-living-in-beautiful-well-designed-cities-makes-people-happy.

to activate a neglected neighborhood: Jason Roberts, "How to Build a Better Block," TEDxOU, February 2012, http:// betterblock.org/better-block-at-tedx.

League of Creative Interventionists: League of Creative Interventionists, "Interventions," http://www.creativeinterven tionists.com/.

"transcend the 'place' to forefront the 'making' ": Susan Silberberg, et al., "Places in the Making: How Placemaking Builds Places and Communities," white paper, Massachusetts Institute of Technology, 2013.

for his eponymous law firm: James Creekmore, in conversation with the author, February 2015.

"they were just as happy, thank you very much": Susan Mattingly, in conversation with the author, May 2015.

"a place for everyone in the project": Kate Nevin, in conversation with the author, March 2015.

Chapter Eleven: Stay Loyal

one of the most toxic places on earth: Holly Morris, "Ukraine: A Country of Women," *More,* April 2011, http://www .more.com/chernobyl-women-nuclear-holly-morris. For haunting pictures of Chernobyl and Pripyat, see Lane Turner, "The Big Picture: Chernobyl Disaster 25th Anniversary," *Boston Globe,* April 25, 2011, http://www.boston.com/bigpicture/2011/04/chernobyl_disaster_25th_annive.html; "Chernobyl Then and Now: 28 Haunting Images from Nuclear Disaster," RT.com, April 26, 2014, http://www.rt.com/news/155072-chernobyl-images-now-then/; Daniel Dalton, "Chilling Photos of Chernobyl 28 Years Later," *Buzz-Feed,* April 25, 2014, http://www.buzzfeed.com/danieldalton/chilling-photos-chernobyl-28-years-later#.nfA4eyOb4; and "Last Season's Fruit," *Laughing Crow Permaculture* (blog), June 6, 2010, https://laughingcrowpermaculture.wordpress.com/2010/06/06/last-seasons-fruit/.

in a sterile Kyiv high-rise: Holly Morris, in conversation with the author, March 2015; and Holly Morris, "Ukraine: A Country of Women."

"are dying of sadness": Holly Morris, "Why Stay in Chernobyl? Because It's Home," talk delivered at TEDGlobal 2013, June 2013, https://www.ted.com/talks/holly_morris_why_stay_in_chernobyl_because_it_s_home?language=en.

"their world was abruptly taken away":

Mindy Thompson Fullilove, *Root Shock: How Tearing Up City Neighborhoods Hurts America, and What We Can Do About It* (New York: Ballantine, 2005).

"This is so very real and raw for them": Holly Morris, in conversation with the author, March 2015.

then quickly recover normalcy afterward: For a good overview of 100 Resilient Cities' mission, see 100 Resilient Cities, "What Is Urban Resilience?" http://www.100resilientcities.org/resilience#/-_/.

"failed to understand the stresses it was facing": Andrew Salkin, in conversation with the author, April 2015.

"huge range of issues that each city is dealing with": Victoria Salinas, in conversation with the author, April 2015.

from zero to almost 10 percent: Ben Dooley, "Community Bonds, Not Seawalls, Key to Minimizing Deaths: 3/11 Study," *Japan Times,* April 16, 2014, http://www.japantimes.co.jp/news/2014/04/16/national/community-bonds-not-seawalls-key-to-minimizing-deaths-311-study/#.

Each town's level of social connection: Daniel P. Aldrich and Yasuyuki Sawada, "The Physical and Social Determinants of Mortality in the 3.11 Tsunami," *Social*

Science and Medicine 124 (2015): 66–75.

"before the disaster strikes": Daniel Aldrich, in conversation with the author, March 2015.

about their chances of handling future disasters: The Associated Press-NORC Center for Public Affairs Research, "Two Years after Superstorm Sandy: Resilience in Twelve Neighborhoods," http://www .apnorc.org/PDFs/Sandy/Sandy%20 Phase%202%20Report_Final.pdf.

can build social capital and resilience: Center for Resilient Cities, "Badger Rock Center," http://www.resilientcities.org/ projects-programs/badger-rock-center/.

"space for individuals to contribute": Victoria Salinas, in conversation with the author, April 2015.

ills of the inner city: Emaleigh Doley, in conversation with the author, April 2015.

neighbors into caring about each other: Malcolm Gladwell describes the broken windows idea of policing in depth in *The Tipping Point: How Little Things Can Make a Big Difference* (New York: Back Bay, 2002).

"if you participate in this project": You can learn more about Grow This Block at the Doleys' website, the W Rockland St. Project, http://rocklandstreet.com/.

"can create a lot of energy": Depending on your neighborhood, you may need city permits to put planters on the sidewalk. Call your city's planning and building office to find out.

"the scales would have tipped to the point of no return": Emaleigh Doley, in conversation with the author, April 2015.

where Sandy's ravages were most devastating: The Associated Press-NORC Center for Public Affairs Research, "Two Years After Superstorm Sandy."

"It's not all like this": Beth Riley, in conversation with the author, January 2015.

Kübler-Ross stages of grief in reverse: Christine Bowenkamp, "Coordination of Mental Health and Community Agencies in Disaster Response," *International Journal of Emergency Mental Health* 2, no. 3 (2000): 159–65.

envision themselves living on the beach someday: Stacy Jones, "3 in 5 Want to Retire Somewhere Else," Bankrate, March 23, 2015, http://www.bankrate.com/finance/retirement/survey-who-wants-to-retire-elsewhere.aspx.

feel depression lowering like a scrim: Bruce Tolar, in conversation with the author, December 2014.

less poverty than the ones they left: Corina Graif, "(Un)natural Disaster: Vulnerability, Long-Distance Displacement, and the Extended Geography of Neighborhood Distress and Attainment after Katrina," *Population and Environment,* published online ahead of print, August 2015.

impossible to reenter their old lives: David S. Kirk, "A Natural Experiment on Residential Change and Recidivism: Lessons from Hurricane Katrina," *American Sociological Review* 74 (June 2009): 484–505.

better off than those who returned: Malcolm Gladwell, "Starting Over," *New Yorker,* August 24, 2015, http://www.newyorker.com/magazine/2015/08/24/starting-over-dept-of-social-studies-malcolm-gladwell.

herculean effort to return to their hometown: Raj Chetty, et al., "Where Is the Land of Opportunity?: The Geography of Intergenerational Mobility in the United States," Working Paper No. 19843, National Bureau of Economic Research, January 2014, http://www.nber.org/papers/w19843.

"This is my home": Emily Chamlee-Wright and Virgil Henry Storr, " 'There's No Place Like New Orleans': Sense of

Place and Community Recovery in the Ninth Ward after Hurricane Katrina," *Journal of Urban Affairs* 31, no. 5 (2009): 615–34.

a lawyer in town named Alwyn Luckey: Alwyn Luckey, in conversation with the author, December 2014.

yet 8.4 million Americans are still happy to live there: Marc Yearsley, "New York City Has Been Destroyed 34 Times On Screen," Gothamist, March 19, 2014, http://gothamist.com/2014/03/19/new_york_city_has_been_destroyed_34.php.

"drove the process of resilience there": Daniel Aldrich, in conversation with the author, March 2015.

has a very bad day once in a while: Beth Riley, in conversation with the author, January 2015.

"foundational building block" for towns: Jeff Coates, in conversation with the author, March 2015.

family letters, newspaper clippings, and journal entries: The biographies on Virginia Tech's We Remember site were particularly helpful. See https://www.weremember.vt.edu/.

he wandered home: Scott and Joyce Hendricks, in conversation with the author, April 2015.

"just a community feeling": Joyce Hendricks, in conversation with the author, April 2015.

Chapter Twelve: Settle Down

between May and August: United Van Lines, "Americans Move to Chicago, Washington D.C. and Atlanta," news release, September 9, 2014, http://www.unitedvanlines.com/about-united/news/summer-long-distance-moving-trends-study.

hurtling toward my third anniversary in Blacksburg: Katherine Loflin, in conversation with the author, November 2014.

"its perfection was not working for my narrative": Ibid.

general sense of geography-related unworthiness: Greg Tehven, in conversation with the author, September 2014.

three-mile loop of closed downtown streets: Rory Beil, in conversation with the author, August 2014. Look at http://www.dakmed.org/cass-clay-alive/streets-alive/ for details.

in a derelict downtown alleyway: Look at AlleyFair.com for more details.

Communal living for entrepreneurs:

See http://www.fargostartuphouse.com/.

dinners for city visitors: See DinnerTies .com.

"it just happened in the last ten years": Mike Williams, in conversation with the author, August 2014.

creating the city where they live: Ethan Kent, in conversation with the author, April 2015.

"the weird kid among my friends": Nick Arnett, in conversation with the author, September 2015. Also Adrienne Westenfeld, "Charting Vision: 20-Year-Old Community Developer Nick Arnett's Journey," Das Fort, http://www.dasfort.com/nick-arnett/.

die-hard place fan would be hard to find: Kyle Sandler, "Twelve Cities Founder and Thiel Fellowship Liason [*sic*] Nick Arnett on Three Themes for Building Great Cities," Serious Startups, August 6, 2013, http://seriousstartups.com/2013/08/06/twelve-cities-founder-thiel-fellowship-liason-nick-arnett-themes-building-great-cities/.

but they moved anyway: Tonya Beeler, in conversation with the author, March 2015.

probably move on from West Rockland Street: Emaleigh Doley, in conversation with the author, April 2015.

"never thought the equation was worth it": Susan Mattingly, in conversation with the author, May 2015.

"Why not try another?": Helen Nearing, *Loving and Leaving the Good Life* (White River Junction, Vt.: Chelsea Green, 1993), 119.

For further resources, visit MelodyWarnick .com.

INDEX

612